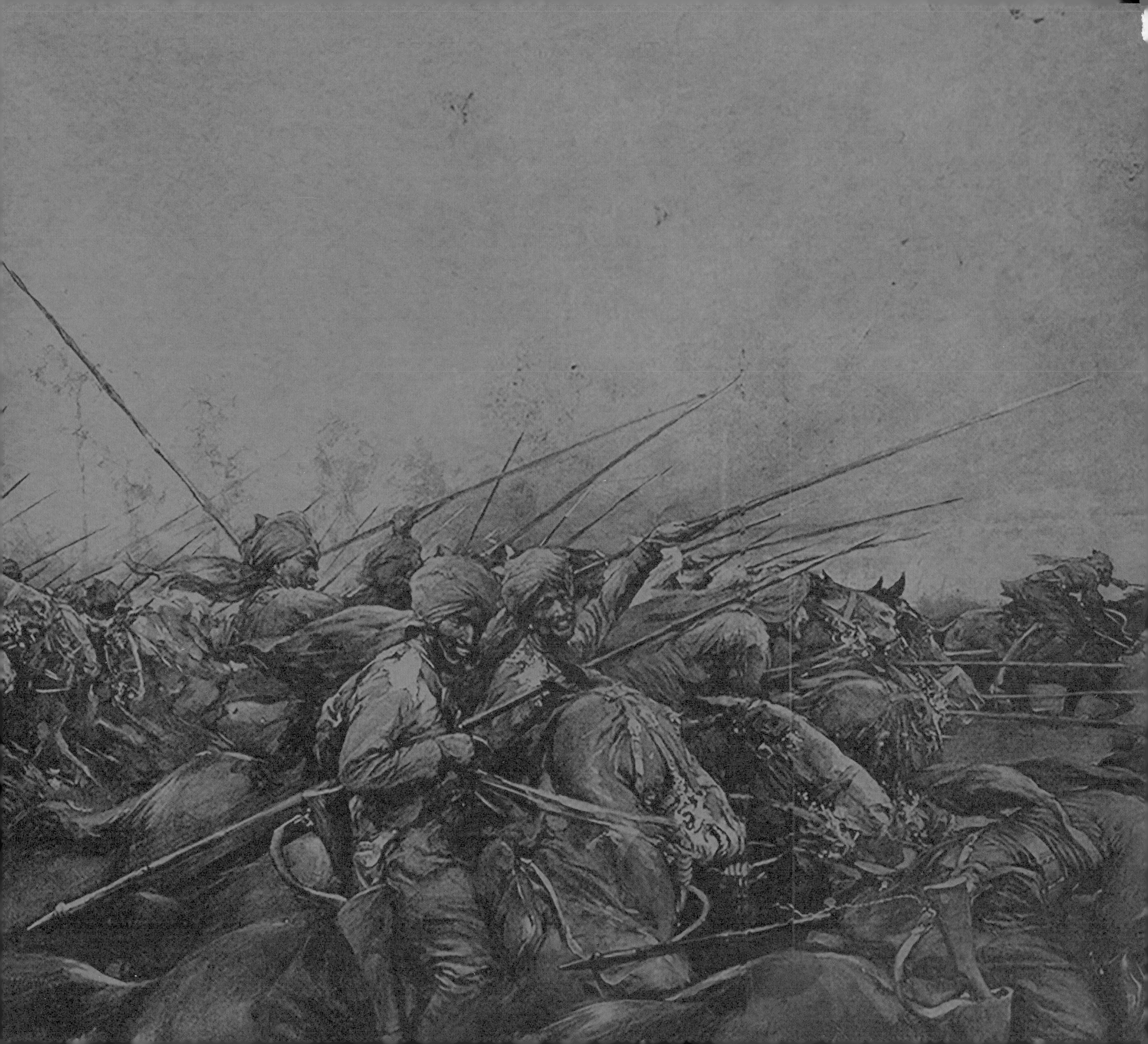

The Sikh roars like a lion on the field of battle
and yields up his life as a sacrifice;
Whoever is fortunate enough to be born a Rajput
never fears the foe in battle;
He gives up all thought of worldly pleasure
and dreams only of the battlefield;

He who dies on the field of battle,
His name never dies, but lives in history;
He who fronts the foe boldly in battle
has God for his protection;
Once a Sikh takes the sword in hand
He has only one aim - victory.

Daffadar Nathan Singh, 2nd Lancers France April 18, 1916

The incident illustrated here was related by an eye witness in "The Daily Telegraph" as follows:

"The German plan seemed to be to break our line at the point where they guessed our men to be the most exhausted. Supported by artillery, a brigade of their infantry was flung at us, and we braced ourselves for what we thought was coming. Our fire was hot enough in all consequence, but it did not seem hot enough to stop those Germans. Just when they were halfway towards our trenches the Bengal Lancers, who had arrived the day before and were anxious to get into it, were brought up. Splendid fellows they looked as they passed us on their fine chargers, and we broke into cheers. They smiled back grimly, with their eyes glancing ahead and their fingers nervously feeling their lance shafts. At the word of command they swept forward, only making a slight detour to get out of our line of fire, and they swept into the Germans from the left like a whirlwind. The enemy were completely taken aback. The Turcos they knew, but these men with their flashing eyes, dark skin, and white gleaming teeth, not to mention their terribly keen-edged lances, they could not understand, the Lancers did not give them much time to arrive at an understanding. With a shrill yell they rode right through the German infantry, thrusting right and left with their terrible lances, and bringing a man down every time. The Germans broke and ran for their lives, pursued by the Lancers for about a mile. When they came back from their charge they were cheered wildly all along our line, but they did not think much of what they had done."

Illustration & Text :
The lightning rush of the Bengal Lancers right
through the lines of the German Infantry
The Sphere December 19, 1914

there be lions

Magni Mogolis Imperium: Abridged Map of The Mughal Empire of North India
Publication: Gerard Mercator's Atlantis Novi Atlas (French Edition 1639)

Depicted on the map:

(1) The river Indus marks the boundary between Persia and India

Since the time of the ancient Greeks, the inhabitants of the lands in the Indus river basin and east of the river had been known to the West as 'Indians'. Their country, as denoted by the Indo-Persian suffix of 'Sthan' meaning 'place of' became known as Hindustan and the religion of these 'Hindus' would become to be known as Hinduism. East of the river Indus and its five tributaries, flows the Yumana river which historically demarked the people of the northern Indian subcontinent as people of the Indus, and those of the eastern regions as the people of the Ganges river belt. The basin of land around the tributaries of the Indus named from west to east as the Jhelum, Chenab Ravi, Beas and Satluj rivers became known in Persian as 'Punjab' the land of the five rivers (Punj meaning 'five' and Aab meaning 'waters'). Punjab first came under Muslim domination in the tenth century with the arrival of successive waves of Arab, Turk and Persian invaders culminating by the 16th century in the conversion of many natives to Islam and the establishment of the Turkic/Persian Islamic dynasty of the Mughals.

(2) The lands of the Indus are embellished with an image of a lion

While the north Indian lion would be hunted to extinction by the 19th century, its renown, however, lives on through the name 'Singh', the Sanskrit derivation of the word lion, adopted by the warriors of North India. In the 11th century, Hindus bestowed these warriors with the title of Rajputs meaning 'son of kings', conferring upon them nobility and galvanising them to confront the Islamic invasion as the sword arm of the subcontinent. In the Punjab the rise of Sikhs throughout the 16th and 17th century culminated in 1699 in the formation of the Khalsa - the 'Brotherhood of the Pure' who would pick up the fight against religious oppression and the defence of the weak as a religious calling. In the proclamation of the birth of the Khalsa, Guru Gobind Singh, warrior, spiritual leader and tenth Guru of the Sikhs mandated all Sikhs to adopt the name Singh in place of their surnames, regardless of caste or nobility.

In the Great War 1914-1918 the warriors of the Punjab would become known as the 'Black Lions' of the east.

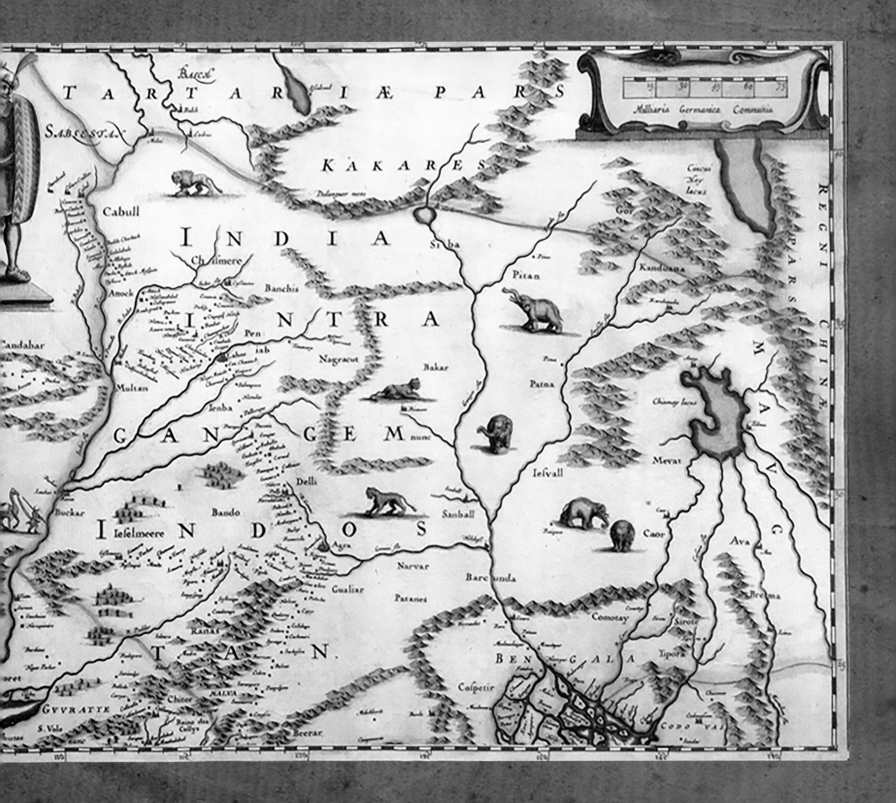

T A R T A R I Æ   P A R S

Baccal

S. ABCESTAN

KAKARES

Cabull

I N D I A

Si ba

Gor

Cenini Noy lacus

Chalmere

Banchis

Pitan

Kanduana

Amock

I N T R A

Pen iab

Nagracut

Bakar

Patna

Multan

Jenba

G A N G E M   *nunc*

Iesuall

Mevat

Chiamay lacus

Delli

Buckar

Ieselmeere   N   D   O   S

Bando

Sanball

Caor

Ava

Agra

Narvar

Barcunda

Brema

Gualiar

Patanes

Comotay

Siroté

Tipora

Ranas

B E N   G A L A

Chitor   MALVA

T A N.

Colpetir

Codo vai

GVVRATTE

S. Vale

Beerar

Milliaria Germanica Communia

RECNI   CHINÆ PARS

M A V G

IN HONOUR

PANJAB

498,560

1914 - 1918

FIRST IN & LAST OUT
UNSUNG & UNTOLD

Victory & Valour

V

100

Remembrance

DUTY, HONOUR & IZZAT

FROM GOLDEN FIELDS TO CRIMSON - PUNJAB'S BROTHERS IN ARMS IN FLANDERS

PUREWAL - RAWLINS

RENEGADE ARTS ENTERTAINMENT

Acknowledgements

During the 2014 - 2018 Centennial of the First World War, the Duty, Honour & Izzat exhibition was featured in over 60 exhibition based programs as part of municipal, provincial and national commemorative events across Canada (www.IMFC.org). These projects could not have been completed without the support of a great number of people. On behalf of myself and the Indus Media Foundation I would like to thank, first and foremost, my wife Zeena and our three children, Sophini, Angelyca and Tzari for making room in their lives and home for this project. I am indebted to Savinder Singh Purewal, Chris Rawlins, Manjinder Sidhu, Jan Robertson, Christopher Trevelyan, Parm Bains, Paul Mann, Bob Mann, Tarik Kiani, Mickey Klota, Gurjinder Jhaj for all their support along the way. A special thank you goes to Mr. Trevelyan for his expert editing of my manuscript and for authoring the teacher's lesson plans to be found at www.DutyHonourIzzat.ca. I am grateful to our public education partners for their enduring support, at Simon Fraser University: Stephen Dooley & Navinder Chima; at the University Fraser Valley: Satwinder Bains, Sharanjit Sandhra, Rajnish Dhawan; at the Royal BC Museum: Scott Cooper, Tzu-i Chung, Janet MacDonald, Lorne Hammond; at the National War Museum: Stephen Quick, Caroline Dromaguet, Andrew Burtch, Tony Glen; at School District 34: Jasbir Singh; at School District 36: Neder Dhillon, Rob Rai, Mandish Saran and teachers Annie Ohana and Gurpreet Bains for hosting our exhibit in the various programs at LA Matheson High School. Thank you also to the Museums of Surrey, Delta, Richmond, Coquitlam, Pit Meadows, Kelowna and Surrey Central Library for hosting our events. My thanks go out also to Inspector Baltej Dhillon(RCMP), Jasinder Gill, Harjot Guram, Jobhan Johal, Captain Robert J Macdonald (BC Regiment) for participating as speakers at our lecture events. It has also been my honour to work with the gentlemen officers of the Indian Ex-Servicemen's association: Col Darshan Singh Sidhu (Artillery), Col Santokh Singh Hundal (RVC), Capt Mohinder Singh Jaswal (Engineers), Sub Sarwan Singh Khaira (Signals), W/O Devinder Singh Dhami (Indian Air Force), Sgt Sukhdev Singh Gadri (Indian Air Force), Sub Gurdev Singh Kanwar (Signals), Sub Joginder Singh Gill (SIKH REGIMENT), Sub Kewal Singh Purewal (SIKH REGIMENT), Flight Lt Gian Singh Saini (Indian Air Force), Sub/Maj Arjan Singh Sandhu (Ordnance), Capt Rachhpal Singh Sraw (Signals), Lt Harpal Singh Brar (Indian Navy). And a special thank you to Brigadier (retired) Indrajeet Singh Gakhal (Indian Army) of 1st Battalion Sikh Regiment (14th Sikhs - 'The Bravest of the Brave') for contributions to our website.

For helping us reach out to our youth and community I would like to thank the Kids Play Foundation: Kal Dosanj & Kiran Toor; the Bhai Kanhaiya 3300 Cadets of the British Columbia regiment: Lt Col Ted Hawthorn, Captain Karamjeet Nagra and Harminder Palak; Gian Singh Gill of Gurdwara Sahib Dasmesh Darbar Surrey, Balbir Singh of Sri Guru Singh Sabha Surrey, Manny Johal, Baljit & Sabrina Gill (Veerhood) and Sergeant Jag Khosa of CFSEU-BC. Thank you also to our project supporters in local media for their event coverage, participation and awards: Harpreet Singh (Joy TV), Gurvinder Hundal & Ramneek Dhillon (Darpan), Pary Dulai & Sukhi Kaur (Channel Punjabi), Bali Deol, Tarannum Thind (Omni), Bhupinder Singh Hundal, Randip Janda, Harpreet Pandher, Kash Heed, Vijay Saini, Rena Heer, Gurpreet Sahota, Dupinder Kaur Saran, Gurlal Singh & Kuldip Singh.

To Punjabi heritage champions, far and wide, thank you all for your inspirational work: Pardeep BoxSingh Nagra III, Gurmit Syndicate Singh, Balwant Sanghera, Nadeem Parmar, Mo Dhaliwal, Moninder Lalli, Harbhajan Gill, Kulvinder Shergill, Arjan Manhas, Gurmeet Singh Sandhu, Amandeep Madra & Parmjit Singh(UK), Avtar Bahra(UK), Gurinder Singh Mann (UK), Amarpal Singh Sidhu(UK), Narinder Singh Desai (UK), Jay Singh Sohal (UK), Irfan Malik (UK), Bhupinder Singh Holland (Netherlands) Kulveer Singh (India), Captain Amarinder Singh (India), Rana Chinna (India), Harchand Singh Bedi (Malaysia), Harjit Singh (Australia). I would like to highlight and thank the non-Punjabi historians who in their work have taken up the cause of the Indian soldier: David Gray (Canada), Gordon Corrigan (UK), Geroge Morton-Jack, Tony McClenaghan (UK), Dominiek Dendooven (Belgium), Andrew Periozi (USA), Mark Higton(UK) and Nick Britton (UK). Thank you also to Amanda Shatzko in Vernon B.C. for producing the first Canadian WW1 memorial inclusive of a turbaned soldier and Norm Crerar (Vernon Tattoo) and Kanwar Nijjer (Canadian Armed Forces) for putting us front and centre at their multicultural military events.

Indus Media Foundation gratefully acknowledges the financial support of the Province of British Columbia during the term of 2014 to 2017 and assistance from Premier Christy Clark, Minister Amrik Virk and Minister Peter Fassbender towards the installation of a permanent tribute to the Punjabi Defenders of the Crown at the BC legislature in 2016. Our thanks also go out to the Lieutenant Governor of British Columbia, Judith Guichon and her Honour's staff who helped to make a corresponding permanent display at Government House a reality. We are grateful for the many words of encouragement received from Canada's Ministers of Defence Jason Kenney (2014-15) and Harjit Singh Sajjan (2015 -).

I remain indebted to the many friends and supporters who have generously donated funds in support of the project, specifically: Mr. A.P. Singh & Family, Dalvir & Ranvir Nahal (Sunterra Custom Homes), Tara Singh and Bakhshish Nahal (Vernon), Mr Balkar Gill (Wood West Associates), Amrik Sahota (Amson Group), Balbir Singh (Sri Guru Singh Sabha Surrey); Federation of Sikh Societies: Mota Singh Jheeta, Davinder Singh Ghatoura, Kirpal Singh Garcha.

Steven Purewal, Surrey, BC. November 2018

This book is produced as a legacy publication for the Duty, Honour & Izzat WW1 Centennial project (2014-2018). This printing was made possible by the kind support of the following sponsors : Lindsey Houghton at the Combined Forces Special Enforcement Unit (CFSEU-BC), Jagmohan Singh at Primus Law (Surrey BC) , Ravi Sidoo at East India Carpets (Vancouver BC) , Satnam Johal at The Canadian Sikh Study and Teaching Society (Vancouver BC), Pardeep Nagra at Sikh Heritage Museum Canada (Toronto ON) and the sangats of the India Cultural Centre of Canada (Richmond BC), Khalsa Diwan Society (Vancouver BC) and the Akali Singh Society (Vancouver BC).

Acknowledgement

This book was written on the unceded territories of the Coast Salish Nations of the Kwantlen, Katzie, and Semiahmoo Nations. As a publication that revives the identities of the over one million South Asian soldiers that contributed to the commonwealth's First World War effort, as settlers of these lands we recognise that soldiers of the First Nations' also fought honourably under one crown in keeping with their warrior traditions.

In a land where settlers removed First Nations' children to place them in residential schools where deaths were commonplace, denied the right to vote, and their cultural practices banned, First Nations upheld their tradition of serving alongside British troops as brothers-in-arms in the War of 1812, the Seven Years War and the Boer War. We recognise that in the Great War they enlisted beyond their numbers and participated in all of the major battles in which Canadian troops fought, distinguishing themselves as brave and gallant soldiers.

In parallel to the history depicted within these pages, we recognise that the governments of the British & Canadian Crown refused to value the humanity of BIPOC soldiers appropriating their honourable cultures only to further their colonial aspirations. That their stories of courage have been purposefully erased as part of assimilative and racist processes perpetrated against marginalised people and that in Canada their land was plundered to be given to returning white soldiers while their sacrifices went unrecognised. We stand with those who are reclaiming their stories, their heritage, their land and their honour. To those who came before us, Rest In Power. To those who exist today, Power to the People. All Our Relations.

Duty, Honour & Izzat

Written by Steven Purewal - Illustrated by Christopher Rawlins
Edited by Alexander Finbow

The short story 'A Question of Honour' is a work of fiction. Names, characters, businesses, places, events, locales, and incidents are either the products of the author's imagination or used in a fictitious manner. Any resemblance to actual persons, living or dead, or actual events is purely coincidental.

Renegade Arts Entertainment books can be purchased for educational purposes through our Education Market Channels

Renegade Arts Canmore Ltd
President: John Finbow
Publisher: Alexander Finbow
Business Development: Luisa Harkins
Marketing: Sean Tonelli
Reporting & Asset Management: Emily Pomeroy
www.renegadeartsentertainment.com

Office of business:
Renegade Arts Canmore Ltd, 25 Prospect Heights, Canmore, Alberta T1W 2S2 email: contact@renegademail.com

First edition
Hardcover ISBN : 9781988903477
ebook ISBN: 9781988903576

Printed in Canada by Friesens

Supported by the Government of Alberta

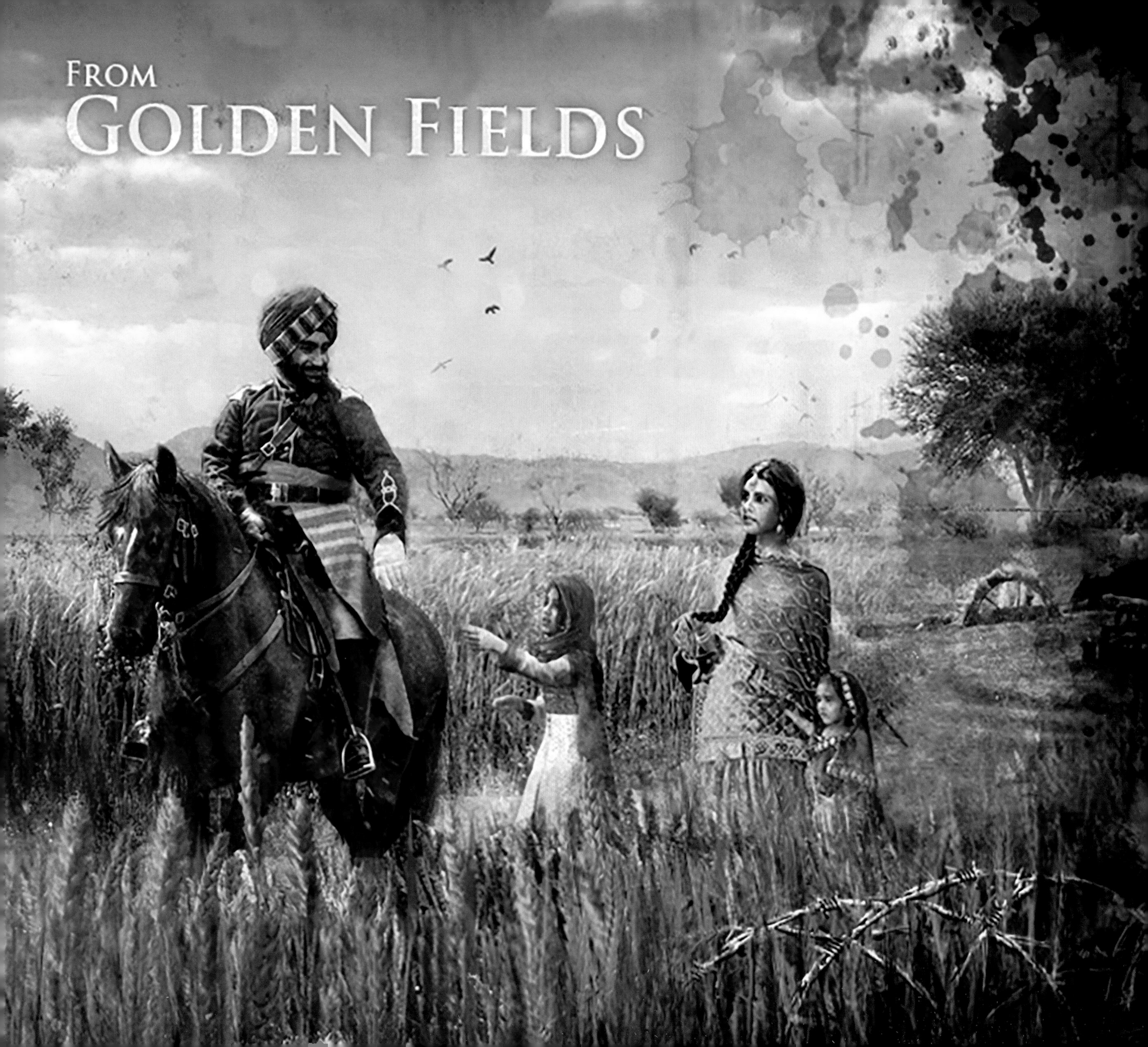
FROM
GOLDEN FIELDS

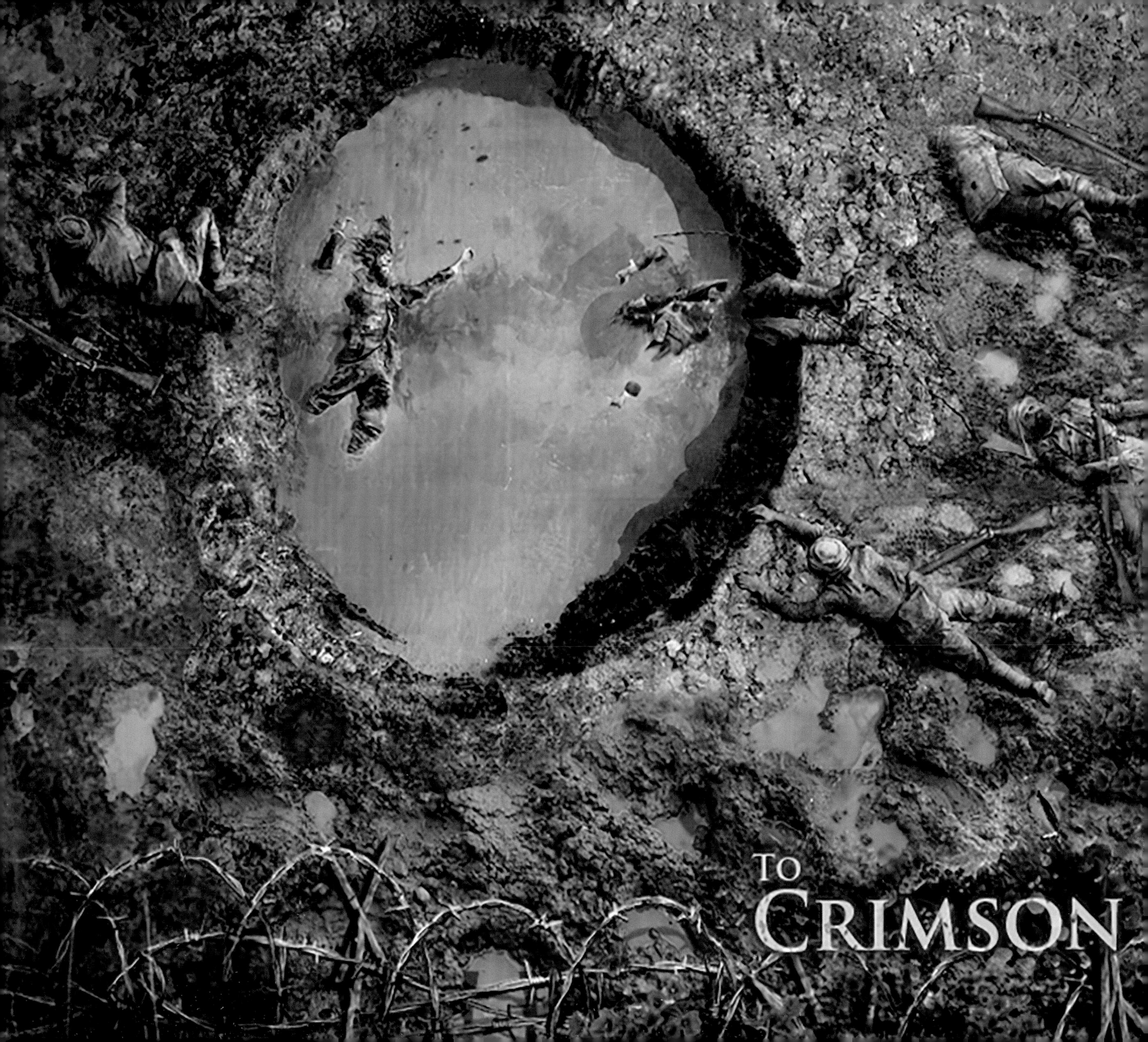
To
Crimson

Shattered

Trenches and barbed wire fences are the only shield,
out on the ruthless gory battlefield.
But once commanded to go over the top,
there is no looking back, every man has to fight nonstop.

Sons of India charge into battle, their turbaned heads held high.
As bombs fall like the monsoon rains from an Indian sky.
One by one shattered bodies crumble and fall,
the survivors triumphantly yelling their battle call.

They were lions, fighting in battlefields of mud,
until their roars were forever silenced,
they lay still in a graveyard of blood.
Duty was their commander, they would not retreat,
they fought to the end, never to accept defeat.

Brothers from far away lands,
once came together to answer the sovereign's call.
But sadly, many would never see these brave strong men again.
Why did you leave your village to join a distant war?
These fathers, husbands, sons, and brothers are no more.

Countless families were shattered awaiting their arrival,
alas they were no more than forgotten bodies,
lying in Flanders fields side by side with their rivals.
These loyal soldiers of the king should now be remembered by all,
while staring death in the eye they stood united and tall.

If the tale of a million Indian warriors is lost to history,
their sacrifice will fade as a myth,
their lives will forever pose a mystery.
When heroes are forgotten and we erase their story,
a debt is neglected, and all that then remains,
are their shattered dreams of glory.

Words: Sophini Purewal (Grade 7)
November 2014
Picture: Angelyca (Grade 5) & Tzari Purewal (Grade 2)
Erma Stephenson Elementary - Surrey School District 36

Contents

*In loving memory of my father
Teja Singh Purewal
8/11/1937 - 4/10/2012
who left village Shankar, Jalandhar,
Punjab in 1961 to establish a life in
the West.*

Dedicated to the men from village Shankar, Jalandhar, in united Punjab, who served as combatants in the Great War (1914-1918): Mangal Singh 34th (Sikh Pioneers), Rur Singh (21st Punjabis), Jiwan Jhiwar (21st Punjabis), Mulkha Singh (Son of Bir Singh) (14th Sikhs), Mulkha Singh (Son of Wazira Brahman) (14th Sikhs), Brothers Uttam Singh (14th Sikhs) & Arjun Singh (26th Punjabis), Rulia Moch (14th Sikhs), Arjun Singh (14th Sikhs) Harcharan Singh (26th Punjabis), Rahmat Ullah Arain (54th Sikhs Frontier Force), Brothers Sant Singh & Lahora Singh (32nd Sikh Pioneers), Kabal Singh (37th Dogras) Mehnga Udasi (37th Lancers), Bishn Singh (56th Punjabi Rifles Frontier Force) (KIA)

Foreword

I am grateful to Steve for the opportunity to contribute the foreword to this well thought out and compelling narrative that highlights the honours and sacrifices of the Punjabi community in the line of duty. The short story presented carefully weaves the experiences of the many souls that served during the First and Second World Wars, to reveal a dramatic insight of those who made the ultimate sacrifice and those who survived to tell the tale. The story of Hari, who served at the Battle of Monte Cassino and Ed Jones, a comrade that he saved with peril to his own life, is splashed with scenes from different times in history that speak to the extensive contributions made by those of the Sikh faith from India that honoured their word and commitment to the Crown shared with Canada, prior to India becoming a Republic in 1947.

Today, through inclusive Centennial Commemorations of the First World War, such as Steve's Duty, Honour & Izzat exhibitions, I have begun to more fully understand this rich military history and contributions towards world peace made by my own community; many facts have now emerged that were not readily known by most, including myself. In my own journey of uniform and duty, I have come across sentiments that were shared by "Hari" in the story, from fellow Canadians. These angry and foul sentiments certainly were not consistent with what one would expect when weighed against the contributions made by the Sikhs in the World Wars as loyal defenders of the Crown - and that too in a country that remains under the reign of the monarchy. I chalk all of it up to ignorance and not knowing. Those who understood history, the sacrifices, the loyalty, the pride, the honor displayed in the face of extraordinary odds, rejoiced and shared congratulatory notes when I received the approval to serve as a member of the RCMP on August 30th 1990 to become the first turbaned officer of the Royal Canadian Mounted Police.

And so it was on attending an inclusive Vimy Ceremony on April 6th 2017 at L. A. Matheson Secondary in Surrey B.C., an event dedicated to honoring Sikh WW2 veterans and the descendants of soldiers from WW1, and commemorating the Battle of Vimy Ridge that I listened intently to retired Captain John MacDonald of the British Columbia Regiment, a regiment historian, recount the origins of the RCMP uniform and its musical ride tradition. Over the years it was already established that the RCMP Stetson was not a Canadian hat, but rather borrowed from our neighbours to the south. This fact alone nullified the argument, that by allowing practising Sikhs to wear their turbans while serving in the ranks of the RCMP, we would erode the essence of the uniform and in turn Canadian symbols. Captain MacDonald's lecture, however, revealed that the first iteration of the RCMP like uniform was actually donned by Punjabi Cavalry under the British Empire; that the long boots, breeches and Sam Browne belt were inventions of the cavalry of the Indian Army; the lance was adopted by British forces after encountering the Khalsa (Sikh) Cavalry in battle in the first Anglo-Sikh war, and the famous musical ride itself had its basis in the exhibition riding of that Sikh Cavalry. Then he went on to say that those who were opposed to the RCMP turban on the basis of tradition had it wrong: that in fact to maintain tradition the turban should be the approved headdress and not the Stetson. When I heard his words, it changed the perspective I personally held these past years, which was that I was given an "exemption" rather than being "entitled" to wear my turban.

This is why this book and the stories within are so important. We owe our ancestors this duty to ensure that their contribution, loyalty to duty, incredible sacrifices and victories are remembered and shared with our society and our youth. The sense of pride that comes from knowing our place and the military contributions made towards world peace allows us to experience a feeling of entitlement to do more and be more in our lives. I can certainly relate directly to this feeling, and I hope that on learning more about our rich traditions in 'to protect and serve' roles, through stories like Hari's that more of our youth will be inspired to feel the same way.

We must share these historical and heroic events with our children to anchor them into understanding the strong legacy they belong to, give them role models that inspire courage and honor, give them examples of perseverance and self-sacrifice which will allow our youth to be armed with pride, self-respect, honor and integrity to face their own battles of being pulled into criminality, gangs and other destructive lifestyles as depicted in this short story that is more truth than fiction. Many other police officers and I have unfortunately sat with too many of our youth whom we had failed, who had fallen into a criminal lifestyle, had committed heinous crimes and were now facing a lifetime in prison. These may have been the lucky ones, their victims, on the other hand, had their young lives end violently and were leaving behind grieving families and pain that will remain for generations.

I would like to end my comments in appreciation of Steve's passion, dedication and efforts towards this project and his continued commitment in rejuvenating the episodes of military history that were instrumental in shaping the world we live in today and the freedoms we enjoy. I wish him continued success in these efforts and encourage our educators, youth workers, community centers and parents to take advantage of this book and share the writings through discussion and discourse with our children.

Baltej Dhillon
Surrey, BC
November, 2018

Part I
Based On True Events

Introduction

In Flanders Fields

The fields of northern France and Belgium have over the centuries rendered an illustrious stage for the clash of European empires. In 1815 Wellington defeated Napoleon at Waterloo and secured peace for Western Europe that would last nearly 100 years. In 1914, these fields once again teemed with European blood, but this time it would be a German army that the British would have to confront on the Flanders horizon. Within weeks of being despatched to the continent, the British Expeditionary Force was overrun by a million German soldiers cutting a murderous path through central Belgium. And on the verge of a British collapse, Germany set her eyes on the French port of Calais to cut off any hope of a lifeline from Britain.

Then on an autumn day, in fields barely 200 miles from the Seat of Empire in London – an Imperial fighting force would arrive to thwart this race to the sea. Despatched from distant shores within days of the declaration of war - they would, as fate would have it, arrive at the grimmest hour to confront the German invasion and save Calais. This wall of khaki cemented the last stretch of the Allied front line - the Western Front - a series of trenches stretching from the northern Belgian-Franco seaboard to Switzerland. This line in the sand would soon decay into a quagmire of mud and blood, swallowing the legions of dead who were to never know a grave, shifting little for the next four years despite the efforts of the earth's mightiest nations.

That an army would arrive from distant shores to Britannia's defence from her white colonies of Canada, Australia, South Africa and New Zealand would surprise no one least of all Germany for in 1914 Britain was at the height of her glory, controlling a quarter of the world's population. But the Imperial army that would defy Germany's war machine, depriving them of their last chance to win the war early, was an army of 'black lions' - the men of an Indian Expeditionary Force. At the vanguard of this British Indian Army were the Punjabis of the Lahore Division. As the first of the Crown's colonial forces to land in Europe, they held their ground as metal rain reduced men to a pink mist in the winter snow of 1914.

Why these imperial subjects would raise their battle cries in a land far distant from their own and for an emperor not of their kin is a testament to the character of both the British officers and the 'Martial Races' they commanded. It was not the first time a ruler and the ruled would fight alongside each other, for had not the Roman legions done the same when men from across that empire's dominions having taken the salt were then bound to take to the battlefield. And in the 18th & 19th centuries, the Irish and the Scots, once fearsome enemies of the English, flew their banners in the vanguard of Britannia's armies including the "Thin Red Line" at Balaclava. And so it was with Punjabis, whose recruitment into a vast imperial enterprise began immediately upon the annexation of the Punjab into the British Empire.

By the time the world was sucked into the vortex of the Great War, the Indian Army had already served the Crown loyally for decades. Atop the battlements of the Northwest frontier and across the battlefields of the Orient and Africa men of different races and religions lived, fought, bled, and died together and forged a close fellowship – camaraderie perhaps unrivalled in the history of armies. When Kipling first wrote The Ballad of East and West, it became famous for the refrain from its first line "East is East, and West is West, and never the twain shall meet", but the honour codes of these fighting men did find a nexus when they confronted a common foe. Through countless daring deeds of courage a culture of familiarity developed from these shared experiences, men developed a sense of kinship through which they drew strength from each other. Unfortunately, the poem has often been quoted to ascribe racism; only if you were to read on would you know the full refrain offers a celebration of the bonds forged between brave men.

Over the years, like the first line of that poem, WW1 texts have not depicted the war experience of the Western Front as being multicultural. While it's often said that there's nothing good about war, there is good to be found in why they were fought and in the men that fought them. And in that respect, little has been said of why men of the Indus would take up the quarrel of those that fell on distant shores. For that, the men of the Punjab should perhaps look to another bard of the English language who penned the words "Life every man holds dear; but the brave man holds honour far more precious than life". Ultimately, in the First World War, for the band of men of the British Indian Army, whether for Duty, Honour, Izzat or glory, the mouth of the cannon, the gauntlet of the Great War, would know no colour but red. Lest we forget these Brothers-in-Arms, this is their story.

Steven Purewal
Curator Duty, Honour & Izzat
Indus Media Foundation

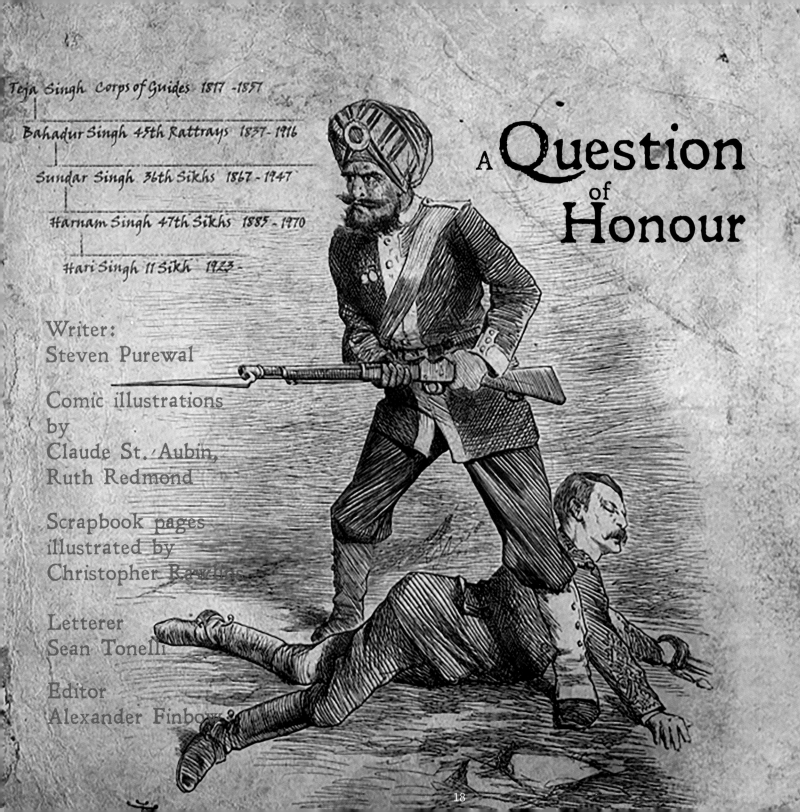

Teja Singh Corps of Guides 1817 - 1857

Bahadur Singh 45th Rattrays 1837 - 1916

Sundar Singh 36th Sikhs 1867 - 1947

Harnam Singh 47th Sikhs 1885 - 1970

Hari Singh 11 Sikh 1923 -

A Question of Honour

Writer:
Steven Purewal

Comic illustrations
by
Claude St. Aubin,
Ruth Redmond

Scrapbook pages
illustrated by
Christopher Rawlins

Letterer
Sean Tonelli

Editor
Alexander Finbow

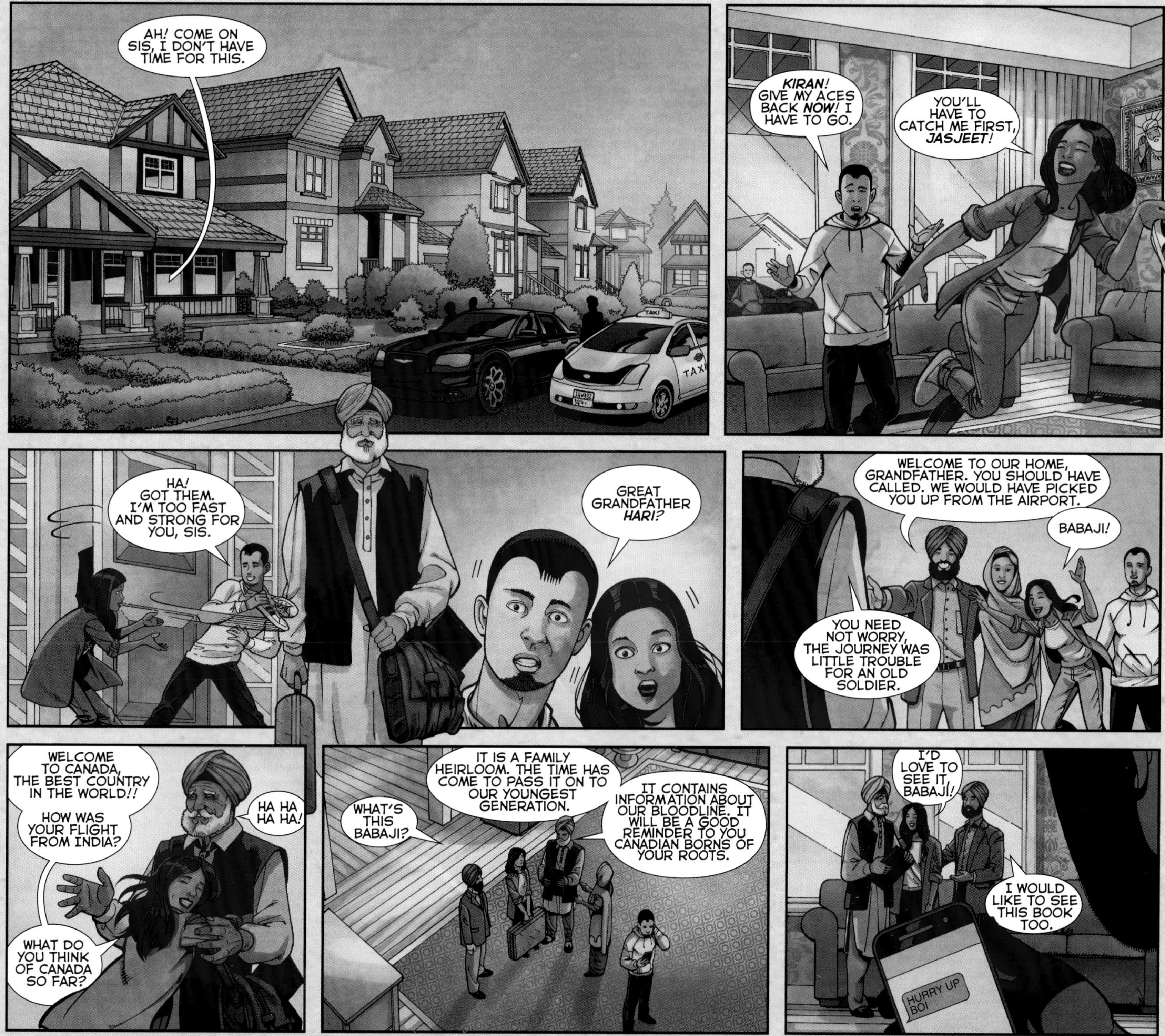
AH! COME ON SIS, I DON'T HAVE TIME FOR THIS.
KIRAN! GIVE MY ACES BACK NOW! I HAVE TO GO.
YOU'LL HAVE TO CATCH ME FIRST, JASJEET!
HA! GOT THEM. I'M TOO FAST AND STRONG FOR YOU, SIS.
GREAT GRANDFATHER HARI?
WELCOME TO OUR HOME, GRANDFATHER. YOU SHOULD HAVE CALLED. WE WOULD HAVE PICKED YOU UP FROM THE AIRPORT.
BABAJI!
YOU NEED NOT WORRY, THE JOURNEY WAS LITTLE TROUBLE FOR AN OLD SOLDIER.
WELCOME TO CANADA, THE BEST COUNTRY IN THE WORLD!!
HOW WAS YOUR FLIGHT FROM INDIA?
HA HA HA HA!
WHAT DO YOU THINK OF CANADA SO FAR?
WHAT'S THIS BABAJI?
IT IS A FAMILY HEIRLOOM. THE TIME HAS COME TO PASS IT ON TO OUR YOUNGEST GENERATION.
IT CONTAINS INFORMATION ABOUT OUR BLOODLINE. IT WILL BE A GOOD REMINDER TO YOU CANADIAN BORNS OF YOUR ROOTS.
I'D LOVE TO SEE IT, BABAJI!
I WOULD LIKE TO SEE THIS BOOK TOO.
HURRY UP BOI

WHAT'S THAT ONE ABOUT, BABAJI?

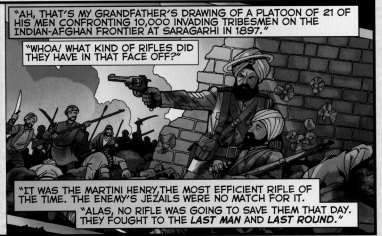

"AH, THAT'S MY GRANDFATHER'S DRAWING OF A PLATOON OF 21 OF HIS MEN CONFRONTING 10,000 INVADING TRIBESMEN ON THE INDIAN-AFGHAN FRONTIER AT SARAGARHI IN 1897."

"WHOA! WHAT KIND OF RIFLES DID THEY HAVE IN THAT FACE OFF?"

"IT WAS THE MARTINI HENRY, THE MOST EFFICIENT RIFLE OF THE TIME. THE ENEMY'S JEZAILS WERE NO MATCH FOR IT.

"ALAS, NO RIFLE WAS GOING TO SAVE THEM THAT DAY. THEY FOUGHT TO THE *LAST MAN* AND *LAST ROUND*."

THOSE GUYS WERE SAVAGE!

HURRUP!!!!!

MAN RELAX

STFD!!!!!

FIT

CHILDREN! LET BABAJI EAT. HE HAS HAD A LONG JOURNEY.

STAY AWAY FROM THOSE BOYS YOU GOT INTO TROUBLE WITH LAST WEEK. AND REMEMBER YOUR *CURFEW*.

YEAH, YEAH, YEAH!

WHAT'S UP WITH YOU BRO? YOU KNOW IT'S NOT A GOOD IDEA TO KEEP JIMMY WAITING?

SORRY GUYS, LET'S GO.

THEM SMOKIN MANNY, JUST MEANS THERE'S MORE TO GO AROUND FOR US WHEN WE TAKE WHAT'S THEIRS, 'G'.

IT'S TIME TO SHOW THEM WE ARE ALL BUSINESS.

WHO GOT THE *LAST ROUND*?

LET ME GET THIS. DUDE, HAVE I GOT A STORY ABOUT SOME HARDCORE GOONDAS AND THEIR *LAST ROUND*.

WELL, ED JONES, I'M FINALLY HERE! I'VE PLANNED THIS VISIT EVER SINCE I LEARNED MY FAMILY WAS GOING TO SETTLE IN YOUR HOMETOWN.

NOW WHERE DID YOU TELL ME THAT YOU SPENT YOUR DAYS...

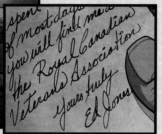

spent of most days you will find me at the Royal Canadian Veterans Association

Yours truly
Ed Jones

"AH, YES. A BRANCH OF THE ROYAL CANADIAN VETERANS ASSOCIATION. A MOST SUITABLE ESTABLISHMENT FOR OUR REUNION."

A BIG NIGHT OUT INDEED, JASJEET.

BABAJI! PHEW, I THOUGHT YOU WERE DAD.

I COULDN'T SLEEP, JET LAG, NO DOUBT.

UH HUH.

BETAH, WHERE IS THE ASSOCIATION? I HAVE TO MEET AN OLD FRIEND. CAN YOU TAKE ME TOMORROW?--

I GUESS.

WHAT KIND OF WORK DO THESE FRIENDS THAT DRIVE SUCH NICE CARS DO? I PRAY THEY ARE NOT INTO DRUGS.

THAT IS ALL I'VE HEARD THIS EVENING OVER DINNER AND ON THE TV NEWS.

THEY DON'T KNOW NOTHING ABOUT WHAT'S REALLY GOING ON.

COME, LET'S TALK OUTSIDE. WE DON'T WANT TO WAKE YOUR FATHER.

POPS, LET'S JUST SAY WE ARE SOLDIERS WHO FIGHT FOR WHAT'S OURS.

KAKA, INTERESTING CHOICE OF WORDS. MURDER AND MAYHEM ARE NOT THE WORK OF A SOLDIER, NOR IS IT WARMONGERING. THAT IS THE WORK OF POLITICIANS.

TELL ME WHO COMMANDS YOU IN YOUR WORTHY CAUSE?

YOU INDIAN SOLDIERS WERE PUPPETS IN A GAME. EVEN DAD SAYS YOU WERE *SLAVES* OF THE BRITISH FIGHTING SOMEONE ELSE'S WAR. IN TODAY'S GAME THE PLAYERS ARE THOSE WITH THE *COURAGE* TO TAKE WHAT THEY WANT. THE MAN DON'T TELL US A THING. THAT'S WHAT GETS US *RESPECT* ON THE STREETS.

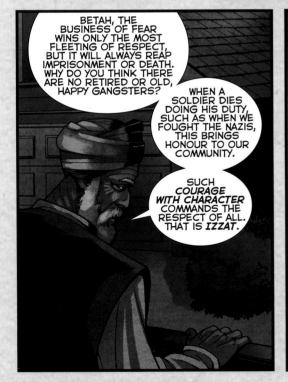

BETAH, THE BUSINESS OF FEAR WINS ONLY THE MOST FLEETING OF RESPECT, BUT IT WILL ALWAYS REAP IMPRISONMENT OR DEATH. WHY DO YOU THINK THERE ARE NO RETIRED OR OLD, HAPPY GANGSTERS?

WHEN A SOLDIER DIES DOING HIS DUTY, SUCH AS WHEN WE FOUGHT THE NAZIS, THIS BRINGS HONOUR TO OUR COMMUNITY.

SUCH *COURAGE WITH CHARACTER* COMMANDS THE RESPECT OF ALL. THAT IS *IZZAT*.

POPS, WW1 OR WW2 I'VE NEVER SEEN ANY STATUES TO ANY OF YOU HERE!

THAT IS TRUE. HOWEVER, COME WITH ME TO THE VETERANS ASSOCIATION TOMORROW. I SHALL SHOW YOU TRUE RESPECT. THE BONDS OF BROTHERHOOD, *THAT'S ALL THE RESPECT SOLDIERS NEED.*

I CAN SEE YOU ARE UNDER THE INFLUENCE. GO TO BED BEFORE YOUR FATHER WAKES TO CATCH YOU LIKE THIS.

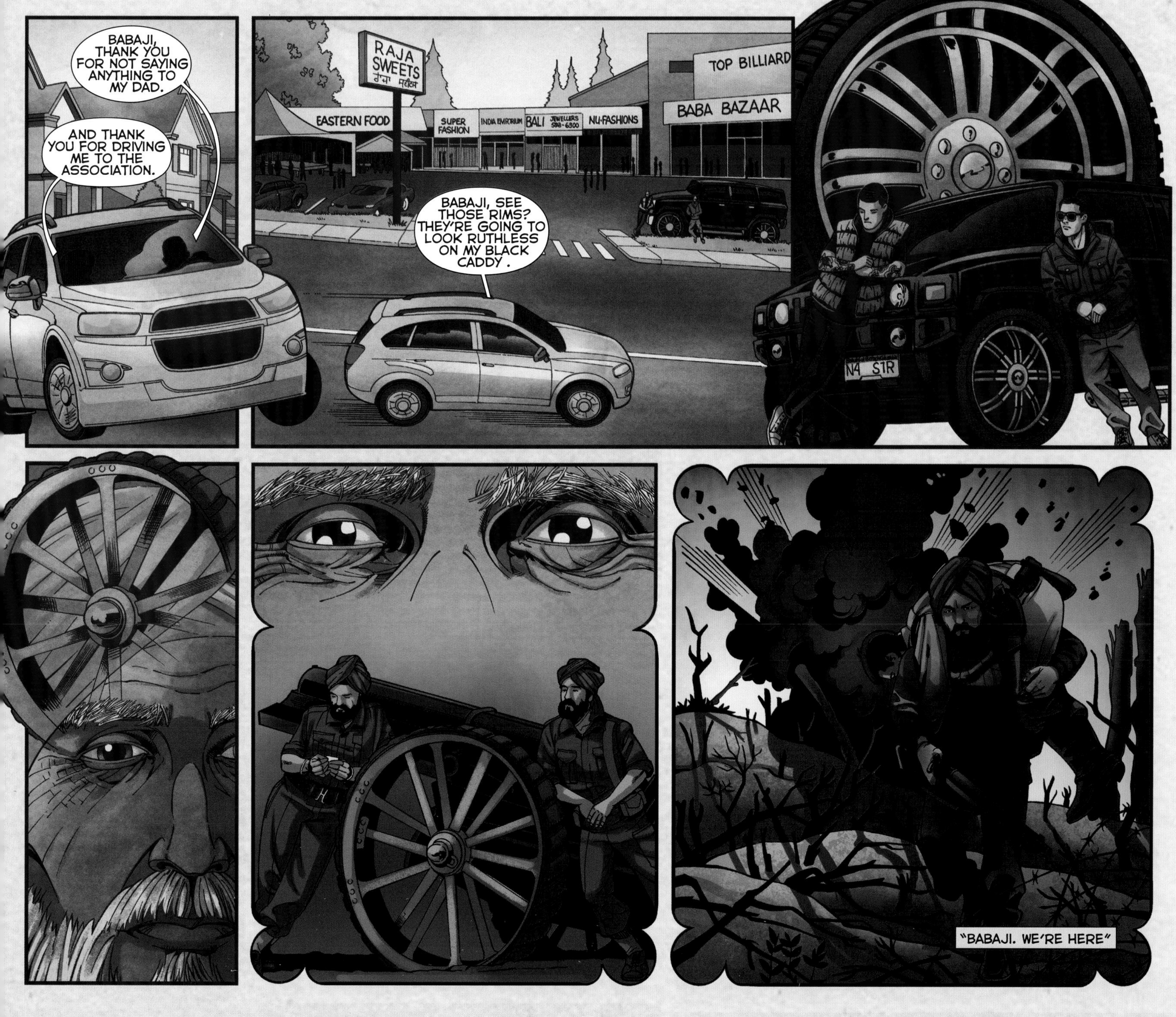
BABAJI, THANK YOU FOR NOT SAYING ANYTHING TO MY DAD.
AND THANK YOU FOR DRIVING ME TO THE ASSOCIATION.
RAJA SWEETS
EASTERN FOOD
SUPER FASHION
INDIA EMPORIUM
BALI JEWELLERS
NU-FASHIONS
TOP BILLIARD
BABA BAZAAR
BABAJI, SEE THOSE RIMS? THEY'RE GOING TO LOOK RUTHLESS ON MY BLACK CADDY.
"BABAJI. WE'RE HERE"

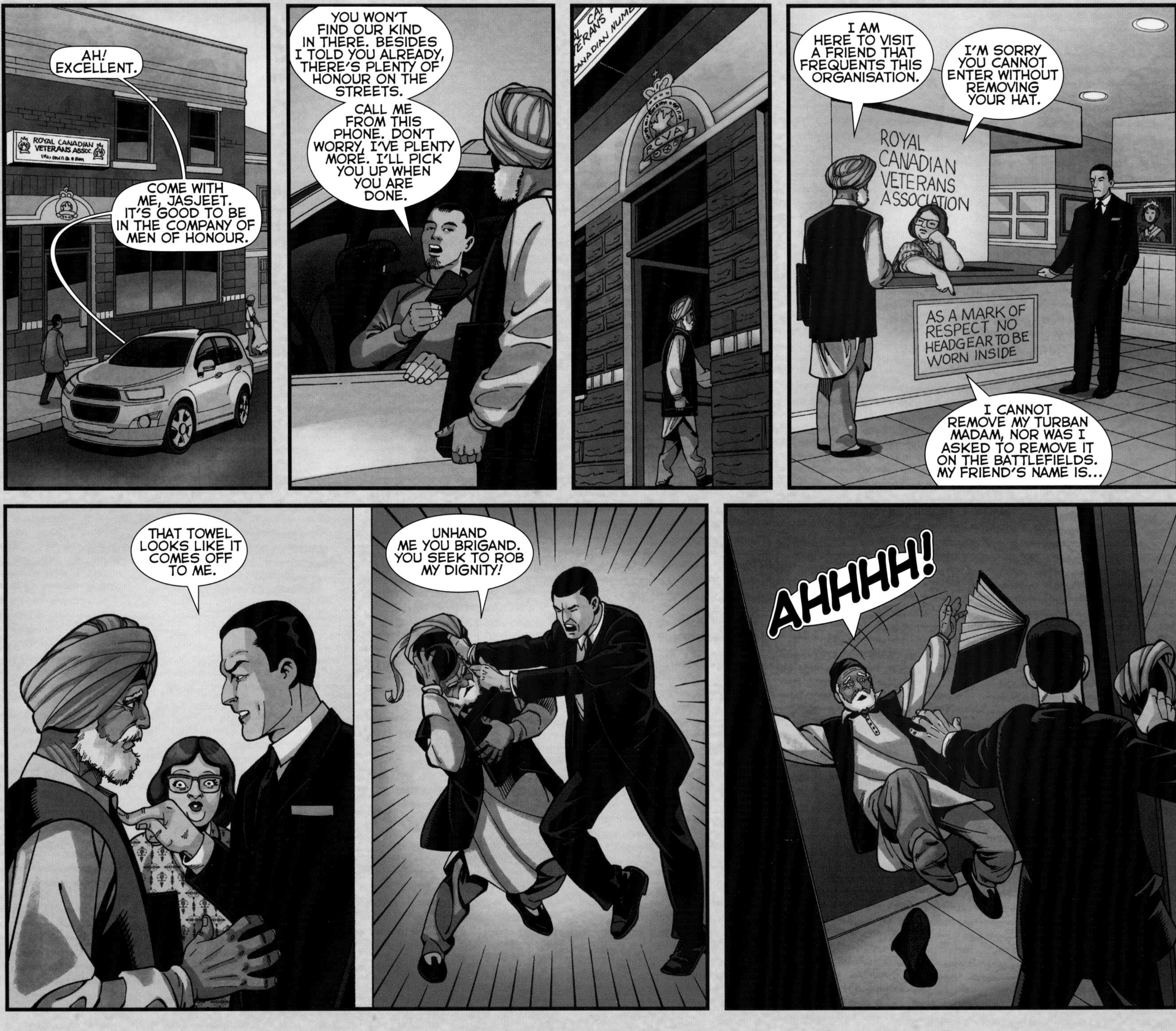

AH! EXCELLENT.
ROYAL CANADIAN VETERANS ASSOC.
COME WITH ME, JASJEET. IT'S GOOD TO BE IN THE COMPANY OF MEN OF HONOUR.
YOU WON'T FIND OUR KIND IN THERE. BESIDES I TOLD YOU ALREADY, THERE'S PLENTY OF HONOUR ON THE STREETS.
CALL ME FROM THIS PHONE. DON'T WORRY, I'VE PLENTY MORE. I'LL PICK YOU UP WHEN YOU ARE DONE.
RCVA
I AM HERE TO VISIT A FRIEND THAT FREQUENTS THIS ORGANISATION.
I'M SORRY YOU CANNOT ENTER WITHOUT REMOVING YOUR HAT.
ROYAL CANADIAN VETERANS ASSOCIATION
AS A MARK OF RESPECT NO HEADGEAR TO BE WORN INSIDE
I CANNOT REMOVE MY TURBAN MADAM, NOR WAS I ASKED TO REMOVE IT ON THE BATTLEFIELDS. MY FRIEND'S NAME IS...
THAT TOWEL LOOKS LIKE IT COMES OFF TO ME.
UNHAND ME YOU BRIGAND. YOU SEEK TO ROB MY DIGNITY!
AHHHH!

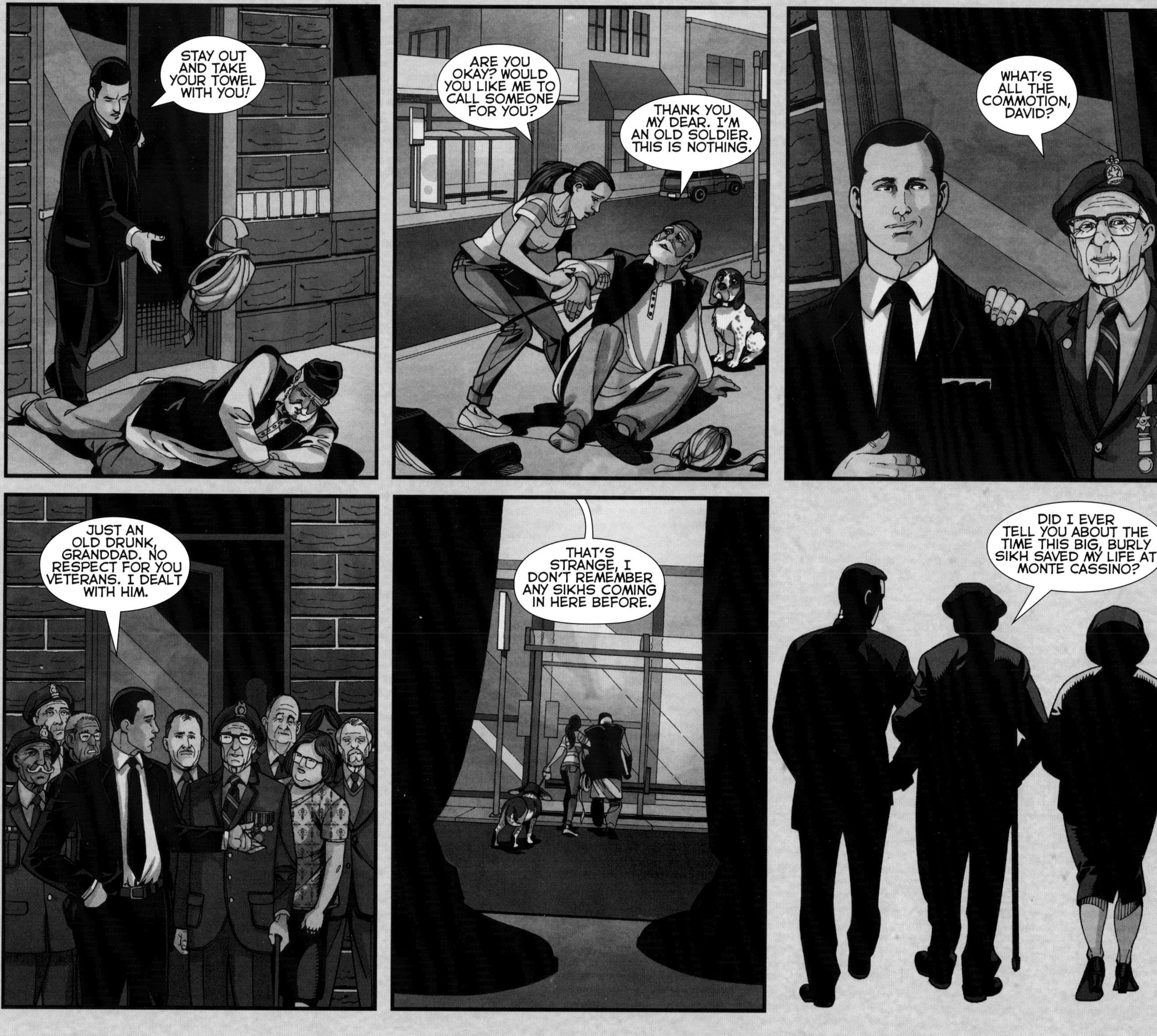
STAY OUT AND TAKE YOUR TOWEL WITH YOU!
ARE YOU OKAY? WOULD YOU LIKE ME TO CALL SOMEONE FOR YOU?
THANK YOU MY DEAR. I'M AN OLD SOLDIER. THIS IS NOTHING.
WHAT'S ALL THE COMMOTION, DAVID?
JUST AN OLD DRUNK, GRANDDAD. NO RESPECT FOR YOU VETERANS. I DEALT WITH HIM.
THAT'S STRANGE, I DON'T REMEMBER ANY SIKHS COMING IN HERE BEFORE.
DID I EVER TELL YOU ABOUT THE TIME THIS BIG, BURLY SIKH SAVED MY LIFE AT MONTE CASSINO?

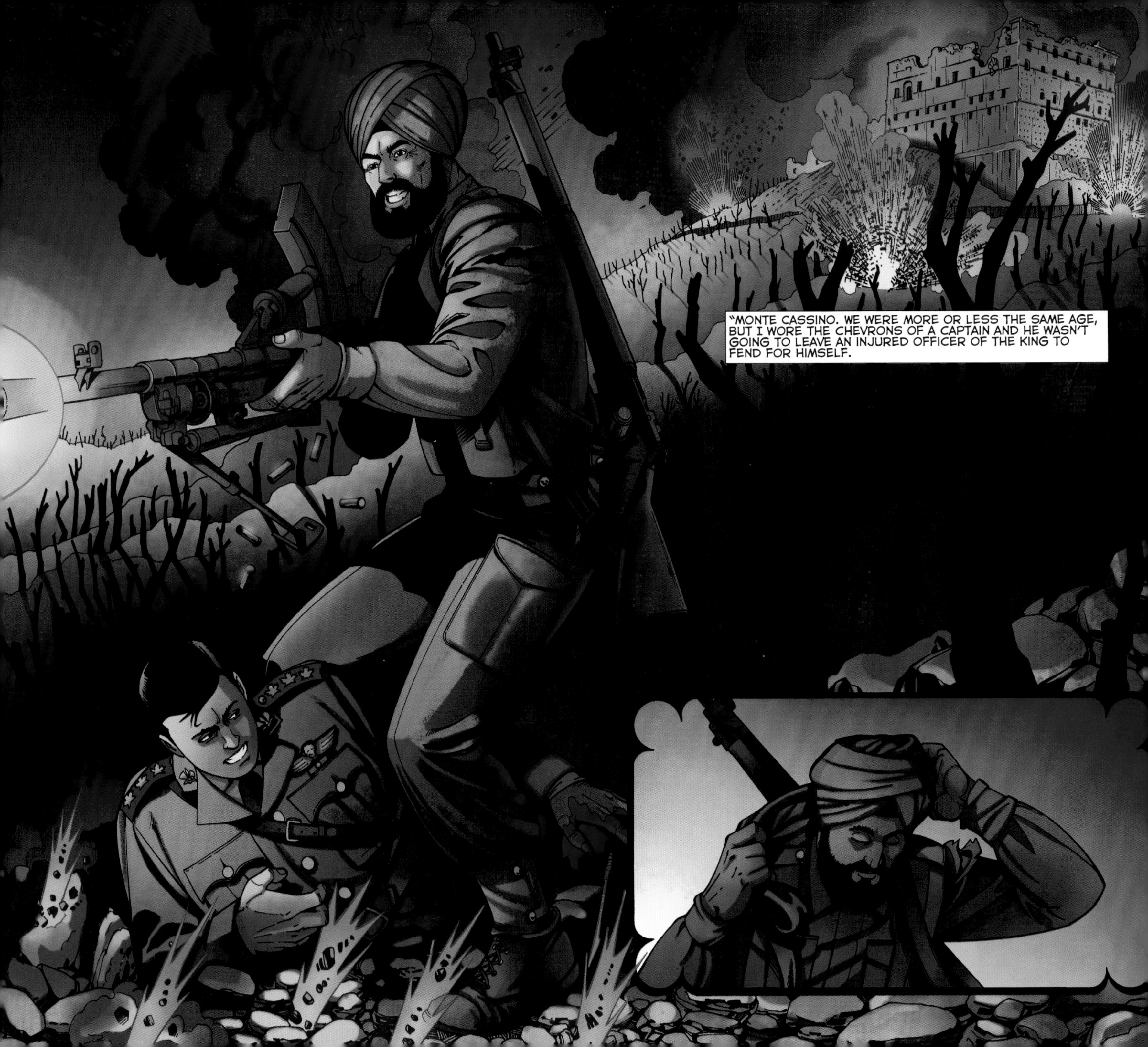
"MONTE CASSINO. WE WERE MORE OR LESS THE SAME AGE, BUT I WORE THE CHEVRONS OF A CAPTAIN AND HE WASN'T GOING TO LEAVE AN INJURED OFFICER OF THE KING TO FEND FOR HIMSELF.

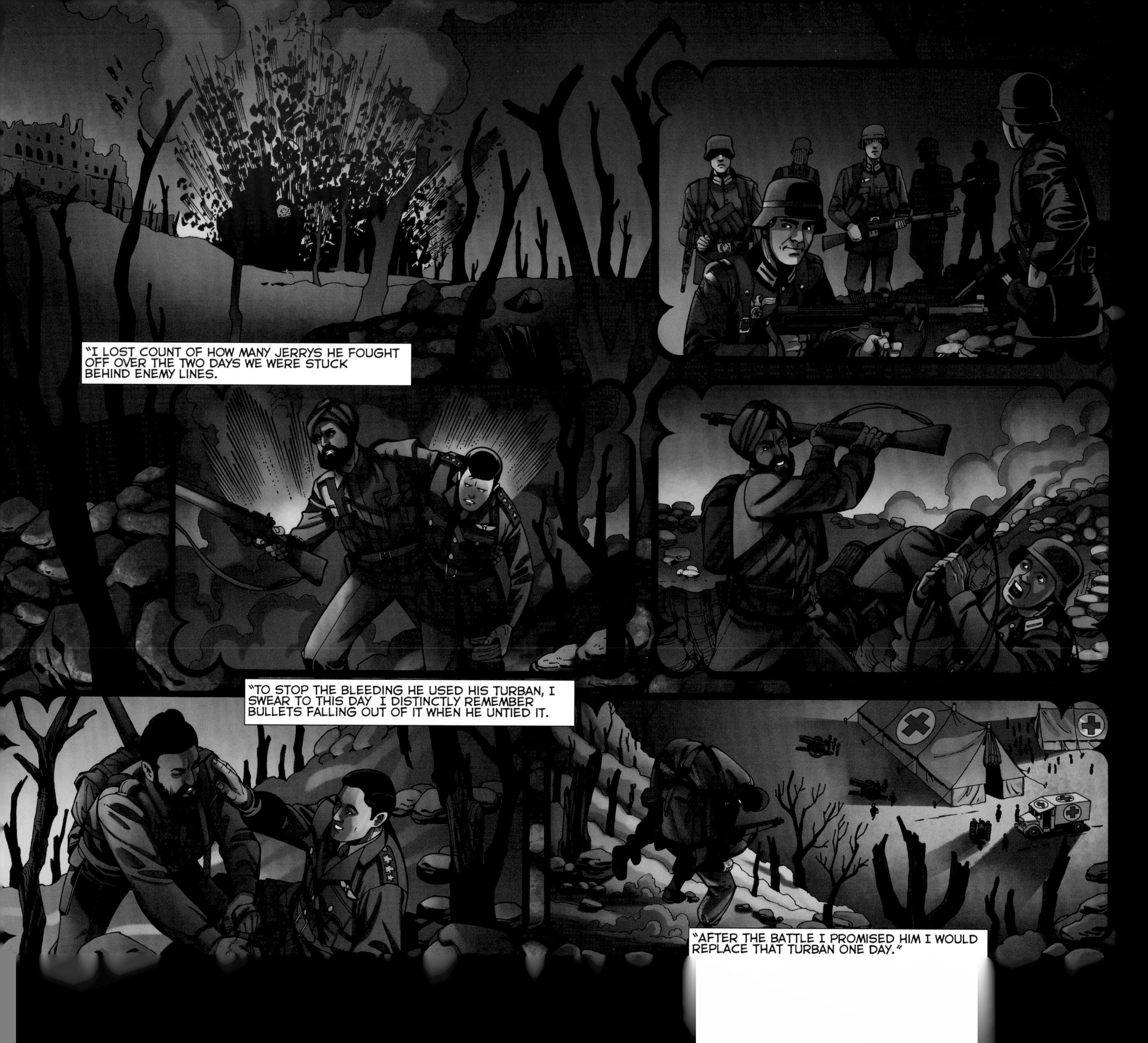
"I LOST COUNT OF HOW MANY JERRYS HE FOUGHT OFF OVER THE TWO DAYS WE WERE STUCK BEHIND ENEMY LINES.
"TO STOP THE BLEEDING HE USED HIS TURBAN, I SWEAR TO THIS DAY I DISTINCTLY REMEMBER BULLETS FALLING OUT OF IT WHEN HE UNTIED IT.
"AFTER THE BATTLE I PROMISED HIM I WOULD REPLACE THAT TURBAN ONE DAY."

WHEN I MOVED TO SURREY, YOU KNOW THE FIRST THING I BOUGHT WAS A TURBAN FOR HIM. THAT WAS 1980, IT'S AT HOME AWAITING HIM.

WE KEPT IN TOUCH FOR A WHILE AFTER THE WAR. HE TOLD ME HE HAD FAMILY HERE NOW AND I OFFERED TO LEAVE THE TURBAN WITH THEM.

HE SAID NONSENSE. I COULD GIVE IT TO HIM MYSELF WHEN HE CAME TO VISIT. IF I WAS 1/2 THE MAN HE WAS, I WOULD HAVE GONE OUT TO INDIA AND GIVEN THE TURBAN TO HIM THERE.

BUSINESS ALL DONE BABAJI?

MY FRIEND WAS NOT THERE. I DOUBT HE WOULD EVER FREQUENT THIS PLACE. I MUST HAVE GOT MY INFORMATION WRONG.

BABAJI, YOU DON'T LOOK SO GOOD. ARE YOU OKAY?

I'M AN OLD SOLDIER. YOU NEED NOT WORRY ABOUT ME. TELL ME ABOUT YOURSELF, I WANT TO KNOW EVERYTHING ABOUT MY GRANDDAUGHTER. HOW IS SCHOOL?

I LOVE MATH IT'S MY FAVOURITE SUBJECT, BUT I ALSO HAVE SOCIALS THIS SEMESTER. IT'S THE MOST BORING CLASS AND IT HAS THE MOST HOMEWORK.

I'VE GOT TO WRITE AN ESSAY ABOUT THE FIRST WORLD WAR TONIGHT, AND I DON'T KNOW WHERE TO START.

THE BEGINNING WOULD BE ADVISABLE, WHEN THE FIRST OF THE KINGS COLONIAL TROOPS LANDED IN FRANCE IN 1914. IT WAS A MOST EXTRAORDINARY SET OF CIRCUMSTANCES.

HOLD UP BABAJI. WE LEARNT THAT THE CANADIANS DIDN'T LAND THERE UNTIL 1915.

I WAS SPEAKING OF PUNJAB'S LAHORE DIVISION, THE DIVISION OUR FAMILY SERVED IN DURING THE WAR.

I DIDN'T EVEN KNOW THE INDIANS FOUGHT IN WW1. DID YOU FIGHT IN THE WAR? DAD TOLD ME WE HAD FAMILY IN THE ARMY BUT HE NEVER REALLY TALKED ABOUT THEM.

IT WAS MY FATHER, HARNAM SINGH, WHO FOUGHT IN THE FIRST WORLD WAR. I HAVE HIS SCRAPS IN MY BOOK. MY FATHER WAS SO PROUD OF BEING AN OFFICER.

THAT'S WHY I JOINED THE ARMY. SEE THE WORLD, GAIN RESPECT AND EARN AN HONEST LIVING.

LET ME FIND MY FATHER'S CHAPTER ON THE GREAT WAR.

BABAJI YOUR ENGLISH IS SO GOOD. DID YOU LEARN IT IN THE ARMY?

YES, BUT EVEN BEFORE OFFICER TRAINING, MY FATHER DRILLED ME IN THE LANGUAGE OF THE SIRKAR* AS A CHILD.

*BRITISH INDIAN GOVERNMENT

IT IS WAR!

August 4th

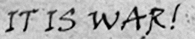

Aug 8th – Division ordered to mobilise destination unknown all ranks recalled – all rejoined

12th – Destination defined 'abroad' for Expeditionary Force 'A' speculation = Europe

18th – regiments entrained at Jullundur 23rd – King's message for all ranks

28th – board SS Akbar destination Suez Sept 13th – Joyous news destination now announced as France!

26th Landed! Splendid welcome by all inhabitants of franceville! 1st point of business H.V. Mark rifle rearmament - sighting & target practice to be obtained in the line –

"AH THE ARRIVAL IN MARSEILLE IN SEPTEMBER 1914. WHEN THE SOVEREIGN CALLED THE INDIAN ARMY ANSWERED!"

"I BET MANY OF THEM DIDN'T WANT TO GO TO FIGHT FOR THE BRITISH CROWN, BABAJI."

"IT WAS INDIA AND CANADA'S CROWN TOO, JASJEET. YES, THERE WAS A HUE AND CRY - MANY PEOPLE DIDN'T WANT US TO GO - BUT ANY MAN WORTH HIS SALT HAVING TAKEN THE KING'S SHILLING IN GOOD TIMES WAS NOW DUTY BOUND."

"AMONGST THESE RANKS OF MEN WERE REGIMENTS THAT TRACED THEIR BLOOD LINES BACK TO THE KHALSA ARMY DISBANDED AT THE END OF THE ANGLO-SIKH WARS. FOR THEM AND MY FATHER'S NEWLY RAISED *PALTAN, TO FIGHT IN EUROPE ON THE WORLD'S GRANDEST STAGE WOULD BE A BATTLE HONOUR SECOND TO NONE, THE RAPTUROUS WELCOME BY THE LOCALS SOON DROWNED OUT THE VOICES OF DISSENT."

*REGIMENT

27th encamp at Boreli 30th –
entrained for place of assembly for the
India Corps Oct 18th - left Orleans for
the front.

Early arrival of Division anxiously
awaited by Headquarters - arrived
With Manta's regiment 15th
Ludhianas others with us in
Jullundur Brigade 59th Scinde Rifles
(FF) / Manchester Regiment (Angrezis)

23rd – welcomed by the enemy
24th - 47th companies despatched to
La Bassee and Neuve Chapelle
Ferozepor dispatched north
into Belgium

"BUT THERE WAS LITTLE TIME TO ENJOY THE FESTIVITIES. THEY WERE IMMEDIATELY TRANSPORTED TO NORTHERN FRANCE WHERE THE SITUATION IN THE BRITISH SECTOR WAS MOST GRAVE. THEY ARRIVED TO FIND 4/5THS OF THE BRITISH FORCE HAD ALREADY BEEN LOST AND THE GERMANS WERE ADVANCING ON THE LIFELINE OF THE CHANNEL PORTS - THEY WERE GOING IN FOR THE KILL.

TO TURN BACK THE INVADER, A BATTALION OF YOUR BABAJI'S REGIMENT WAS COMMANDED TO RECAPTURE A STRATEGIC VILLAGE IN SOUTH FLANDERS CRITICAL TO THE DEFENCE OF VERY IMPORTANT TRANSPORTATION ROUTES."

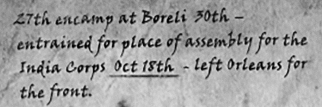

EXCELSIOR
Journal Illustré Quotidien

Trois types de nos alliés

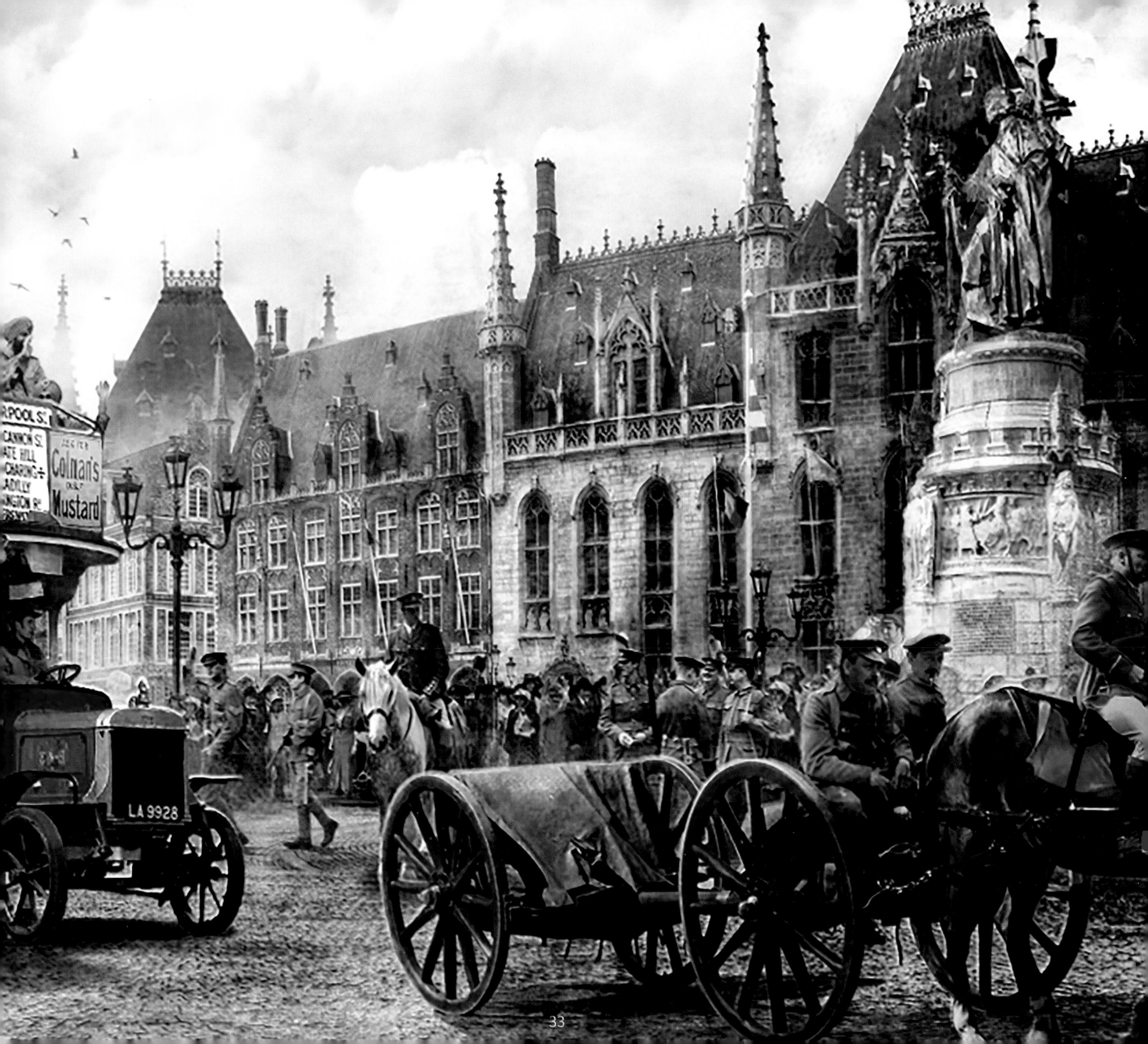
CANNON St.
Colman's
Mustard
LA 9928

Subedar Thakur Singh was among the
first of all the King's officers to receive
the Military Cross - for gallantry on
October 27 at Neuve Chapelle

created December 1914 for exemplary
gallantry during active operations
against the enemy.

Military Cross

Mons Star

Awarded to British and Indian
Expeditionary Forces in action in
France or Belgium between 5
August and close of the First
Battle of Ypres 22 November 191

The Sydney Mail, November 4, 1914

The Dashing Indians.

An eye-witness relates an incident which took place at La Bassee. The Germans had heavily shelled the British trenches, also a line of miners' cottages running to the northwards. There was nothing to indicate their intention to rush any particular point, though aviators reported that they were massing several brigades behind artillery in different positions. Suddenly an avalanche of men was let loose. The section line of British infantry outwinged the enemy rank after rank, but the rush was irresistible. The British defenders held their ground to the last. Reinforcements were hurried up, but before they could repair the broken line further hordes of Germans appeared. For a while the situation was dangerous. The Germans were confident that at last they had found a way to the coast, but were rudely deceived. The Indian troops were supporting the British. This was the first time they had been in action. For days they had been watching bursting shrapnel, and thirsting to prove their quality. Now they were ordered to move forward with the bayonet. The forces met and clashed. In an instant the issue was decided. The German advance was not merely checked; it was beaten and broken. The Indians ran through them, pushing the foe back to receive, right and left, the fire of the British infantry. The Indians were not content with recapturing the trench, but leaping from it they pursued the Germans downhill until the officers recalled them. A staff officer estimated that 20,000 dead and wounded Germans were left on the field at La Bassee, while the British losses did not exceed 2000.

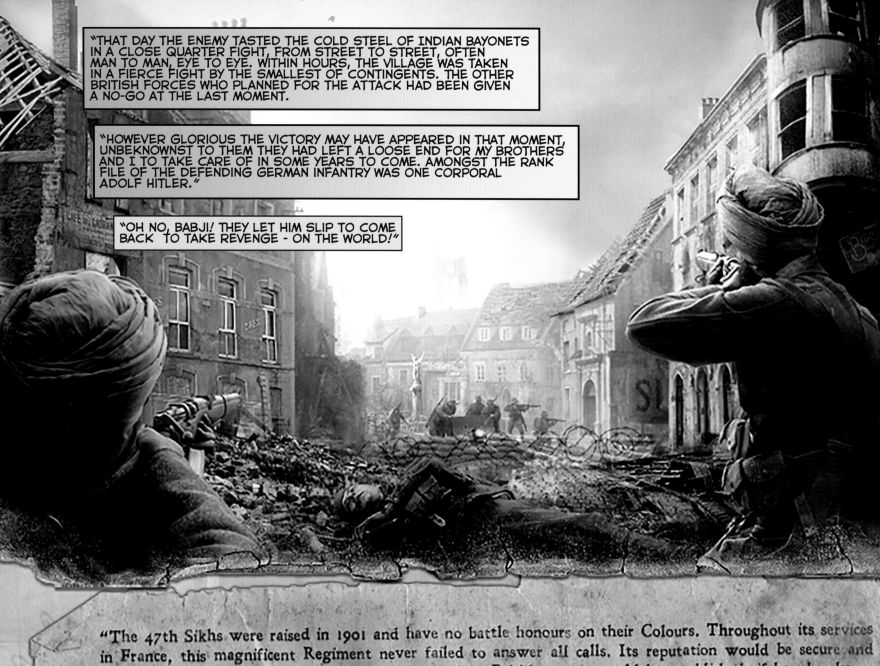

"THAT DAY THE ENEMY TASTED THE COLD STEEL OF INDIAN BAYONETS IN A CLOSE QUARTER FIGHT, FROM STREET TO STREET, OFTEN MAN TO MAN, EYE TO EYE. WITHIN HOURS, THE VILLAGE WAS TAKEN IN A FIERCE FIGHT BY THE SMALLEST OF CONTINGENTS. THE OTHER BRITISH FORCES WHO PLANNED FOR THE ATTACK HAD BEEN GIVEN A NO-GO AT THE LAST MOMENT.

"HOWEVER GLORIOUS THE VICTORY MAY HAVE APPEARED IN THAT MOMENT, UNBEKNOWNST TO THEM THEY HAD LEFT A LOOSE END FOR MY BROTHERS AND I TO TAKE CARE OF IN SOME YEARS TO COME. AMONGST THE RANK FILE OF THE DEFENDING GERMAN INFANTRY WAS ONE CORPORAL ADOLF HITLER."

"OH NO, BABJI! THEY LET HIM SLIP TO COME BACK TO TAKE REVENGE - ON THE WORLD!"

"The 47th Sikhs were raised in 1901 and have no battle honours on their Colours. Throughout its services in France, this magnificent Regiment never failed to answer all calls. Its reputation would be secure and its right to fight shoulder to shoulder with our best British troops would be established, if based only on the record of Neuve Chapelle, but this action was only one of many in which the 47th distinguished themselves. The history of Indian Army contains few nobler pages that that of the 28th October 1914.

W.B. Merewether Official Historian of the Indian Corps in France

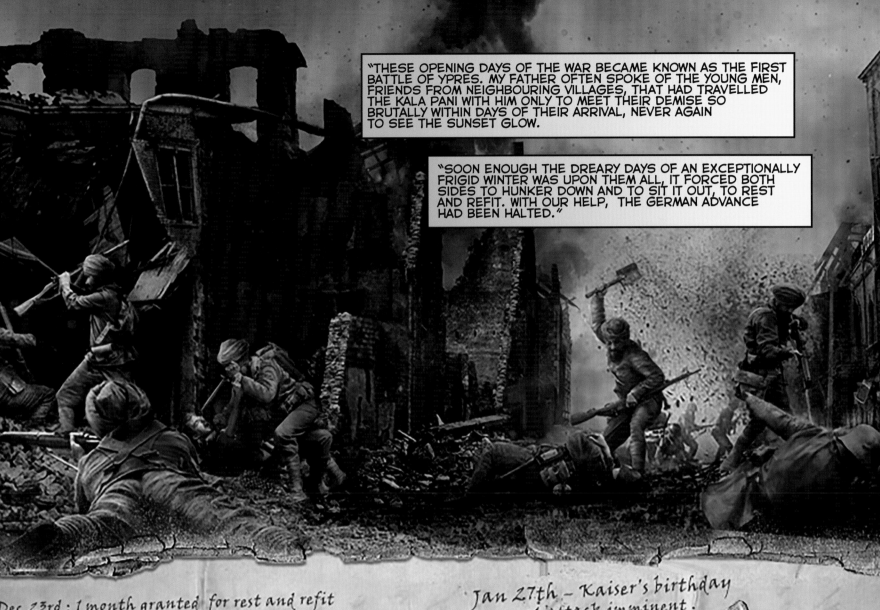

"THESE OPENING DAYS OF THE WAR BECAME KNOWN AS THE FIRST BATTLE OF YPRES. MY FATHER OFTEN SPOKE OF THE YOUNG MEN, FRIENDS FROM NEIGHBOURING VILLAGES, THAT HAD TRAVELLED THE KALA PANI WITH HIM ONLY TO MEET THEIR DEMISE SO BRUTALLY WITHIN DAYS OF THEIR ARRIVAL, NEVER AGAIN TO SEE THE SUNSET GLOW.

"SOON ENOUGH THE DREARY DAYS OF AN EXCEPTIONALLY FRIGID WINTER WAS UPON THEM ALL, IT FORCED BOTH SIDES TO HUNKER DOWN AND TO SIT IT OUT, TO REST AND REFIT. WITH OUR HELP, THE GERMAN ADVANCE HAD BEEN HALTED."

Dec 23rd : 1 month granted for rest and refit
Dec 25th: Christmas day is quiet
Dec 26th: Reservists from four ink battalions 35/36th Sikhs arrive under Jemadar Waryam Singh from our depot in India
Jan 16th: We start for our frontline barracks at LACOUTURE front is quiet because of inclement weather – heavy rains country is waterlogged and trenches full of ice cold water – no trench boots yet - White 'nightshirts' issued for snow camo on the 1st line

Jan 27th – Kaiser's birthday general attack imminent.

... Damn the mud, clogging up the rifles !

37

Feb - holding the line from Givenchy to Neuve Chapelle. Only 335 originals now present.

New draft of 83 men of the 87th Punjabis received & trained: trench warfare, bombing, mortars, rifles grenades, assault, clearing and occupation of enemy trenches - Mar 7th training complete

March 8th - newly trained Canadian colonials arrive - attached to British 1st Army

Mar 9th a sahib suggests the day is coming when we should return to the East.

Mar 10/11 we give the naysayers a glorious reply - our 'replacements' are given duties more befitting their position.

of the S........ ...s or No. 3454

"For the first time the British Army has broken the German Line and struck the Germans a blow which they will remember to the end of their lives. It is the revelation of the fact that the much-vaunted German army-machine on which the whole attention of mighty nation has been lavished for four decades is not invincible."

The Times 19 April 1915

Read this London!

"ONCE WINTER RELEASED ITS GRIP, THE BRITISH ATTACKED FIRST. THEY TOOK THE FIGHT BACK TO NEUVE CHAPELLE, WHERE THE INDIAN CORPS, MORE THAN 1/2 OF THE BRITISH FORCE IN THIS BATTLE, ONCE AGAIN PROVED ITS METTLE BY BREAKING THE GERMAN LINE WITHIN AN HOUR. IT APPEARED THE LONG AWAITED DAY OF RECKONING FOR THE HUN HAD ARRIVED.

"DURING FIRESIDE TALKS AFTER THE WAR MY FATHER OFTEN REVELLED IN HOW THESE GRAND OLD SOLDIERS HAD ONCE REPELLED A COUNTER ATTACK BY GERMANS LED BY OFFICERS ON HORSEBACK. THE MEN WERE DELIGHTED WITH THE UNUSUALLY FINE TARGETS OFFERED BY DENSE MASSES OF THE ENEMY IN SUCH CLOSE ORDER.

"BUT THIS BANQUET TOO WAS CUT SHORT. A DEARTH OF BRITISH ARTILLERY SHELLS STALLED OUR ADVANCE. THE SHORTAGE HELPED BRING DOWN THE GOVERNMENT IN VILAYET*."

*BRITAIN

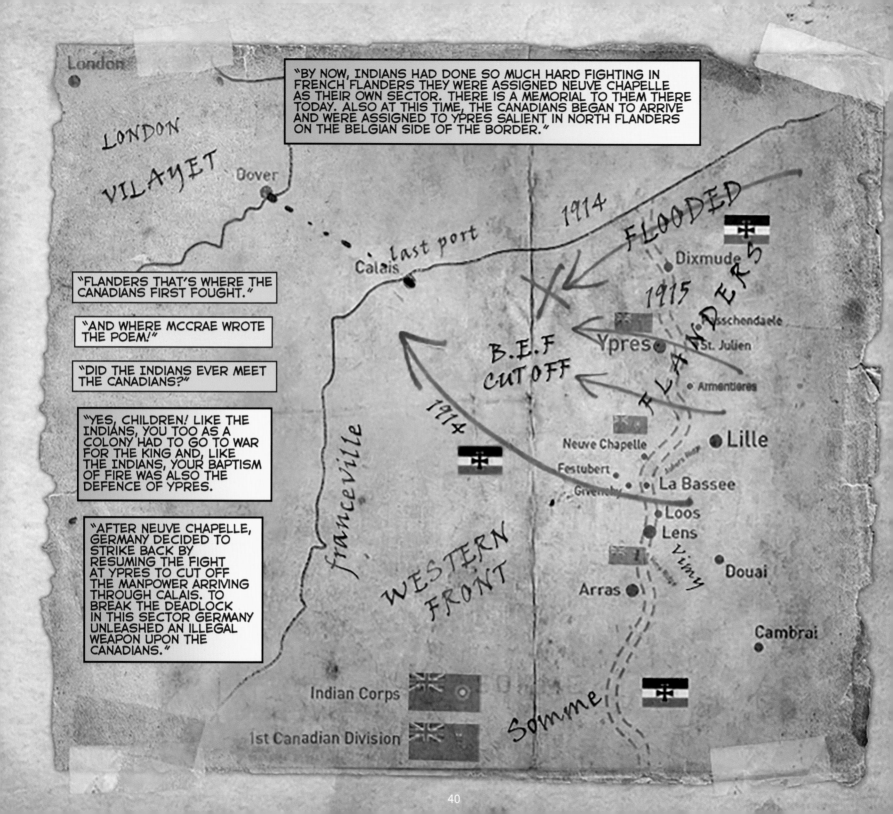

"BY NOW, INDIANS HAD DONE SO MUCH HARD FIGHTING IN FRENCH FLANDERS THEY WERE ASSIGNED NEUVE CHAPELLE AS THEIR OWN SECTOR. THERE IS A MEMORIAL TO THEM THERE TODAY. ALSO AT THIS TIME, THE CANADIANS BEGAN TO ARRIVE AND WERE ASSIGNED TO YPRES SALIENT IN NORTH FLANDERS ON THE BELGIAN SIDE OF THE BORDER."

"FLANDERS THAT'S WHERE THE CANADIANS FIRST FOUGHT."

"AND WHERE MCCRAE WROTE THE POEM!"

"DID THE INDIANS EVER MEET THE CANADIANS?"

"YES, CHILDREN! LIKE THE INDIANS, YOU TOO AS A COLONY HAD TO GO TO WAR FOR THE KING AND, LIKE THE INDIANS, YOUR BAPTISM OF FIRE WAS ALSO THE DEFENCE OF YPRES.

"AFTER NEUVE CHAPELLE, GERMANY DECIDED TO STRIKE BACK BY RESUMING THE FIGHT AT YPRES TO CUT OFF THE MANPOWER ARRIVING THROUGH CALAIS. TO BREAK THE DEADLOCK IN THIS SECTOR GERMANY UNLEASHED AN ILLEGAL WEAPON UPON THE CANADIANS."

London

LONDON

VILAYET

Dover

Calais   last port

1914   FLOODED

Dixmude

1915

Passchendaele

B.E.F   Ypres   St. Julien

CUT OFF

FLANDERS

Armentieres

1914

Neuve Chapelle   Lille

Festubert   Aubers Ridge

franceville   Givenchy   La Bassee

WESTERN   Loos

FRONT   Lens   Vimy   Douai

Arras

Cambrai

Somme

Indian Corps

1st Canadian Division

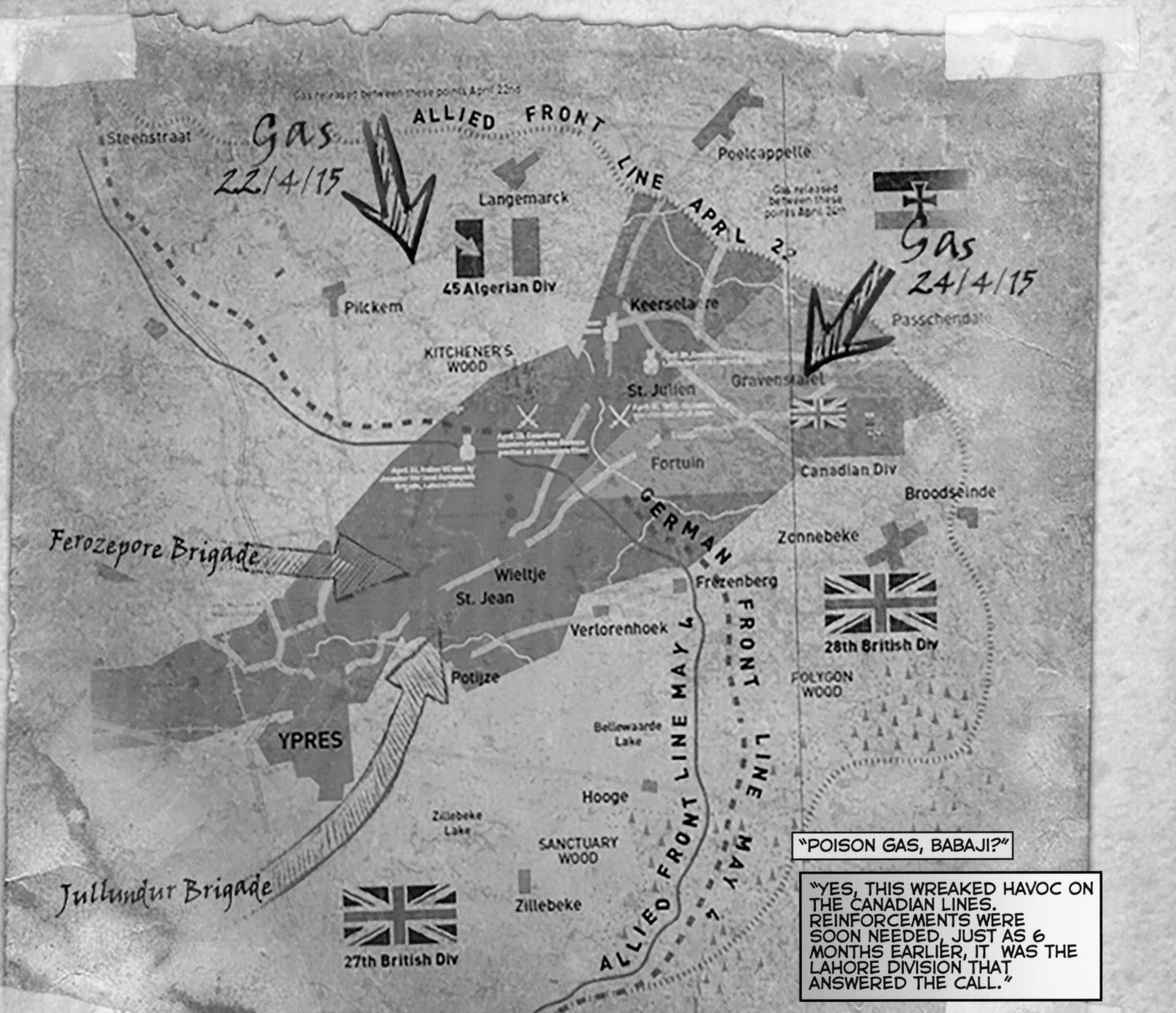
Gas released between these points April 22nd
Steenstraat
Gas 22/4/15
ALLIED FRONT LINE APRIL 22
Poelcappelle
Langemarck
Gas released between these points April 24th
Gas 24/4/15
45 Algerian Div
Pilckem
Keerselaere
Passchendale
KITCHENER'S WOOD
St. Julien
Gravenstafel
Fortuin
Canadian Div
Broodseinde
GERMAN FRONT LINE MAY 4
Zonnebeke
Ferozepore Brigade
Wieltje
Frezenberg
St. Jean
Verlorenhoek
28th British Div
Potijze
POLYGON WOOD
YPRES
Bellewaarde Lake
ALLIED FRONT LINE MAY 4
Hooge
Zillebeke Lake
SANCTUARY WOOD
Zillebeke
Jullundur Brigade
27th British Div
"POISON GAS, BABAJI?"
"YES, THIS WREAKED HAVOC ON THE CANADIAN LINES. REINFORCEMENTS WERE SOON NEEDED, JUST AS 6 MONTHS EARLIER, IT WAS THE LAHORE DIVISION THAT ANSWERED THE CALL."

Our 1st Visit to Ypres 1914
Reason: to Honour the Sirkar's
obligation to defend Belgian liberty
& life - cost: 9,000 Indian casualties

The Rape of Belgium!

<u>Duty calls</u>
The Hun has shot civilian hostages
and pillaged scores of towns across
Belgium - refugees to:
Holland 700,000 France 200,000
Britain 100,000

"THE 35 MILE MARCH FROM THEIR SECTOR TO YPRES WAS HARD GOING. RAIN HAD MADE THE COBBLED ROADS TREACHEROUSLY SLIPPERY. MARCHING CONDITIONS WERE AT THEIR WORST.

"THE OVERHEAD WHISTLES AND SCREAMS OF A CONTINUOUS BARRAGE OF 42CM SHELLS TURNED INTO DISTANT THUNDER UPON FINDING THEIR MARK AMIDST THE TOWERS AND SPIRES OF THE LAST REMAINING FREE TOWN OF THE BELGIANS, REDUCING IT TO RUINS."

FRIENDS IN NEED, ARE FRIENDS INDEED.

"THE MARCH, ALTHOUGH BECOMING SLOW MOVING, AS IT WOUND THROUGH AN EXODUS OF REFUGEES, PERMITTED NO REST. LIKE THE CANADIANS, THE INDIANS HAD LEFT DISTANT SHORES FOR THE DEFENCE OF THIS DEVASTATED NATION'S LIBERTY.

"IT WAS TIME TO STEP INTO THE BREACH ONCE MORE..."

"WHEN THEY ARRIVED THEY FOUND THE RANKS OF THE CANADIANS SHATTERED BY 4 DAYS OF HARD FIGHTING. THEY HAD LOST 1/2 OF THEIR NUMBER. THEN THEY WERE GREETED WITH THE NEWS THE HUN HAD POSSESSED ST. JULIEN AND WAS READYING TO MAKE THE FINAL ATTACK ON YPRES ITSELF. THE NEW CANADIAN DIVISION HAD MADE YOUR YOUNG COUNTRY PROUD. THEY HAD FOUGHT BRAVELY WITHOUT RESPITE TO HOLD THE LINE.

"SURPASSING THE MEAGRE EXPECTATIONS OF BRITISH COMMAND THEY HAD EVEN COUNTER ATTACKED THE ENEMY TO STEM THE ADVANCE AND BUY TIME FOR REINFORCEMENTS."

The Butcher's Bill April 22-25 1915 more than 6,000 Canadian casualties

British Colonial Flags.

Ensign.   CANADA.   Jack.

THREE CHEERS FOR CANADA!

Casualties, &c.   Rank

"OH CANADA!"

"YES, KIRAN. BUT, THEY HAD SUFFERED TOO GREAT AN INJURY TO CONTINUE, SO THEY HANDED THE TORCH TO THE INDIANS. ANY DIFFERENCES OVER THE TREATMENT OF PUNJABIS IN CANADA WAS PUT ASIDE. PUNJAB'S MEN OF HONOUR COULD NOT BREAK FAITH WITH THEIR BROTHERS-IN-ARMS."

British
Colonial Flags.

Ensign.   INDIA.   Jack.

INDIA ALL HAIL!

April 26 - May 1st
Lahore Division losses :
133 British officers
+ 64 Indian officers + 1620 British
and 2070 Indian other ranks casualties,
30% of our infantry strength engaged

45

Valour's reward

1911 Indian Order of Merit
1st class becomes Victoria Cross

Indian Order
of Merit
2nd Class
(Silver)

Indian Order of Merit
Jemadar Sucha Singh 47th Sikhs

On April 26th, 1915 during the 2nd battle of Ypres, Sucha Singh took command of his company when all the British Officers were killed or wounded.

Sucha Singh was a native of Lahore.

Indian Order of Merit
Jemadar Mangal Singh 57th Wilde's Rifles (Punjab Frontier Force)

Mangal Singh received his award for gallantry during the 2nd Battle of Ypres, on 26th April 1915:

"On recovering consciousness after being gassed, in spite of intense suffering, he went out time after time and helped to bring in the wounded under fire".

Mangal Singh was a native of Amritsar

Foreign Service, see Sec.
XIX., para. 142, Regulations, 1881.

"WITHOUT ANY REST, PAPAJI'S BRIGADE WAS HURLED INTO A COUNTERATTACK TO TAKE BACK THE LOST GROUND. OPENING THE ATTACK, THE JALANDAR AND FEROZEPOR BRIGADES, PARADED SIDE BY SIDE ONTO GROUND STREWN WITH THE BLOATED BODIES OF CANADIANS. IN THE HELLSCAPE THAT UNFURLED BEFORE THEM, SINISTER FUMES WAITED TO EMBRACE THEIR SORELY TIRED BODIES."

Army F
3 4

Jemadar Mir Dast, I.O.M., 55th Coke's Rifles Punjab Frontier Force, attached 57th Wilde's Rifles Punjab Frontier Force

For most conspicuous bravery and great ability at Ypres on 26th April, 1915, when he led his platoon with great gallantry during the attack, and afterwards collected various, parties of the regiment (when no British) Officers were left and kept them under his command until the retirement was ordered. Jemadar Mir Dast subsequently on this day displayed remarkable courage in helping, to carry eight British and Indian Officers into safety, whilst exposed to very heavy fire.

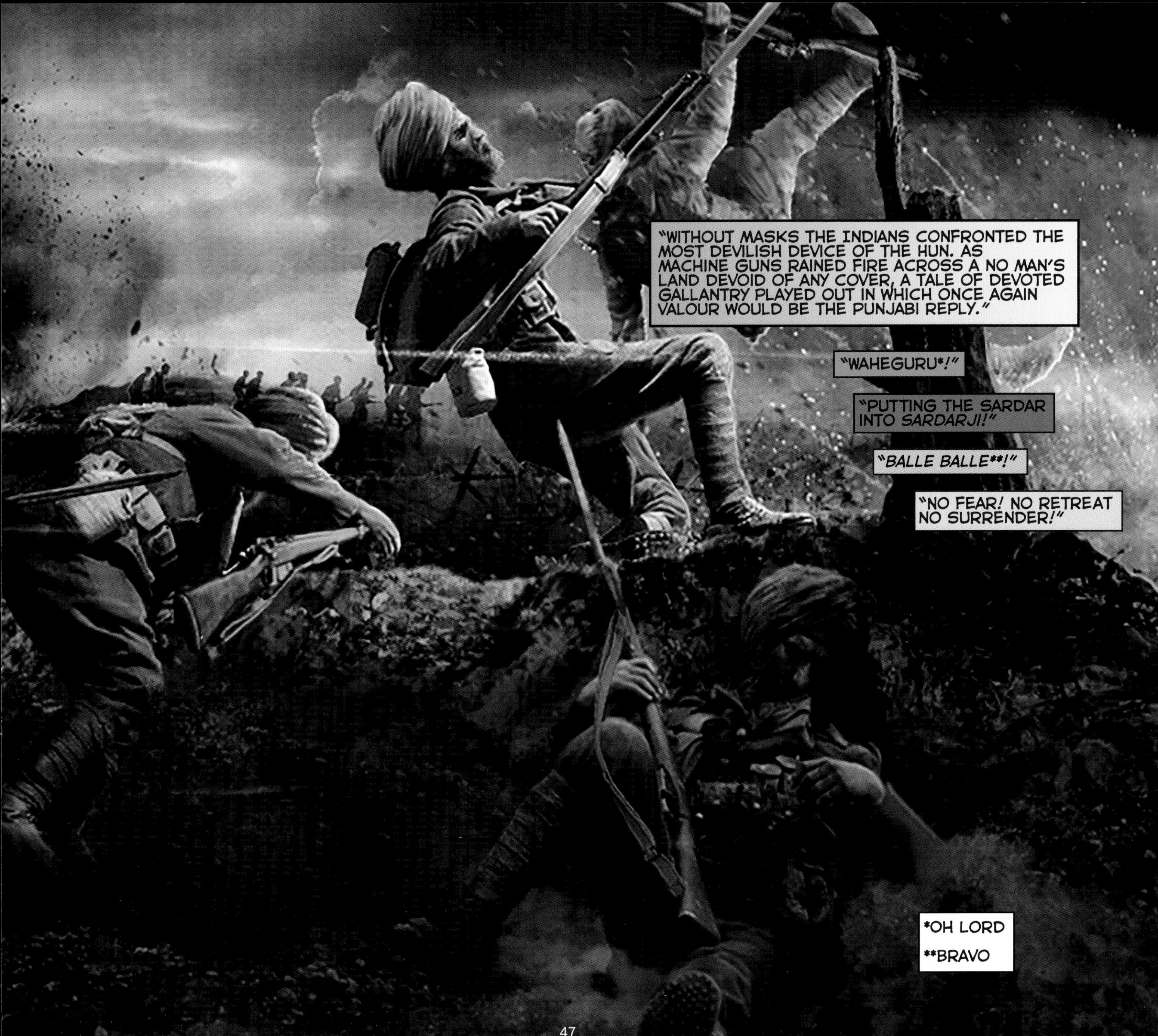
"WITHOUT MASKS THE INDIANS CONFRONTED THE MOST DEVILISH DEVICE OF THE HUN. AS MACHINE GUNS RAINED FIRE ACROSS A NO MAN'S LAND DEVOID OF ANY COVER, A TALE OF DEVOTED GALLANTRY PLAYED OUT IN WHICH ONCE AGAIN VALOUR WOULD BE THE PUNJABI REPLY."
"WAHEGURU*!"
"PUTTING THE SARDAR INTO *SARDARJI!*"
"*BALLE BALLE***!"
"NO FEAR! NO RETREAT NO SURRENDER!"
*OH LORD
**BRAVO

"ALAS, THE MARCH WAS DOOMED FROM THE START. ROW UPON ROW OF MEN FELL IN AN ILL PREPARED ATTACK AGAINST A WELL POSITIONED AND NUMERICALLY SUPERIOR ENEMY. OVER 1,000 CASUALTIES WERE SUFFERED BY THE LEADING THREE BATTALIONS. THE JULLUNDUR BRIGADE, PAPAJI'S REGIMENT, LOST 4/5 OF THEIR MEN."

"... insufficient Artillery preparation, on our side, and an open, glacis —like slope to advance over in the face of over-whelming shell, rifle, and machine—gun fire, and the employment of poisonous gasses by the enemy, and that in spite of these disadvantages, the troops, although only partially successful in wrenching ground from the enemy, effectually prevented his further advance, and thus ensured the safety of Ypres."

General Sir Horace Smith—Dorrien, Commander British Second Army at 2nd Ypres

Donkeys leading lions
Smith-Dorrien
- General relieved of command after
April 26th attack!

"AS THE ATTACK OF THE LAHORE DIVISION UNFOLDED, THE INDIANS, ALONG WITH ACCOMPANYING BRITISH REGIMENTS, SUSTAINED OVER 4,000 CASUALTIES ON A FRONT OF LITTLE MORE THAN A MILE. MEN FROM ALL OVER THE PUNJAB LAY IN CRUMBLED HEAPS ACROSS THE CRIMSON FIELDS OF FLANDERS. EUROPEAN LIBERTY WOULD NOT BE CHEAP."

Gefecht mit Indern.

BEWARE!

Chlorine and phosgene gases attack the lungs / mustard gas attacks sensitive skin - eyes, armpits, and groin causing searing blisters and horrific pain. Designed to terrify and kill - made illegal by 1899 Hague Convention

War Crime!

AMBALA: BAKHTAWAR SINGH,31ST PUNJABIS,SEPOY,4074,47TH SIKHS, OF SOHALI, KHARAR, DEYA SINGH,15TH LUDHIANA SIKHS,SEPOY,510, SON OF UMR SINGH, OF TAPPARIAN, KUPAR, INDAR SINGH,47TH SIKHS,SEPOY,1637, SON OF GOPAL SINGH, OF PANJOKHRA. JAHANGIR KHAN,18TH INDIAN INFANTRY,HAVILDAR,1182, SON OF HAKIM ALI KHAN, OF BHABNARAH, ROPAR. KARTAR SINGH,14TH KING GEORGE'S OWN FEROZEPORE SIKHS, SEPOY,4589,15TH LUDHIANA SIKHS, SON OF CHATTAR SINGH, OF RAIPUR, KHARAR, MUNSHI KHAN,18TH INDIAN INFANTRY,HAVILDAR,1260, SON OF IMAMUDDIN KHAN, OF BAIRAKH, KHARAR, NIZAMDIN KHAN,18TH INDIAN INFANTRY,SEPOY,1855, SON OF GULAB KHAN, OF KEKAVT, ROPAR, AMRITSAR: BADHAWA SINGH,QUEEN VICTORIA'S OWN CORPS OF GUIDES INFANTRY JEMADAR, 57TH WILDE'S RIFLES, SON OF GURMUKH SINGH, OF PANDORI RANSI, TARN TARAN.BELA SINGH, 57TH WILDE'S RIFLES,SEPOY,2507, SON OF ATAR SINGH, OF RAYA KHURD. BHAGAT SINGH,QUEEN VICTORIA'S OWN CORPS OF GUIDES INFANTRY, SEPOY, 5140,57TH WILDE'S RIFLES, SON OF HAKIM SINGH, OF GALA PANDORI, TARN TARAN. FATEH SINGH,QUEEN VICTORIA'S OWN CORPS OF GUIDES INFANTRY, SEPOY, 257,57TH WILDE'S RIFLES, SON OF SUDH SINGH, OF LALPUR, TARN TARAN. HARNAM SINGH,47TH SIKHS,SEPOY,1896, SON OF JAGAT SINGH, OF KASEL, TARN TARAN. JAGAT SINGH,57TH WILDE'S RIFLES, SEPOY,3284, SON OF HAKIM SINGH, OF ADHIWALA, AGNALA. JANMEJA SINGH,57TH WILDE'S RIFLES, HAVILDAR, 2397, SON OF KATHA SINGH, OF CHUBAL, TARN TARAN. SHAM SINGH,35TH SIKHS, NAIK, 1623,47TH SIKHS, SON OF CHET SINGH, OF KHUTRA, AJNALA. SOHAN SINGH,47TH SIKHS,HAVILDAR,606, SON OF PANJAB SINGH, OF MAKHOWAL, AJNALA. SURAIN SINGH,47TH SIKHS, HAVILDAR,1648, SON OF LEHNA SINGH, OF KALA, TARN TARAN. OF MUHAMMAD KHAN, OF TRAP, TALAGANG, CAMPBELLPUR, KHAN ZAMAN,57TH WILDE'S,SEPOY,,, SON OF MIAN MUHAMMAD, OF DHERMOND, TALAGANG, CAMPBELLPUR, KIRPA SINGH,57TH WILDE'S RIFLES, JEMADAR, OF BANGOLI, HARIPUR, CAMPBELLPUR, FIROZPUR: JAIMAL SINGH,35TH SIKHS,SEPOY,3389,47TH SIKHS, SON OF NANAK SINGH, OF TURKI KHEL, KHYBEE. KAMMAU KHAN, 18TH INDIAN INFANTRY,SEPOY,27 , SON OF JUMMA KHAN, OF BARWARI, ZIRA. NUR MUHAMMAD KHAN,18TH INDIAN INFANTRY,SEPOY,2718, SON OF PIR BAKHSH, OF GHODELWALA. SUCHE KHAN,18TH INDIAN INFANTRY, SEPOY,2741, SON OF JALU KHAN, OF THAMAN, MOGA. GUJRANWALA: JAGAT SINGH,57TH WILDE'S RIFLES, SEPOY, 3516, SON OF NARAYAN SINGH, OF KALOKE, KHANGA DOGRA. MALA SINGH,19TH PUNJABIS, LANCE NAIK, 662,15TH LUDHIANA SIKHS, SON OF MIHAN SINGH, OF CHANDIANWALI, KHANGAH DOGRAN. SUNDAR SINGH,47TH SIKHS, HAVILDAR,422, SON OF GANDA SINGH, OF MATTA. GUJRAT: PIARA SINGH,40TH PATHANS, SEPOY,4806, SON OF CHARTA, OF KOTLI. GURDASPUR: CHET SINGH, 32ND SIKH PIONEERS,SEPOY,4593,34TH SIKHS, SON OF DALEL SINGH, OF CHAK SARJR, HARNAM SINGH, 55TH COKE'S RIFLES, SEPOY,2379,57TH WILDE'S RIFLES, SON OF KHUSHAL SINGH, OF DHARIWAL, BATALA. JAGAT SINGH,45TH RATTRAY'S SIKHS,SEPOY,1053,15TH LUDHIANA SIKHS, SON OF CHANDA SINGH, OF GILLAN WALI, BATALA. KEHR SINGH,57TH WILDE'S RIFLES, NAIK,2672, SON OF NAR SINGH, OF SOGI, SHAKAR GARH, HISSAR: MALUK SINGH,15TH LUDHIANA SIKHS,SEPOY,752, SON OF PHUMAN SINGH, OF TAKHAT, SIRSA. HOSHIARPUR: MAL SINGH,34TH SIKH PIONEERS, HAVILDAR, 1607, SON OF DIWAN SINGH, OF MASITPALKOT, GARHDEWALA. MUL SINGH,47TH SIKHS,SEPOY,2212,SON OF HIRA SINGH, OF MADIANI, GARHSHANKAR, TEJA SINGH, 34TH SIKH PIONEERS, SEPOY,30 , SON OF SANT SINGH, OF TAHLI, URMAR TANDA. UMAR DIN KHAN, 18TH INDIAN INFANTRY,SEPOY,2472, SON OF BUTA KHAN, OF KALUBAHAR, JULLUNDUR: AMAR SINGH,21ST PUNJABIS, SEPOY, 4944,9TH BHOPAL, SON OF ACHEL SINGH, OF FATEHPUR, BADAN SINGH, 36TH SIKHS,SEPOY,2556,47TH SIKHS, SON OF PREM SINGH, OF KANDOLA. CHAGAT SINGH,47TH SIKHS,HAVILDAR,277, SON OF LAL SINGH, OF RERAM, NAKODAR, HARI SINGH,35TH SIKHS, SEPOY, 3025,47TH SIKHS, SON OF INDAR SINGH, OF HAPPU WAL, NAWAN SHAHAR, KISHN SINGH,INDIAN ARMY,SEPOY,577, SON OF SUNDAR SINGH, OF BAL KHURD, OGHLSEWA SINGH,47TH SIKHS,SEPOY,2065, SON OF WAZIR SINGH, OF BAL NAKODAR, SUCHET SINGH,19TH PUNJABIS, SEPOY ,1301,15TH LUDHIANA SIKHS, SON OF ISAR SINGH, OF MANKO. JHELUM: ALLAH DITTA 40TH PATHANS,SEPOY,2926, SON OF MEHDI KHAN, OF KATIAM. JAWAN KHAN,40TH PATHANS, SEPOY, 3830, SON OF SHARAF DIN, OF BAROR, KARAM ILAHI,40TH PATHANS,LANCE NAIK,3922, SON OF NUR DIN, OF CHAK JALO. KANGRA: GURDIAL SINGH,57TH WILDE'S RIFLES, SEPOY, 2570, OF CHHUMI PALAMPUR, RANJA SINGH, 57TH WILDE'S RIFLES, HAVILDAR, 187, OF BARJAL. LAHORE: HARNAM SINGH, 47TH SIKHS, SEPOY,212, SON OF HER SINGH, OF MARI. SONE KHAN,18TH INDIAN S INFANTRY, SEPOY,2498, SON OF BHAGGA KHAN, OF LILIANI, KASUR. LUDHIANA: BISHN SINGH,QUEEN VICTORIA'S OWN CORPS OF GUIDES INFANTRY, SEPOY,4972,57TH WILDE'S RIFLES.

Narwan Singh, 47TH Sikhs, Sepoy,
son of Her Singh of Zira

Dalel Singh, 36TH Sikhs, Sepoy,
son of Her Singh of Garhdewala

Wazir Singh, 47TH Sikhs, Sepoy,
son of Her Singh of Doara

Jawan Singh, 45TH Sikhs, Sepoy,
son of Chanda Singh of Batala

Ranja Singh, 34TH Sikhs, Sepoy
son of Isar Singh of Manko

 T Sikhs, Havildar
ingh of Tando

Harnam Sin , 47TH Sikhs, Sepoy,
son of Her Singh of Mari

Gurdial Singh, Indian Infantry
Sepoy, son of Prem Singh of Ba

SON OF NÁTHÁ SINGH, OF BHÁI KI MALSIÁN, JAGRÁON. INDÁR SINGH, QUEEN VICTORIA'S OWN CORPS OF GUIDES INFANTRY,SEPOY,370,57TH WILDE'S RIFLES), SON OF JAIMAL SINGH, OF SUJÁNPUR, JÁGRÁON. MAKHE KHÁN,18TH INDIAN INFANTRY, LANCE NAIK,1848, SON OF NATHU KHÁN, OF DHÁNAULA. PARTÁB SINGH,31ST PUNJÁBIS, NÁIK, 3394,47TH SIKHS, OF BAGROR, SAMRÁLA. PARTÁB SINGH, 35TH SIKHS, SEPOY, 2662,47TH SIKHS, SON OF DHYÁN SINGH, OF GULÁB, JÁGRÁON. SÁNTA SINGH, 25TH LUDHIÁNA SIKHS, HÁVILDÁR,4273, SON OF SÁWAI SINGH, OF LÁLTON BÁDL SOBHÁ SINGH,15TH LUDHIÁNA SIKHS, SEPOY,273, SON OF HAZÁRÁ SINGH, OF PHÁLEWÁL. MIRPUR; SUCHET SINGH, 40TH PÁTHANS, SEPOY,3815, SON OF SÁHIB SINGH, OF BATÁLA, BHIMBER, PATIÁLA; BÁGA SINGH,47TH SIKHS, SEPOY,568, SON OF THÁMMAN SINGH, OF LADHA, DHURI. BHÁGGU KHÁN,18TH INDIAN INFANTRY, SEPOY,1916, SON OF RUHELA KHÁN, OF CHAK, BARNÁLA. CHUR SINGH,55TH COKE'S RIFLES, SEPOY, 2035, 57TH WILDE'S RIFLES, SON OF RÁMDIT SINGH, OF NÁURA, MALOH, NÁBHA STATE. GANDA SINGH,47TH SIKHS, SEPOY,697, SON OF KHÁZÁN SINGH, OF THULIWÁL, DHURI. ISHÁR SINGH,57TH WILDE'S RIFLES ,SEPOY,2724, SON OF MOTI SINGH, OF SÁNGAT, BHÁTINDA. JIWÁN KHÁN,18TH INDIAN INFANTRY, SEPOY,2473, SON OF ISMÁIL KHÁN, OF DORÁHA, PAYAL. MÁGHAR SINGH,24TH KING GEORGE'S OWN FEROZEPORE SIKHS,SEPOY,978,25TH LUDHIÁNA SIKHS, SON OF SUHEL SINGH, OF SAUDÁRÁ, BHÁTINDA. RAJA SINGH,31ST PUNJABIS, SEPOY, 4298,47TH SIKHS, SON OF LEHNA SINGH, OF KHERI, BANAUR, SÁNTA SINGH,55TH COKE'S RIFLES, SEPOY, 2524,57TH WILDE'S RIFLES, SON OF PREM SINGH, OF HINDIAYA, BARNÁLA, SHÁDI KHÁN,18TH INDIAN INFANTRY,SEPOY,2466, SON OF BÁRKAT KHÁN, OF THADRA, DHÁNAULA, NÁBHA. WÁRYAM SINGH,47TH SIKHS,HAVILDAR,462, SON OF DIWÁN SINGH, OF UPLI, DHODE. RAWÁLPINDI; AMIR ALI,57TH WILDE'S RIFLES, SEPOY,3366, SON OF RAJ WALI, OF SKOT, KAHUTA. FATEH-JANG,57TH WILDE'S RIFLES,SUBÁDÁR, HUSBAND OF NUR BEGUM, OF MATOR VILLAGE, KAHUTA. GUL KHÁN, 40TH PÁTHANS,SEPOY, 3087, SON OF PUR BAKHSH, OF GUFF, KAHUTA; HARI SINGH, 57TH WILDE'S RIFLES, HÁVILDÁR,2126, OF JHÁNGI JALAL, GUJAR KHÁN. MEHR KHÁN,40TH PÁTHANS,LANCE NAIK,3821, SON OF AMIR KHÁN, OF RUKA BHÁITH. NÁTHÁ KHÁN, 40TH PÁTHANS, SEPOY, 2765, SON OF FAUJDÁR KHÁN, OF MOARA, KAHUTA. ZAMAN ALI,40TH PÁTHANS,BUGLER,3907, SON OF JÁFAR, OF MATORE, KAHUTA. SÁNGRUR; SANT SINGH, QUEEN VICTORIA'S OWN CORPS OF GUIDES INFANTRY, SEPOY, 252,57TH WILDE'S RIFLES, SON OF HIRÁ SINGH, OF KHERI KHURD, DHURI. SIÁLKOT; BUTÁ SINGH, 35TH SIKHS, SEPOY, 3263,47TH SIKHS, SON OF KYÁNHAIYA SINGH, OF POONG TALWANDI, RAIYA. DEWA SINGH,47TH SIKHS, SEPOY,1597, SON OF NIHÁL SINGH, OF KAPURWÁLI. LAL SINGH, 47TH SIKHS,SEPOY, 1679, SON OF CHET SINGH, OF GUJÁRKE, DASKA. SUNDAR SINGH, 35TH SIKHS, SEPOY, 3418,47TH SIKHS, SON OF JHANDA SINGH, OF SÁDHÁR WÁLI ZAFAR WAL. SUNDAR SINGH, 35TH SIKHS,SEPOY, 2644,47TH SIKHS, SON OF GANDÁ SINGH, OF SÁLUKI, DASKA.

In Flanders fields the poppies blow
Between the crosses, row on row,
That mark our place; and in the sky
The larks, still bravely singing, fly
Scarce heard amid the guns below.

We are the Dead. Short days ago
We lived, felt dawn, saw sunset glow,
Loved and were loved, and now we lie
In Flanders fields.

Take up our quarrel with the foe:
To you from failing hands we throw
The torch; be yours to hold it high.
If ye break faith with us who die
We shall not sleep, though poppies grow
In Flanders fields.

After fresh attacks a sleeping army lies in front of one of our brigades; they rest in good order, man by man, and will never wake again — Canadian Divisions. The enemy's losses are enormous.

Rudolf Binding
Jungdeutschland Division
April 27·1915
Published January 1929

First published Punch Magazine (London) December 8th 1915

★ written without attribution to Lieut. Col John McCrae

★★ First written May 3rd 1915 during the second battle of Ypres

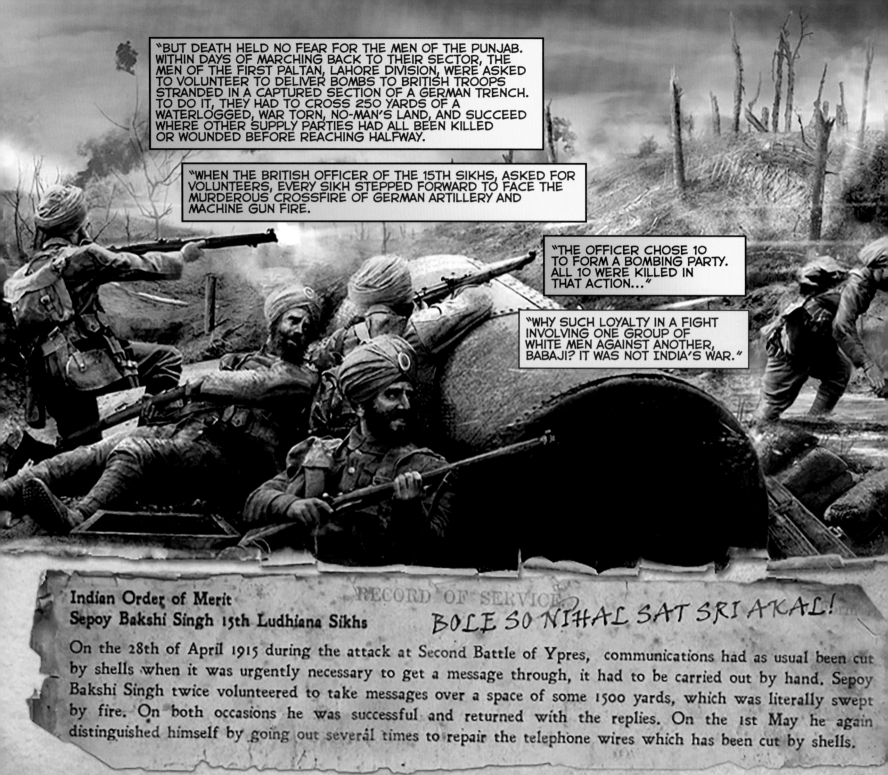

"BUT DEATH HELD NO FEAR FOR THE MEN OF THE PUNJAB. WITHIN DAYS OF MARCHING BACK TO THEIR SECTOR, THE MEN OF THE FIRST PALTAN, LAHORE DIVISION, WERE ASKED TO VOLUNTEER TO DELIVER BOMBS TO BRITISH TROOPS STRANDED IN A CAPTURED SECTION OF A GERMAN TRENCH. TO DO IT, THEY HAD TO CROSS 250 YARDS OF A WATERLOGGED, WAR TORN, NO-MAN'S LAND, AND SUCCEED WHERE OTHER SUPPLY PARTIES HAD ALL BEEN KILLED OR WOUNDED BEFORE REACHING HALFWAY.

"WHEN THE BRITISH OFFICER OF THE 15TH SIKHS, ASKED FOR VOLUNTEERS, EVERY SIKH STEPPED FORWARD TO FACE THE MURDEROUS CROSSFIRE OF GERMAN ARTILLERY AND MACHINE GUN FIRE.

"THE OFFICER CHOSE 10 TO FORM A BOMBING PARTY. ALL 10 WERE KILLED IN THAT ACTION..."

"WHY SUCH LOYALTY IN A FIGHT INVOLVING ONE GROUP OF WHITE MEN AGAINST ANOTHER, BABAJI? IT WAS NOT INDIA'S WAR."

Indian Order of Merit
Sepoy Bakshi Singh 15th Ludhiana Sikhs

RECORD OF SERVICE

BOLE SO NIHAL SAT SRI AKAL!

On the 28th of April 1915 during the attack at Second Battle of Ypres, communications had as usual been cut by shells when it was urgently necessary to get a message through, it had to be carried out by hand. Sepoy Bakshi Singh twice volunteered to take messages over a space of some 1500 yards, which was literally swept by fire. On both occasions he was successful and returned with the replies. On the 1st May he again distinguished himself by going out several times to repair the telephone wires which has been cut by shells.

May 18th Wrote letter to Manta now residing at the grand Brighton hospital in Vilayet. Informed him of Bakshi Singh.

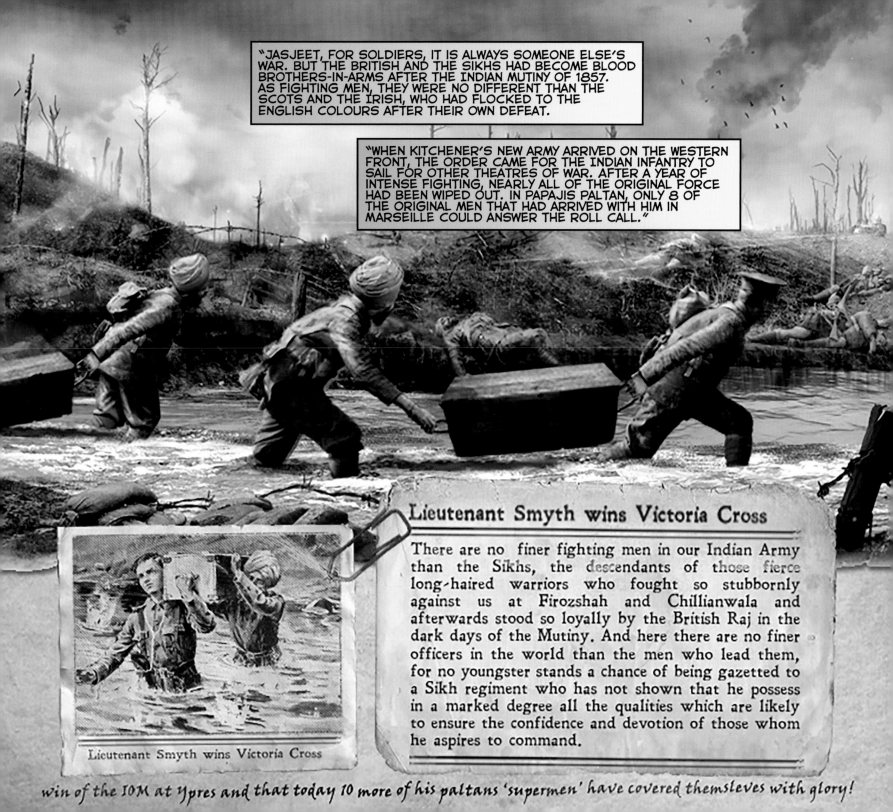

"JASJEET, FOR SOLDIERS, IT IS ALWAYS SOMEONE ELSE'S WAR. BUT THE BRITISH AND THE SIKHS HAD BECOME BLOOD BROTHERS-IN-ARMS AFTER THE INDIAN MUTINY OF 1857. AS FIGHTING MEN, THEY WERE NO DIFFERENT THAN THE SCOTS AND THE IRISH, WHO HAD FLOCKED TO THE ENGLISH COLOURS AFTER THEIR OWN DEFEAT.

"WHEN KITCHENER'S NEW ARMY ARRIVED ON THE WESTERN FRONT, THE ORDER CAME FOR THE INDIAN INFANTRY TO SAIL FOR OTHER THEATRES OF WAR. AFTER A YEAR OF INTENSE FIGHTING, NEARLY ALL OF THE ORIGINAL FORCE HAD BEEN WIPED OUT. IN PAPAJIS PALTAN, ONLY 8 OF THE ORIGINAL MEN THAT HAD ARRIVED WITH HIM IN MARSEILLE COULD ANSWER THE ROLL CALL."

Lieutenant Smyth wins Victoria Cross

Lieutenant Smyth wins Victoria Cross

There are no finer fighting men in our Indian Army than the Sikhs, the descendants of those fierce long-haired warriors who fought so stubbornly against us at Firozshah and Chillianwala and afterwards stood so loyally by the British Raj in the dark days of the Mutiny. And here there are no finer officers in the world than the men who lead them, for no youngster stands a chance of being gazetted to a Sikh regiment who has not shown that he possess in a marked degree all the qualities which are likely to ensure the confidence and devotion of those whom he aspires to command.

win of the IOM at Ypres and that today 10 more of his paltans 'supermen' have covered themsleves with glory!

Salute! To Hardit Singh Malik engaging the enemy in the sky!

First Sikh fighter pilot of the Royal Flying Corp

First not permitted to fly then fought in the Battle of Passchendaele against the Red Baron's Flying Circus with Canadian Victoria Cross winner Major William Barker.

Oct 18th, 1917

ACE! Hardit's Sopwith Camel hit 400 times - and while shot through both legs he got his man

SIDOR MALLOC SINGH

Avg life expectancy of a pilot is 10 days

"THAT'S LEGENDARY STUFF, BABAJI! I HAD NO IDEA PUNJABI INFANTRY HAD FOUGHT IN FLANDERS."

"PUNJABIS FOUGHT IN ALL ARMS OF THE SERVICE. THEY WERE THE BACKBONE OF THE INDIAN ARMY MAKING UP NEARLY 1/2 OF INFANTRY AND 2/3 OF CAVALRY AND 4/5 OF THE ARTILLERY. AFTER THE INFANTRY WAS MOVED, THESE ARMS CONTINUED THEIR SERVICE IN FRANCE. THEN LATER IN THE WAR, A SIKH EVEN FLEW IN THE ROYAL FLYING CORP, IN THE 3RD BATTLE OF YPRES."

"HE FOUGHT UNDER THE WING OF YOUR COUNTRY'S MOST DECORATED SOLDIER IN HISTORY, MAJOR BILLIE BARKER. TOGETHER, THEY FOUGHT THE INFAMOUS RED BARON. BUT THAT STORY WILL HAVE TO WAIT, I'M AFRAID..."

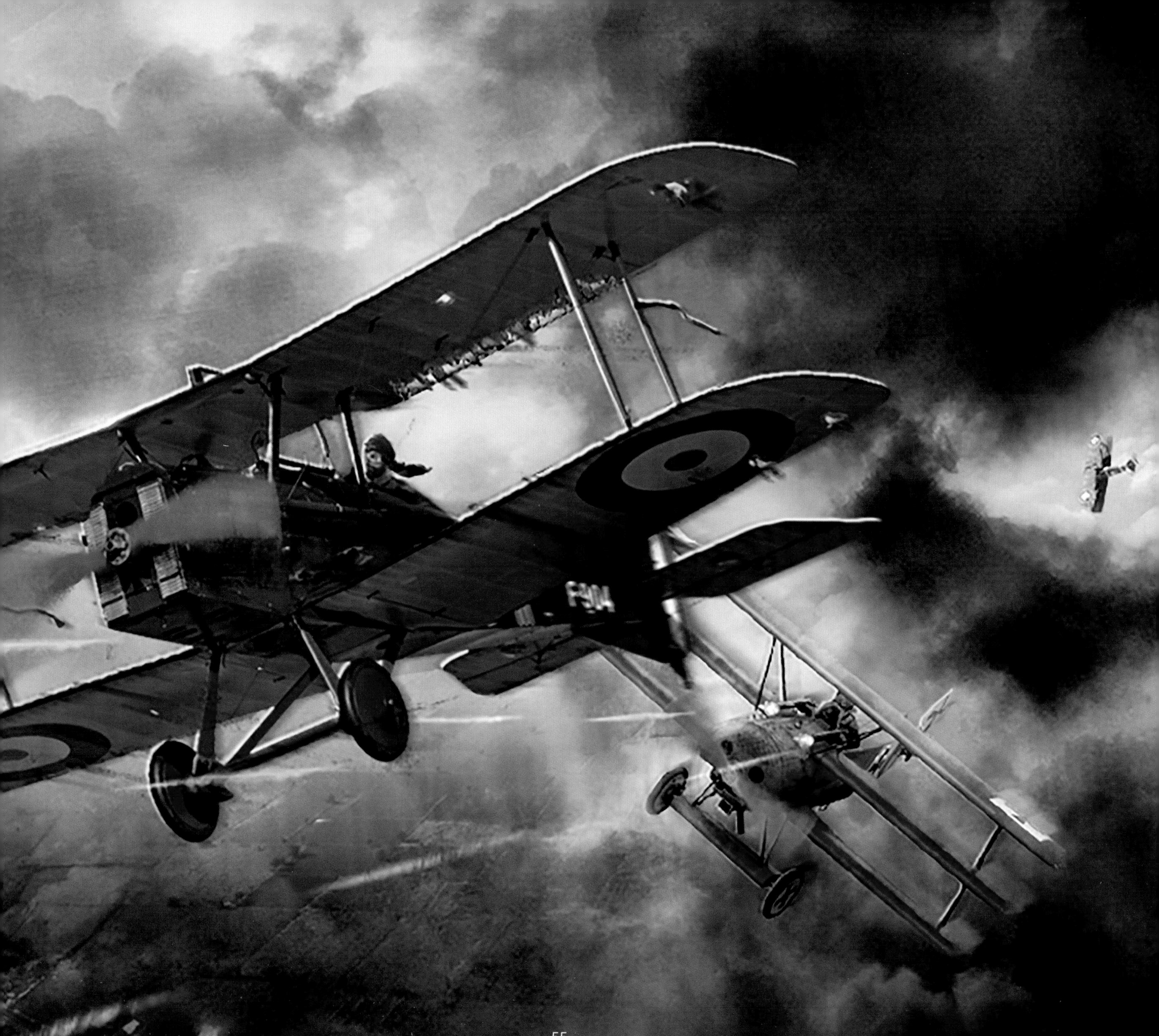
F904

I'M FEELING A LITTLE DIZZY, PERHAPS I HAVE NOT HAD ENOUGH SLEEP. I SHALL RETIRE EARLY. I SHALL TEACH YOU MORE ABOUT OUR FAMILY TOMORROW.

GOODNIGHT BABAJI. I'M GOING TO WRITE ABOUT THIS IN MY SOCIAL HOMEWORK.

BABAJI? GOOD MORNING, WOULD YOU LIKE SOME TEA?

BABAJI, HELLO?

DAD?

HE HASN'T WOKEN UP YET. THE DOCTOR SAID THEY FOUND SOME BRUISING ON THE BACK OF HIS HEAD. I TOLD HIM WE DIDN'T KNOW HOW THAT HAPPENED. HE'S AN OLD MAN...

HE'LL BE FINE, HE'S AN OLD SOLDIER.

‡KNOCK KNOCK‡

JASJEET, GO SEE WHO IS HERE.

EXCUSE ME, BUT I'M HOPING YOU CAN HELP ME. I'M LOOKING FOR AN ADDRESS FOR HARI SINGH IN INDIA. I HAVE A GIFT TO SEND TO HIM. THAT MAN IS A HERO.

WE HAVEN'T SEEN EACH OTHER SINCE 1944. YOUR GRANDDAD IS A HERO. I STILL CAN'T BELIEVE HE'S ACTUALLY HERE IN CANADA.

IF HE WAKES UP, I'M SURE HE'LL BE HAPPY THAT YOU FOUND HIM. I JUST HOPE HE'S OKAY.

HE'S CONSCIOUS NOW, BUT SEEMS TO BE LOST, LIKE HE'S GIVEN UP.

HARI? HARI SINGH? CAN YOU HEAR ME? IT'S ED JONES.

ED JONES? ED? IS THAT REALLY YOU OR AM I HALLUCINATING?

HARI, IT'S ME. LOOK, I NEVER FORGOT WHAT YOU DID. I HAVE YOUR TURBAN AS I PROMISED.

NO... IT CAN'T BE.

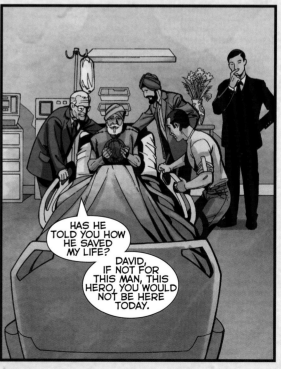

HAS HE TOLD YOU HOW HE SAVED MY LIFE?

DAVID, IF NOT FOR THIS MAN, THIS HERO, YOU WOULD NOT BE HERE TODAY.

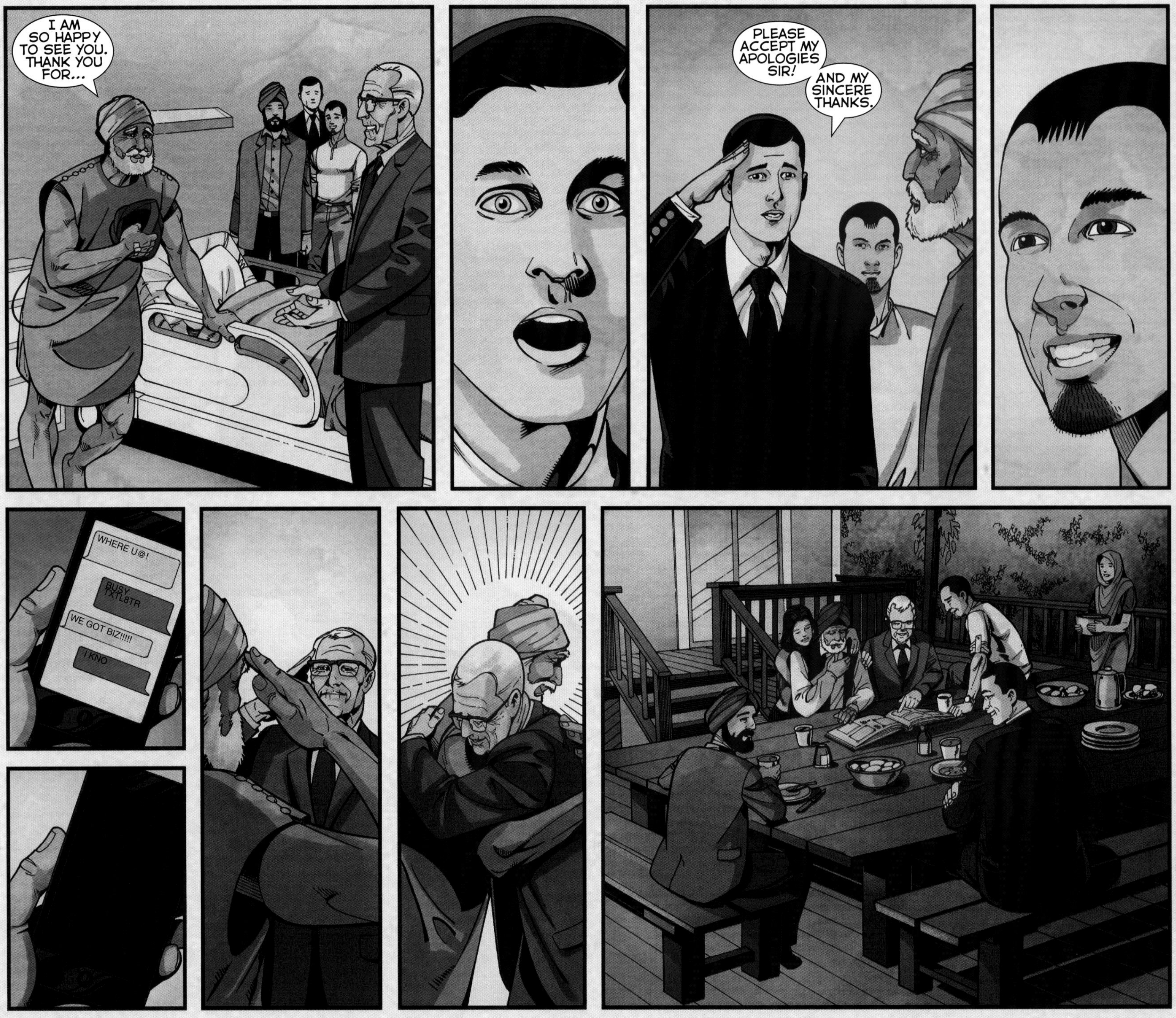
I AM SO HAPPY TO SEE YOU. THANK YOU FOR...
PLEASE ACCEPT MY APOLOGIES SIR!
AND MY SINCERE THANKS.
WHERE U@!
BUSY TXTL8TR
WE GOT BIZ!!!!!
I KNO

Harnam Singh
Soldier of the Raj

Many soldiers named Harnam Singh fought across all the theatres of the Great War. While some like Hari's father returned to tell the tale, many did not.

I

Beneath an ancient pipal-tree, fast by Jhelum's tide,
In silent thought sat Hurnam Singh,
A Khalsa soldier of the King:
He mused on things now done and past,
For he had reached his home at last,
His empty sleeve his pride.

II

Five years before a village lout, beneath the self-same tree,
He met the Havildar, who'd come
With honeyed words and beat of drum,
Cajoling all who glory sought,
And telling how the regiment fought
The Zakha and the Mohmand clans,
With shouts of victory.

III

Wah Guru Ji!! Rang in his ears, the famous battle cry,
And Hurnam Singh had since then seen,
On Flanders plains, from fierce Messines,
To Festubert and Neuve Chapelle,
'Mid festering bogs and scenes of hell,
How Khalsa soldiers die.

IV

The village yokels round him flocked to hearken to his tales,
How he had crossed the Kala sea,
From India's strand past Araby,
Thro' Egypt's sands to Europe's shores,
Where the wild stormy mistral roars,
And anchor'd in Marseilles.

V

"Is it the truth," said one more bold than village yokels be,
"That men with wings ascend on high
And fight with Gods in yonder sky?
That iron monsters belching wrath,
Beneath their wheels of Juggernaut,
Claim victims for Kali?"

VI

"Now list all ye," said Hurnam Singh, "the aged and the youth
The tales they told in bygone days,
Of Gods and Ghouls in ancient lays,
Are true, not false; mine eyes descried,
Mine ears have heard as heroes died,
The Mahabharat's truth.

VII

"The land of France is wide and fair, the people brave and free,
I fain would tell, but orders came,
'Push on, the foe awaits the game'
The game of death; the Khalsa cry,
The warriors' welkin, rent the sky,
Fateh Wah Guri Ji!

VIII

"The Sahibs face told their tale; no craven thought or sloth
In those brave hearts, as we had learned
When Gujerat the tide had turned,
And left the names of Aliwal
And Chillianwala as a pall
Of glory to us both.

IX

"And thus the sons of Hindustan, from Himalaya to Scinde,
From Hindu Kush to Deccan plains,
Rent in a day the ancient chains
Which isolated class from clan,
And joined in battle as one man,
To die for Mata Hind.

X

"Hur Mahadeo! Guru Ji! And Allah's sacred name,
Shri Gunga Jai! From brave Nepal,
Re-echoed loud through wild Garhwal;
From Dogra vale, Afridi clan,
To the proud homes of Rajistan,
Was lit the martial flame.

XI

"As pitiless the bullets rained, 'mid angry storm and flood,
Khudadad Khan! Immortal name,
Stood by his gun, for India's fame
Was in his hands; the Huns advance,
Recoil; Retire; the soil of France
Is richer with his blood."

XII

And Hurnam paused as he recalled, one dark November morn,
When twice three thousand foes had rushed
Our trenches, powdered into dust,
And bayonet point and Kukry blade
Avenging retribution made,
Before the break of dawn.

XIII

"Garhwal will tell," he said, "with pride her children oft recite,
How Durwan Negi, lion-heart!
Was first and foremost from the start;
He led the charge which won the day,
Oh, brothers, 'twas a glorious fray,
For victory came with light."

XIV

Shabash! Shabash! From every tongue, and mothers' hearts stood still,
As sons stepped forth and made demand
They too should join the glorious band,
They too should hear the battle's din,
Or purge the soul of every sin,
If such were Ishwar's will.

XV

Hurnam went on: "At Neuve Chapelle, at Festubert, we bled,
On Wipers field, at Moulin Pietre,
We heard the German hymn of hate;
Above our lines the war-ships soared,
Our trenches rocked while cannon roared
The requiem of the dead."

XVI

The Jhelum's bank had witnessed oft her waters stained with gore,
Had heard the tramp of countless feet,
Had known both triumph and defeat,
But never had her waters swirled
A prouder message to the world
Than Hurnam's story bore.

XVII

For India's sons had sealed their oath, according to their laws;
Sealed it with blood across the sea,
From Flanders to Gallipoli,
On Tigris' banks, on Egypt's sands,
'Mid Afric's swamps and hinterlands,
And died in England's cause.

XVIII

For ages long the Mullah's cry, the temple bells shall wile,
And call to prayer for those who died,
The father, mother, son, and bride,
Descendants of the loyal brave
Who rest in warrior's simple grave,
And need no marble pile.

Harnam Singh
By General Sir James Willcocks
Commander of the Indian army in France
Published July 1917

2ND LANCERS (GARDNER'S HORSE)

SOWAR HARNAM SINGH OF BAMB, BATALS, GURDASPUR. DOD: 17-JUN-1918. EGYPT.

7TH HARIANA LANCERS

SOWAR HARNAM SINGH OF KHAPERKUI, AMRITSAR. DOD: 01-MAR-1917. IRAQ.

11TH KING EDWARD'S OWN LANCERS (PROBYN'S HORSE)

LANCE DAFFADAR HARNAM SINGH OF MAL CHAK, TARN TARAN, AMRITSAR. DOD: 05-NOV-1919. IRAQ.

SOWAR HARNAM SINGH OF CHAGRALI, RAYA, SIALKOT. DOD: 09-JUN-1920. IRAQ.

16TH INDIAN CAVALRY

SOWAR HARNAM SINGH OF JALUR, PATIALA. DOD: 26-NOV-1919. INDIA.

18TH KING GEORGE'S OWN LANCERS

SOWAR HARNAM SINGH OF RAKBA, LUDHIANA. DOD: 17-APR-1917. FRANCE.

SOWAR HARNAM SINGH OF PAKHA, LUDHIANA. DOD: 17-APR-1917. INDIA.

19TH LANCERS (FANE'S HORSE)

SOWAR HARNAM SINGH OF BHAGUPUR, KASUR, LAHORE. DOD: 19-OCT-1918. LEBANON.

20TH DECCAN HORSE

SOWAR HARNAM SINGH OF RATTON, RUPAR, AMBALA. DOD: 21-DEC-1914. FRANCE.

SOWAR HARNAM SINGH OF NANHEDA, AMBALA. DOD: 23-NOV-1917. FRANCE.

SOWAR HARNAM SINGH OF MANDIANI, JAGRAON, LUDHIANA. DOD: 05-JAN-1918. FRANCE.

21ST PRINCE ALBERT VICTOR'S OWN CAVALRY (PUNJAB FRONTIER FORCE) (DALY'S HORSE)

DAFFADAR HARNAM SINGH OF SAYAD KASRAN, GUJAR KHAN, RAWALPINDI. DOD: 14-MAY-1915. FRANCE.

23RD INDIAN CAVALRY (PUNJAB FRONTIER FORCE)

SOWAR HARNAM SINGH DOD: 04-AUG-1914. IRAQ.

SOWAR HARNAM SINGH OF LOKHE, TARN TARAN, AMRITSAR. DOD: 22-JAN-1916. IRAQ.

SOWAR HARNAM SINGH OF CHUHI, TARN TARAN, AMRITSAR. DOD: 04-FEB-1916. IRAQ.

25TH INDIAN CAVALRY (PUNJAB FRONTIER FORCE)

SOWAR HARNAM SINGH OF NANDPUR, GUJRANWALA. DOD: 03-AUG-1916. INDIA.

SOWAR HARNAM SINGH OF NATHU, TARN TARAN, AMRITSAR. DOD: 30-OCT-1920. INDIA.

30TH LANCERS (GORDON'S HORSE)

SOWAR HARNAM SINGH OF PUNDORI RUN SINGH, TARN TARAN, AMRITSAR. DOD: 17-MAY-1919. INDIA.

38TH KING GEORGE'S OWN CENTRAL INDIA HORSE

RISALDAR HARNAM SINGH OF THATTIAN, AMRITSAR. DOD: 28-AUG-1916. FRANCE.

SOWAR HARNAM SINGH OF RAJOKE, KASUR, LAHORE. DOD: 23-OCT-1918. EGYPT.

PATIALA (RAJINDRA) LANCERS

KOT DAFFADAR HARNAM SINGH OF AIHNON, MALERKOTLA. DOD: 16-AUG-1919. INDIA.

1ST KING GEORGE'S OWN SAPPERS AND MINERS

JEMADAR HARNAM SINGH OF SIDHAM, JAGRAON, LUDHIANA. DOD: 23-MAY-1918. INDIA.

3RD SAPPERS AND MINERS

SAPPER HARNAM SINGH OF DIYALPURA MIRZUKA, SANGRUR, JIND. DOD: 17-NOV-1914. IRAQ.

SAPPER HARNAM SINGH OF SINDAVAD, LUDHIANA. DOD: 16-MAR-1917. GERMANY.

4TH PRINCE ALBERT VICTOR'S RAJPU

SEPOY HARNAM SINGH OF ROHTAK. DOD: 05-JAN-1916. INDIA.

6TH JAT LIGHT INFANTRY

SEPOY HARNAM OF SAMLO, JIND. DOD: 23-NOV-1915. INDIA.

SEPOY HARNAM OF DUBALDHAN, JHAJJAR, ROHTAK. DOD: 27-JAN-1916. IRAQ.

7TH DUKE OF CONNAUGHT'S OWN RAJPUTS

SEPOY HARNAM SINGH OF BHIWANI, HISSAR. DOD: 03-MAR-1915. IRAQ.

9TH BHOPAL INFANTRY

HAVILDAR HARNAM SINGH DOD: 30-JUL-1916. GERMANY.

SEPOY HARNAM SINGH OF PANDAURI, HOSHIARPUR. DOD: 16-JAN-1916.

SEPOY HARNAM SINGH OF NANKI, SAMRALA, LUDHIANA. DOD: 16-MAR-1917. IRAQ.

12TH INDIAN PIONEERS

SEPOY HARNAM SINGH OF DULCHIPURA, SHARAKPUR, SHEIKHUPURA. DOD: 02-JAN-1917. IND.

14TH KING GEORGE'S OWN FEROZEPORE SIKHS

SEPOY HARNAM SINGH OF CHHAPAR, LUDHIANA. DOD: 09-MAY-1915. TURKEY.

SEPOY HARNAM SINGH OF DALEWALI, BHIKHI, PATIALA. DOD: 20-MAY-1915. TURKEY.

SEPOY HARNAM SINGH OF JITWAL CHHOTA, MALERKOTLA, LUDHIANA. DOD: 04-JUN-1915. TURK.

SEPOY HARNAM SINGH OF CHAU, LUDHIANA. DOD: 04-JUN-1915. TURKEY.

SEPOY HARNAM SINGH OF DHAULA, DHANAULA, NABHA. DOD: 04-JUN-1915. TURKEY.

SEPOY HARNAM SINGH OF LOHAKHERA, SUNAM, PATIALA. DOD: 04-JUN-1915. TURKEY.

SEPOY HARNAM SINGH OF JASSI BAGWALI, BHATINDA, PATIALA. DOD: 04-JUN-1915. TURKEY.

SEPOY HARNAM SINGH OF KHADIALE, SANGRUR. DOD: 07-AUG-1915. TURKEY.

BUGLER HARNAM SINGH OF KHIALI, LUDHIANA. DOD: 19-SEP-1915. TURKEY.

SEPOY HARNAM SINGH OF SANDAUR, LUDHIANA. DOD: 19-SEP-1915. TURKEY.

SEPOY HARNAM SINGH OF SELWARA, DHANAULA, NABHA. DOD: 02-AUG-1918. IRAQ.

15TH LUDHIANA SIKHS

NAIK HARNAM SINGH OF DAL, JAGRAON, LUDHIANA. DOD: 28-OCT-1914. FRANCE.

LANCE NAIK HARNAM SINGH OF SAHAULI, JAGRAON, LUDHIANA. DOD: 05-NOV-1914. FRANCE.

SEPOY HARNAM SINGH OF SEHLAR, GARHSHANKAR, HOSHIARPUR. DOD: 17-FEB-1915. UNITED KINGDOM.

SEPOY HARNAM SINGH OF CHIMME, SUNAM, PATIALA. DOD: 15-MAR-1915. FRANCE.

SEPOY HARNAM SINGH OF DHARAMKOTE, ZIRA, FEROZEPORE. DOD: 03-APR-1915. FRANCE.

SEPOY HARNAM SINGH OF BADE MAHAL, BARNALA, PATIALA. DOD: 01-FEB-1917. IRAQ.

SEPOY HARNAM SINGH OF BALEH, KHARAR, AMBALA. DOD: 19-DEC-1917. IRAQ.

SEPOY HARNAM SINGH OF BINANG, JULLUNDUR. DOD: 01-MAY-1918. IRAQ.

JEMADAR HARNAM SINGH OF PHULANWAL, LUDHIANA. DOD: 13-MAY-1919. INDIA.

SEPOY HARNAM SINGH OF MARIKE, DHURI, PATIALA. DOD: 31-JUL-1919. INDIA.

16TH RAJPUTS

SEPOY HARNAM SINGH OF BHAO, GURGAON, INDIA. DOD: 07-NOV-1918. IRAN.

19TH PUNJABIS

SEPOY HARNAM SINGH OF BAJWARA, HOSHIARPUR. DOD: 19-MAY-1915. FRANCE.

SEPOY HARNAM SINGH OF HAINARA, JULLUNDUR, INDIA. DOD: 13-APR-1916. IRAN.

SEPOY HARNAM SINGH OF PHERUMAN, AMRITSAR, INDIA. DOD: 25-AUG-1918. IRAN.

SEPOY HARNAM SINGH OF JAJJE, AJNALA, AMRITSAR, INDIA. DOD: 15-SEP-1918. IRAN.

20TH DUKE OF CAMBRIDGE'S OWN INFANTRY (BROWNLOW'S PUNJABIS)

SEPOY HARNAM SINGH OF JODHAY, TARN TARAN, AMRITSAR. DOD: 23-SEP-1915. IRAQ.

SEPOY HARNAM SINGH OF CHAK MANAK, SHAKERGARH, GURDASPUR. DOD: 28-SEP-1915. IRAQ.

NAIK HARNAM SINGH OF KUL BEJWA, PASRUR, SIALKOT. DOD: 17-FEB-1917. IRAQ.

21ST PUNJABIS

SEPOY HARNAM SINGH OF ACHALWALI, SHAKARGARH, GURDASPUR. DOD: 01-MAY-1917. INDIA.

22ND PUNJABIS

SEPOY HARNAM SINGH OF JUTPORE, GARHSHANKAR, HOSHIARPUR. DOD: 01-NOV-1915. IRAQ.

SEPOY HARNAM SINGH OF BABA, BAKALA, AMRITSAR. DOD: 22-NOV-1915. IRAQ.

SEPOY HARNAM SINGH OF BHARNOLI, NURPUR, KANGRA. DOD: 06-APR-1916. IRAQ.

SEPOY HARNAM SINGH OF BAD, HOSHIARPUR. DOD: 05-MAY-1916. IRAQ.

SEPOY HARNAM SINGH OF BUDHI PIND, DASUYA, HOSHIARPUR. DOD: 01-DEC-1917. IRAQ.

SEPOY HARNAM SINGH OF LLANGEWALI, BATALA, GURDASPUR. DOD: 19-DEC-1918. EGYPT.

SEPOY HARNAM SINGH OF NANDPUR, UNA, HOSHIARPUR, INDIA. DOD: 27-MAY-1919. IRAN.

23RD SIKH PIONEERS

SEPOY HARNAM SINGH OF PANDORI RAN SINGH, TARN TARAN, AMRITSAR. DOD: 24-JUN-1916. IRAQ.

SEPOY HARNAM SINGH OF KOKRI, MOGA, FEROZEPORE. DOD: 21-SEP-1917. ISRAEL.

24TH PUNJABIS

SEPOY HARNAM SINGH OF GUMANPURA, AMRITSAR. DOD: 22-NOV-1915. IRAQ.

25TH PUNJABIS

SEPOY HARNAM SINGH OF MANGARH, DASUYA, HOSHIARPUR. DOD: 22-NOV-1916. INDIA.

SEPOY HARNAM SINGH OF SADHAR, AMRITSAR. DOD: 25-JAN-1917. INDIA.

26TH PUNJABIS

HAVILDAR HARNAM SINGH OF TIMOWAL, AMRITSAR. DOD: 08-MAR-1916. IRAQ.

LANCE NAIK HARNAM SINGH OF BAHOWAL, GARHSHANKAR, HOSHIARPUR. DOD: 08-MAR-1916. IRAQ.

SEPOY HARNAM SINGH OF PATAR, UNA, HOSHIARPUR. DOD: 04-JAN-1917. INDIA.

JEMADAR HARNAM SINGH OF SATTOWAL, AMRITSAR. DOD: 26-JAN-1917. IRAQ.

LANCE NAIK HARNAM SINGH OF NAGOKE, AMRITSAR. DOD: 26-JAN-1917. IRAQ.

SEPOY HARNAM SINGH OF CHAK NO. 73, LYALLPUR. DOD: 09-FEB-1917. IRAQ.

27TH PUNJABIS

SEPOY HARNAM SINGH OF NANGAL WANGANWALA, AMRITSAR. DOD: 28-DEC-1915. EGYPT.

SEPOY HARNAM SINGH OF JURIAN MANGAL, BATALA, GURDASPUR. DOD: 17-APR-1916. IRAQ.

28TH PUNJABIS

NAIK HARNAM SINGH DOD: 04-AUG-1914. INDIA.

SEPOY HARNAM SINGH OF SANJOGLA, JULLUNDUR. DOD: 14-OCT-1915. FRANCE.

HAVILDAR HARNAM SINGH OF DHOLOWAL, HOSHIARPUR. DOD: 09-MAR-1917. IRAQ.

SEPOY HARNAM SINGH DOD: 21-APR-1917. IRAQ.

SEPOY HARNAM SINGH OF GAURE, NANGAL, AJNALA, AMRITSAR. DOD: 21-APR-1917. IRAQ.

29TH PUNJABIS

LANCE NAIK HARNAM SINGH DOD: 04-AUG-1914. INDIA.

SEPOY HARNAM SINGH OF GALLAN, NURPUR, KANGRA. DOD: 18-OCT-1917. TANZANIA.

30TH PUNJABIS

HAVILDAR HARNAM SINGH OF TALHE BHILA, AMRITSAR. DOD: 18-OCT-1917. TANZANIA.

SEPOY HARNAM SINGH OF KABULPUR, JULLUNDUR. DOD: 03-AUG-1917. TANZANIA.

SEPOY HARNAM SINGH OF BCHRANWALA, LAHORE. DOD: 03-AUG-1917. TANZANIA.

NAIK HARNAM SINGH OF MONDIAN, HOSHIARPUR. DOD: 11-FEB-1918. INDIA.

31ST PUNJABIS

SEPOY HARNAM SINGH OF ARAICHE, PATIALA. DOD: 21-JUN-1915. FRANCE.

32ND SIKH PIONEERS

LANCE NAIK HARNAM SINGH OF PIPLANWALA, HOSHIARPUR. DOD: 05-NOV-1918. LEBANON.

34TH SIKH PIONEERS

SEPOY HARNAM SINGH DOD: 23-NOV-1914. FRANCE.

SEPOY HARNAM SINGH OF KANJRA, LAHORE. DOD: 23-NOV-1914. FRANCE.

SEPOY HARNAM SINGH OF FATEHGARH, JAGRAON, LUDHIANA. DOD: 23-NOV-1914. FRANCE.

SEPOY HARNAM SINGH OF TODAR MAJRA, KHARAR, AMBALA. DOD: 24-NOV-1914. FRANCE.

SEPOY HARNAM SINGH OF MANKO, JULLUNDUR. DOD: 16-JAN-1917. IRAQ.

HAVILDAR HARNAM SINGH OF DHABAN KHURD, KHANGAH DOGRAN, SHEIKHUPURA. DOD: 25-MAR-1917. IRAQ.

SEPOY HARNAM SINGH OF GOBINDGARH, KHANGAH, DOGRAN, SHEIKHUPURA. DOD: 20-JUN-1919. IRAQ.

35TH SIKHS

SEPOY HARNAM SINGH OF BALASCHANDAR, AMRITSAR. DOD: 12-MAR-1915. FRANCE.

HAVILDAR HARNAM SINGH OF MOHANPUR, LUDHIANA. DOD: 23-AUG-1915. FRANCE.

LANCE NAIK HARNAM SINGH OF MADHO, SHAKARGARH, GURDASPUR. DOD: 15-JAN-1917. IRAQ.

HAVILDAR HARNAM SINGH OF KANGANWAL, MALERKOTLA. DOD: 29-NOV-1917. IRAQ.

36TH SIKHS

SEPOY HARNAM SINGH OF HARIPUR, JULLUNDUR. DOD: 04-AUG-1914. FRANCE.

JEMADAR HARNAM SINGH OF JAMSHER, JULLUNDUR. DOD: 12-APR-1916. IRAQ.

SEPOY HARNAM SINGH OF PATTA, JULLUNDUR. DOD: 12-APR-1916. IRAQ.

LANCE NAIK HARNAM SINGH OF KHURA, MALERKOTLA. DOD: 12-APR-1916. IRAQ.

LANCE NAIK HARNAM SINGH OF MUM, BARNALA, PATIALA. DOD: 01-FEB-1917. IRAQ.

LANCE NAIK HARNAM SINGH OF TAKHALPURA, MOGA, FEROZEPORE. DOD: 02-FEB-1917. IRAQ.

SUBADAR HARNAM SINGH OF RUPOWAL, HOSHIARPUR. DOD: 20-FEB-1917. IRAQ.

SEPOY HARNAM SINGH OF KHARAR, AMBALA. DOD: 04-JUN-1918. IRAQ.

37TH DOGRAS

SEPOY HARNAM SINGH OF KUNERAN, UNA, HOSHIARPUR. DOD: 07-JAN-1916. IRAQ.

41ST DOGRAS

SEPOY HARNAM SINGH OF KUNERAN, UNA, HOSHIARPUR. DOD: 07-JAN-1916. IRAQ.

45TH RATTRAY'S SIKHS

SEPOY HARNAM SINGH OF SEKHA, BARNALA, PATIALA. DOD: 23-JAN-1916. EGYPT.

SEPOY HARNAM SINGH OF DAULATPUR, NAWASHAHR, JULLUNDUR. DOD: 27-MAY-1916. IRAQ.

SEPOY HARNAM SINGH OF KHAPIA, NABHA. DOD: 01-FEB-1917. IRAQ.

SEPOY HARNAM SINGH OF MADYA, AJNALA, AMRITSAR. DOD: 01-FEB-1917. IRAQ.

SEPOY HARNAM SINGH OF THATTA, GURDASPUR. DOD: 01-FEB-1917. IRAQ.

SEPOY HARNAM SINGH OF JASSOWAL, LUDHIANA. DOD: 01-FEB-1917. IRAQ.

SEPOY HARNAM SINGH OF KURAR, DHURI, PATIALA. DOD: 01-FEB-1917. IRAQ.

SEPOY HARNAM SINGH OF CHURAL, SUNAM, PATIALA. DOD: 01-FEB-1917. IRAQ.

SEPOY HARNAM SINGH OF JAITO, PHUL, NABHA. DOD: 22-NOV-1918. IRAQ.

SEPOY HARNAM SINGH OF DALLEKE, AJNALA, AMRITSAR. DOD: 22-AUG-1920. IRAQ.

47TH SIKHS

SEPOY HARNAM SINGH OF BASSI, DASUYA, HOSHIARPUR. DOD: 27-OCT-1914. FRANCE

SEPOY HARNAM SINGH OF PUJWAR, TARN TARAN, AMRITSAR. DOD: 28-OCT-1914. FRANC

SEPOY HARNAM SINGH OF WADALA, AMRITSAR. DOD: 21-DEC-1914. FRANCE.

SEPOY HARNAM SINGH OF MAULI, KHARAR, AMBALA. DOD: 12-MAR-1915. FRANCE.

SUBADAR HARNAM SINGH OF JAGATPURA, NAWANSHAHR, JULLUNDUR. DOD: 13-MAR-1915. FRAN

SEPOY HARNAM SINGH OF KASEL, TARN TARAN, AMRITSAR. DOD: 26-APR-1915. BELGIUM.

SEPOY HARNAM SINGH OF MARI, LAHORE, PUNJAB. DOD: 26-APR-1915. BELGIUM.

SEPOY HARNAM SINGH OF CHAHIL, DASUYA, HOSHIARPUR. DOD: 13-MAY-1917. IRAQ.

HAVILDAR HARNAM SINGH OF CHOHLA, TARN TARAN, AMRITSAR. DOD: 13-MAY-1917. IRAQ

SEPOY HARNAM SINGH OF PURTHIPORE, KAPURTHALA. DOD: 06-NOV-1917. IRAQ.

SEPOY HARNAM SINGH OF NANGAL KHURD, LUDHIANA. DOD: 28-OCT-1918. ISRAEL.

48TH INDIAN PIONEERS

SEPOY HARNAM SINGH OF BHIKOWAL, DASUYA, HOSHIARPUR. DOD: 24-NOV-1914. IRAQ.

BUGLER HARNAM SINGH OF LODHAR, PASRUR, SIALKOT. DOD: 13-APR-1915. IRAQ.

SUBADAR HARNAM SINGH OF NURPUR, JULLUNDUR. DOD: 24-JUL-1915. IRAQ.

SEPOY HARNAM SINGH OF LADIALA, SHARAKPUR, SHEIKHUPURA. DOD: 16-APR-1918. IRAQ.

51ST SIKHS
(PUNJAB FRONTIER FORCE)

SEPOY HARNAM SINGH OF SALINA, MOGA, FEROZEPORE. DOD: 07-JAN-1916. IRAQ.

SEPOY HARNAM SINGH OF TAKHATPUR, SHAKARGARH, GURDASPUR. DOD: 11-MAR-1916. IRA

HAVILDAR HARNAM SINGH OF GULALIPUR, TARN TARAN, AMRITSAR. DOD: 25-DEC-1916. IRAQ.

SEPOY HARNAM SINGH OF MAMIAN, GURDASPUR. DOD: 25-FEB-1917. IRAQ.

SEPOY HARNAM SINGH OF BARA NANGAL, GARHSHANKAR, HOSHIARPUR. DOD: 22-APR-1917. IRAQ.

SUBADAR HARNAM SINGH OF JAGATPUR, NAWASHAHR, JULLUNDUR. DOD: 22-APR-1917. IRAQ.

SEPOY HARNAM SINGH OF NARAIN GARH, SAMRALA, LUDHIANA. DOD: 22-APR-1917. IRAQ.

SEPOY HARNAM SINGH OF THAUR, GURDASPUR. DOD: 08-JUN-1918. EGYPT.

HAVILDAR HARNAM SINGH OF SHERPUR, AGRAON, LUDHIANA, INDIA. DOD: 04-SEP-1918. IRAN.

52ND SIKHS (PUNJAB FRONTIER FORCE)

SEPOY HARNAM SINGH OF KANGWAL, HOSHIARPUR. DOD: 06-NOV-1918. IRAQ.

54TH SIKHS (PUNJAB FRONTIER FORCE)

SEPOY HARNAM SINGH OF SURTYAT, SIRSA, HISSAR. DOD: 15-SEP-1919. EGYPT.

55TH COKE'S RIFLES (PUNJAB FRONTIER FORCE)

SEPOY HARNAM SINGH OF DHARIWAL, BATALA, GURDASPUR. DOD: 26-APR-1915. BELGIUM.

SEPOY HARNAM SINGH OF NESTI, KANGRA. DOD: 17-DEC-1916. INDIA.

55TH COKE'S RIFLES (PUNJAB FRONTIER FORCE)

SEPOY HARNAM SINGH OF DHARIWAL, BATALA, GURDASPUR. DOD: 26-APR-1915. BELGIUM.

SEPOY HARNAM SINGH OF NESTI, KANGRA. DOD: 17-DEC-1916. INDIA.

56TH PUNJABI RIFLES (PUNJAB PUNJAB FRONTIER FORCE)

SEPOY HARNAM SINGH OF IKOLAHA, SAMRALA, LUDHIANA. DOD: 07-JAN-1916. IRAQ.

NAIK HARNAM SINGH OF DALA, MOGA, FEROZEPORE. DOD: 13-JAN-1916. IRAQ.

SEPOY HARNAM SINGH OF KOTLA SARF, BATALA, GURDASPUR. DOD: 28-JAN-1916. IRAQ.

57TH WILDE'S RIFLES (PUNJAB FRONTIER FORCE)

SEPOY HARNAM SINGH OF SALNU, BILASPUR. DOD: 30-NOV-1914. FRANCE.

LANCE NAIK HARNAM SINGH OF NASAR, AMRITSAR. DOD: 28-JAN-1920. INDIA.

58TH VAUGHAN'S RIFLES (PUNJAB FRONTIER FORCE)

SEPOY HARNAM SINGH OF GOZIPORE, BHAWANIGARH, PATIALA. DOD: 13-NOV-1917. EGYPT.

SEPOY HARNAM SINGH OF NAKHLI, BHAWANIGARH, PATIALA. DOD: 26-NOV-1917. EGYPT.

HAVILDAR HARNAM SINGH OF DHADOGAL, DHURI, PATIALA. DOD: 27-APR-1918. EGYPT.

59TH SCINDE RIFLES (PUNJAB FRONTIER FORCE)

SEPOY HARNAM SINGH OF THAKDOBURJI, PASRUR, SIALKOT. DOD: 26-OCT-1914. FRANCE.

SEPOY HARNAM SINGH OF BHAIKI PISHOWR, PATIALA. DOD: 19-DEC-1914. FRANCE.

SEPOY HARNAM SINGH OF GANDIWIND, TARN TARAN, AMRITSAR. DOD: 09-JAN-1917. IRAQ.

SEPOY HARNAM SINGH OF THILLE, RAYA, SIALKOT. DOD: 22-JAN-1919. EGYPT.

RIFLEMAN HARNAM SINGH OF GHUKE, RAYA, SIALKOT. DOD: 22-JAN-1919. ISRAEL.

QUEEN VICTORIA'S OWN CORPS OF GUIDES INFANTRY (PUNJAB FRONTIER FORCE) (LUMSDEN'S)

SEPOY HARNAM SINGH OF KESOWALI, RAYA, SIALKOT. DOD: 19-SEP-1916. KENYA.

JEMADAR HARNAM SINGH OF CHOGAWAN, MOGA, FEROZEPORE. DOD: 14-AUG-1918. EGYPT.

62ND PUNJABIS

NAIK HARNAM SINGH OF DAKHE, LUDHIANA. DOD: 08-MAR-1916. IRAQ.

HAVILDAR HARNAM SINGH OF RETERA, HANSI, HISSAR. DOD: 26-JAN-1917. IRAQ.

66TH PUNJABIS

SEPOY HARNAM SINGH OF CHIMON, SAMRALA, LUDHIANA. DOD: 17-JUL-1916. IRAQ.

67TH PUNJABIS

SEPOY HARNAM SINGH OF BADU, NAKODAR, JULLUNDUR. DOD: 01-MAY-1917. INDIA.

69TH PUNJABIS

SEPOY HARNAM SINGH OF HARSIPINDI, DASUYA, HOSHIARPUR. DOD: 14-NOV-1918. EGYPT.

72ND PUNJABIS

SEPOY HARNAM SINGH DOD: 13-MAR-1916. IRAQ.

SEPOY HARNAM SINGH DOD: 25-JUL-1918. EGYPT.

76TH PUNJABIS

SEPOY HARNAM SINGH OF ROPAR, NAWASHAHR, JULLUNDUR. DOD: 21-JAN-1915. EGYPT.

COLOUR HAVILDAR HARNAM SINGH OF PANDORI, HOSHIARPUR. DOD: 05-JUL-1915. IRAQ.

SEPOY HARNAM SINGH OF BADLIWARA, NAKODAR, JULLUNDUR. DOD: 31-MAR-1917. INDIA.

82ND PUNJABIS

SEPOY HARNAM SINGH OF MADAI, MOGA, FEROZEPORE. DOD: 25-SEP-1915. FRANCE.

84TH PUNJABIS

SEPOY HARNAM SINGH OF RAMPUR BIRLOW, GARHSHANKAR, HOSHAIRPUR. DOD: 30-MAR-1919. IRAQ.

87TH PUNJABIS

SEPOY HARNAM SINGH OF HERIKI, DHURI, PATIALA. DOD: 14-SEP-1917. IRAQ.

89TH PUNJABIS

SEPOY HARNAM SINGH OF TARIGIR, GUJRANWALA. DOD: 05-FEB-1915. EGYPT.

SEPOY HARNAM SINGH OF JOGIWALA, MOGA, FEROZEPORE. DOD: 18-AUG-1915. INDIA.

LANCE NAIK HARNAM SINGH OF GANDIWIND, TARN TARAN, AMRITSAR. DOD: 04-MAR-1916. IRAQ.

HAVILDAR HARNAM SINGH OF DUNA KOT, BARNALA, PATIALA. DOD: 11-MAR-1916. IRAQ.

NAIK HARNAM SINGH OF PAKHO, DHANUA, NABHA. DOD: 12-APR-1916. IRAQ.

90TH PUNJABIS

SEPOY HARNAM SINGH OF DIPHARWALA, GURDASPORE. DOD: 11-MAY-1915. TURKEY.

SEPOY HARNAM SINGH OF KAUSAN, BARNALA, PATIALA. PUNJAB. DOD: 24-JUL-1915. IRAQ.

NAIK HARNAM SINGH OF GANGOHAR, BARNALA, PATIALA. DOD: 07-MAR-1917. INDIA.

NAIK HARNAM SINGH OF KARAKA, TARN TARAN, AMRITSAR. DOD: 29-SEP-1917. IRAQ.

92ND PUNJABIS

SEPOY HARNAM SINGH OF MAGANPUR, SIMLA. DOD: 07-JAN-1916. IRAQ.

SEPOY HARNAM SINGH OF JHALARI, AMRITSAR. DOD: 22-FEB-1917. IRAQ.

93RD BURMA INFANTRY, INDIAN ARMY

SEPOY HARNAM SINGH OF AJNALA, AMRITSAR. DOD: 08-MAR-1916. IRAQ.

HAVILDAR HARNAM SINGH OF BALGARH, JAGRAON, LUDHIANA. DOD: 25-MAR-1917. IRAQ.

SEPOY HARNAM SINGH OF JANDIALA, AMRITSAR. DOD: 30-APR-1917. INDIA.

151ST INDIAN INFANTRY

HAVILDAR HARNAM SINGH OF BACHAWANA, FATEHABAD, HISSAR. DOD: 13-AUG-1918. EGYPT.

BURMA MILITARY POLICE

RIFLEMAN HARNAM SINGH OF GHANINKE, FATEHGARH, GURDASPORE. DOD: 22-AUG-1915. TURKEY.

RIFLEMAN HARNAM SINGH OF DHURKOTE, DEHLON, LUDHIANA. DOD: 09-SEP-1915. TURKEY.

RIFLEMAN HARNAM SINGH OF SADHANWALI, DERABABANANAK, GURDASPORE. DOD: 19-SEP-1915. TURKEY.

LANCE NAIK HARNAM SINGH OF BHAIM, TARN TARAN, AMRITSAR. DOD: 01-FEB-1917. IRAQ.

RIFLEMAN HARNAM SINGH OF RATOKA, AMRITSAR. DOD: 25-MAR-1917. IRAQ.

JEMADAR HARNAM SINGH OF KHIALA, AJNALA, AMRITSAR, INDIA. DOD: 13-MAY-1918. IRAN.

RIFLEMAN HARNAM SINGH OF DAKHA, LUDHIANA, INDIA. DOD: 03-NOV-1918. IRAN.

RIFLEMAN HARNAM SINGH OF HUDIARA, LAHORE, PAKISTAN. DOD: 08-NOV-1918. IRAN.

RIFLEMAN HARNAM SINGH OF PATHAN NANGAL, AJNALA, AMRITSAR, INDIA. DOD: 09-NOV-1918. IRAN.

JIND INFANTRY

SEPOY HARNAM SINGH OF GUJRAN, BHAWANIGARH, PATIALA. DOD: 09-JUL-1915. KENYA.

SEPOY HARNAM SINGH OF KHUDAL, MANSA, PATIALA. DOD: 14-MAY-1917. TANZANIA.

KAPURTHALA INFANTRY (JAGATJIT REGIMENT) :

SEPOY HARNAM SINGH OF BHANDAL, KAPURTHALA. DOD: 19-NOV-1916. KENYA.

1ST PATIALA INFANTRY

SEPOY HARNAM SINGH OF LALRU, RAJPURA, BASSI, PATIALA. DOD: 08-OCT-1915. TURKEY.

FOLLOWER HARNAM SINGH OF BADAUCHHI, BASSI, PATIALA. DOD: 23-OCT-1915. TURKEY.

SEPOY HARNAM SINGH OF KARHALI, PATIALA. DOD: 20-DEC-1918. EGYPT.

ROYAL GARRISON ARTILLERY, INDIAN ARMY

NAIK HARNAM SINGH DOD: 19-MAR-1915. FRANCE.

GUNNER HARNAM SINGH OF HANS, JAGRAON, LUDHIANA. DOD: 29-MAR-1918. EGYPT.

ROYAL HORSE AND FIELD ARTILLERY, INDIAN ARMY

DRIVER HARNAM SINGH DOD: 24-OCT-1918. EGYPT.

INDIAN SIGNAL CORPS

SEPOY HARNAM SINGH DOD: 02-APR-1919. IN

SUPPLY AND TRANSPORT CORP

DRIVER HARNAM SINGH DOD: 11-SEP-1916. IRAQ.

DRIVER HARNAM SINGH OF CHESSLYWAL KASUR, LAHORE. DOD: 13-DEC-1917. IRAQ

CLERK HARNAM SINGH DOD: 03-OCT-1918. IRAN.

SARWAN HARNAM SINGH DOD: 31-OCT-1918. IRAN.

DRIVER HARNAM SINGH DOD: 19-DEC-1919. IRAQ.

INDIAN MOUNTAIN ARTILLER

LANCE NAIK HARNAM SINGH OF THUROO, TARN AMRITSAR, INDIA. DOD: 05-MAR-1915. IRAN

GUNNER HARNAM SINGH OF RUNIAN, MOG FEROZEPORE. DOD: 18-JUN-1916. KENYA.

DRIVER HARNAM SINGH OF RAUNIAN, MOG FEROZEPORE. DOD: 18-JUN-1917. INDIA.

DRIVER HARNAM SINGH DOD: 27-JAN-1918. TANZANIA.

DRIVER HARNAM SINGH OF KOANKH, GUJRAT. DOD: 10-JUN-1919. INDIA.

1914-1918

Beyond The Western Front

The preceding pages memorialise Indian soldiers named Harnam Singh recorded in the Commonwealth War Graves Commission database of First World War Casualties.

In addition to the deployment of the Indian Expeditionary Force A (IEF A) to Europe, Indian Expeditionary Forces were deployed across the globe including German East Africa (IEF B & IEF C), Mesopotamia (IEF D), Egypt and Palestine (IEF E & IEF F), and Gallipoli (IEF G).

By engaging the enemy on several fronts, the Indian Army stretched the resources of the Central Powers and won notable victories. In Egypt in 1915, Indian forces defeated an Ottoman attack on the Suez Canal, and in neighbouring Mesopotamia (Iraq) IEF A joined IEF D to capture Baghdad in 1917.

In Palestine, at the location of the biblical battle of Armageddon, another Anglo-Indian Army launched a devastating offensive in 1918 that defeated a much larger enemy army leading directly to the surrender and collapse of the Ottoman Empire. This battle was also probably the last great cavalry offensive in history, in which hundreds of miles and Damascus itself were captured by massed cavalry alone. The bulk of the infantry and much of the cavalry during the 1918 Palestine campaign were Indian Army regiments.

Indian forces were also retained in many theatres beyond the Armistice of November 1918. Regiments such as the 19th Punjabis saw action, along with other Commonwealth troops, in British missions against the Bolsheviks in Russian and Persian campaigns.

Indian Gallantry at the Front: Saving A Stricken Comrade
The Illustrated London News Dec 12, 1914

The First World War was not the first time soldiers like Harnam Singh fought for the British Empire. During the 19th Century, Great Britain expanded its Empire to become the largest in history. Much of this expansion was in Asia and Africa where the Indian Army saw service in many campaigns winning for itself a reputation of loyalty and effectiveness

SAHIB & SEPOY

BROTHERHOOD OF THE BOLD

Campaigns across the far-flung outposts of Empire served to build a unique camaraderie between the Indian Army 's British officers and the Indian soldier. Without this relationship, the Sepoy would not have followed his commander into battle

Origin of the British Indian Army

The British Indian Army (BIA) began its existence in the early 18th Century as the private soldiers of the British Honourable East India Company (HEIC); a trading company established in London to expand the spice trade between Europe and South Asia. It initially employed a few hundred Indian irregulars to guard a handful of trading posts in India. Ongoing hostilities with foreign competitors (primarily the Dutch, Portuguese, and French) required it to expand its military and administrative capacities aggressively. As a result, the 'Company' evolved into three distinct presidencies, Bengal, Madras and Bombay, each with its own army consisting of British Regiments and Indian Regiments commanded by British officers.

By 1856 the HEIC had grown to become one of India's largest employers, with a force of 214,985 native troops supplemented by 39,375 European soldiers. The Bengal Army was the showpiece unit, boasting the largest contingent of troops. Unlike the other Presidencies, this army recruited only high caste Hindus (Brahmins and Rajputs) and Muslim soldiers previously employed in the Mughal forces. Through these caste exclusions, the Bengal Army encouraged a sense of superiority over other Indian Sepoys (soldiers) and the Indian population in general.

In India, the military profession naturally attracted hereditary soldiers such as the Rajputs. For these groups, being a soldier carried with it prestige, and many preferred it to farm or menial labour. In addition, after the two Anglo-Sikh Wars resulted in the defeat of the Sikhs, the British heavily courted agriculturalist (Jat) Sikhs who had formed the backbone of the Sikh Empire's Khalsa army. British authorities considered the Sikhs the ideal Indian soldier, their shining deeds of noble heroism and sacrifice were attributed to a religious zeal which at its root comprised simple virtues such as tolerance, humility and service as preached by their Gurus.

Anglo-Sikh War: Annexation of the Punjab 1846-49

In the 1830s the only major independent Indian power left in the Indian subcontinent was the Sikh Kingdom in Punjab. The Sikhs and the British had entered into a peace treaty in 1809, but after the death of its founder, Maharaja Ranjit Singh, relations between them had soured to the point of open conflict. Two bloody wars broke out (1st Anglos-Sikh War 1846, 2nd Anglo Sikh War 1849) in which the Punjab was ultimately taken over, but not without great cost to the British. Despite being undermined by a treacherous leadership and self-interested opportunists within their ranks, many British officers felt that the Punjabis had fought better than their own Bengal Army soldiers. As a result, once peace was established, the British courted the ranks of their former opponents to raise two infantry regiments, the 14th Ferozepore Sikhs and 15th Ludhiana Sikhs, as well as a mixed troop of

infantry and cavalry to become the 'Punjab Frontier Force'. These regiments survive to this day, and all served in WW1, the 15th Sikhs, 57th Wilde's Rifles Frontier Force, 58th Rifles (Frontier Force), and 59th Scinde Rifles (Frontier Force) fought in France and Belgium on the Western Front in 1914. The 14th Sikhs served with distinction in Gallipoli in 1915.

Rebellion: The Mutiny of 1857

The recruitment of Punjabis after the Anglo-Sikh Wars threatened the Purbiya's (easterner) monopoly of employment in the Bengal Army. Discontent with service conditions had also been mounting in this army over withdrawn pay allowances and demands for overseas deployment. According to Hindu beliefs, crossing the seas was a taboo that incurred a loss of caste for high-caste Hindus. In the end, an alleged issue of ammunition cartridges being greased with both cow and pig fat insulted Hindu and Muslim Bengali soldiers alike, sparking long-standing seething resentment into open rebellion.

On May 10th, 1857, two Bengal regiments mutinied and murdered their British officers. Soon others followed until much of the Bengal Army was in revolt. The Rebels proclaimed a new Mughal Empire and occupied Delhi as their capital. The British were utterly unprepared for such an event and found themselves outnumbered in northern India by their former soldiers. Little help could be expected from Great Britain for many months, and the loyal Bombay and Madras Presidency Armies further south were too far to help in any significant way. It took over a year for the British and their allies to fully suppress the Mutiny, with the last rebel strongholds falling in June 1858. Many innocent lives, including women and children, were lost on both sides. Despite being severely outnumbered early on, the British triumphed with the support and loyalty of their new Punjabi regiments. Ultimately, the newly recruited Punjabi and Sikh soldiers of the former Khalsa Army had held the balance of power in their hands; if they had chosen to side with the rebels, then a British victory would have been near impossible.

The Punjabis for their part had not forgotten the Anglo-Sikh Wars of only eight years earlier, in which garrisons of Bengal Presidency troops (Purbiyas) had attacked their independent nation as part of the HEIC army, and had boasted openly of their victory despite the British troops having done much of the hard fighting. Given the traditional divide between the peoples of the Indus and those of the Ganges belt, the insult cut deep into the injury. If there was any hesitation amongst Punjabi soldiers over which side to choose during the Mutiny, the rebel proclamation of a new Mughal Empire sealed the matter in Britain's favour. The Mughal Empire of the 17th and 18th Centuries had a long record of persecuting the newly formed Sikh community, to fight to return such a government to power was seen as a far worse option by the Sikhs than siding with the British. In the end, Punjabi soldiers stayed loyal to Britain, and they played a critical role in defeating the rebellion.

Many people considered poor HEIC management of India to be one of the major factors contributing to the Sepoy rebellion. India was now considered too valuable to the growing British Empire to leave in the hands of a commercial enterprise so following the Mutiny, in 1858, the British Government assumed direct control of HEIC territories and formally established India as a colony of the Crown.

The Martial Races

The Mutiny taught the British that their hold on India depended directly on the loyalty of their Indian soldiers. The old Bengal Army was now viewed with distrust which meant that new soldiers would have to be recruited from elsewhere. Because of their courage fighting the British during the two Anglo-Sikh Wars and their loyalty during the Mutiny, soldiers from Punjab began to be recruited heavily. To support this effort, several senior British Officers developed the 'Martial Race' theory. In brief, this theory stated that some races within India made better warriors than others; 18th century beliefs in the influence of the environment had fostered longstanding assumptions that northern 'races' were hardier, more industrious, and more courageous, all thanks to the difficult terrain and cold weather.

In the 19th century, with the sciences of 'race' taking hold of Western imagination, the theory found scientific justification within Darwinist anthropological discussions of colonialism and ethnicity. In India the theory was used to label certain classes and communities as 'warrior' races, possessing attributes of self-sufficiency, physical and moral resilience, orderliness, fighting prowess, and a sense of courage and loyalty. General Sir J.J.H. Gordon argued that Punjabi Sikhs were "a fine martial race" whose admirable traits were "steadfast loyalty, dogged tenacity, and dauntless courage." He added that this was a consequence of "climate, occupation and the northern strain of their character." On the other hand, the suspected lethargy and timidity of other Indians was attributed by many to prolonged exposure to a stiflingly hot climate. Also at this time, the widely reported exploits of Sikhs, Gurkhas, and Scottish Highlanders had forged strong reputations for them as great warriors across the Empire. This success on the battlefield seemed to prove the martial race theory correct in the mind of Victorian Britons.

By 1875, the Indian Army drew 1/3 of its recruits from the Punjab.

In 1879 the Eden Commission, headed by Sir Ashley Eden Lieutenant-Governor of Bengal, looked to reform the Indian Army. It recommended recruiting more soldiers from the northwest of India. The commission's report defined 'the Punjab as the home of the most martial races in India' and that it was 'the nursery of our best soldiers'. A Russian encroachment into Afghanistan during the latter half of the 19th century also presented a new and growing threat, which intensified demand for more local 'Martial Race' recruiting.

Disciples of the Martial Race theory included Indian army commanders Lord Roberts, Lord Kitchener and General Willcocks. All three British Officers knew the Punjabis first hand from having served alongside them in battle.

Lord Roberts VC was an Irishman born in India that served 41 years in the British Indian Army. He rose through the ranks to become the most distinguished soldier of the 19th century, upon his death, he was buried as Queen Victoria's greatest General at St Paul's Cathedral in London. An architect of the Empire's greatest victories he never forgot the staunch support Punjab's loyal soldiers gave him throughout his illustrious career. In 1885, as part of the Eden Commission, he continued the reforms in Indian Army recruitment; Roberts had been Commander-in-Chief of the Madras Army between 1881 and 1885, and this tenure had convinced him of the lack of a fighting spirit in the peoples of Madras. Though retired at the outbreak of WW1, 'Bob's Bahadur' (the brave) would provide an important figurehead for the deployment of India's colonial soldiers into the war effort.

General Sir James Willcocks was born in India, a son of an officer of the HEIC he spent his entire military career with the Indian Army. Willcocks served in the Anglo-Afghan war of 1878 as well as many other North West Frontier campaigns. He had also served as part of the British Indian Army's international campaigns in the Soudan in 1885 and the Burma expedition of 1886-89. In 1898, he was appointed as second-in-command of the West African Frontier Force which he later commanded in 1899-1900, followed by Ashanti Field Force. In 1902, he joined the Field Force in South Africa war and on returning to India in 1908 he commanded with distinction the 1st (Peshawar) Division in the Zakka Khel and Mohamed expeditions. On the outbreak of WW1 Willcocks was appointed commander of the Indian army in France. According to General Willcocks, the Sikhs formed the "backbone of British military prestige in the East".

Lord Horatio Kitchener was a colonial administrator featuring prominently in the major campaigns of the Victorian era including the war in Sudan and Lord Robert's campaigns of the Boar War. He was Commander-in-Chief (1902–09) of the British Indian Army, a role in which he undertook far-reaching reforms to address the threat of Russian encroachment on India. He was appointed Secretary of State for War in the British Government at the outbreak of WW1. Recognising the limits of Britain's standing army he instigated a huge recruitment campaign to form "Kitchener's new army".

The Salt of the Sirkar

Punjab's peasantry had many reasons for joining the British Indian Army. Soldiers were offered guaranteed salaries and retirement benefits which were nearly unheard of at the time. Better living conditions also appealed to those living a harsh life of farming in the less arable districts of the province such as the Salt Plains of West Punjab. However, for the agriculturalist landholding classes of the more fertile regions, the allotment of land became the biggest allure of service in the British forces. The Indian Army offered Jagirs (land grants) for loyal service on retirement and gallantry on the battlefield, which ensured military service would remain prestigious to future generations. Within Punjabi culture ownership of land can be considered to be the most important marker of Izzat. For Jat Sikhs, who were known to be expert farmers and agricultural proprietors, ownership and control of farmland and produce attracted high returns and shaped their Izzat and caste dominance in Punjab. For many such Punjabis, to fight and die in military service was a means to raise the heroic reputation of one's caste and its economic standing.

The BIA was structured on the regimental system; each regiment had their own unique customs, traditions, colours (banners), and recruiting areas. Some regiments were 'one class' formations like the 47th Sikhs or 15th Sikhs which employed only Jat Sikhs while others like the 34th Sikh Pioneers employed only Mazhbi Sikhs. Regiments such as the 24th Punjabis and Frontier Force regiments were mixed regiments, and employed Sikhs, Dogras, Punjabi Muslims, and Afridis (Pashtuns/Pathans). Caste-class unit definitions including the spellings shown here were used by the Government of India in the military's periodic Caste Returns.

Indian Ranks (Infantry/Cavalry)
Subadar-Major / Risaldar-Major = Highest Indian rank.
Subadar / Risaldar = Captain (Senior Indian Officer rank)
Jemadar / Jemadar = Lieutenant (Junior Indian Officer rank)
Havildar / Daffadar = Sergeant (Platoon or section commander command)
Naik / Acting Lance Daffadar = Corporal (Lowest non-commissioned officer rank)
Sepoy / Sowar = Private (Lowest enlisted rank)

Above: Members of the King's Own Cavalry Regiments of the Indian Army who came to the coronation of George V. A coloured lithograph published in The Illustrated London News 1911. The coronation took place at Westminster Abbey London, and was commemorated in Delhi 6 months later with the crowning of the Sovereign as Emperor of India. Over 26,000 silver Delhi Durbar Medals were awarded to the men and officers of the British and Indian Armies who participated in the Durbar.

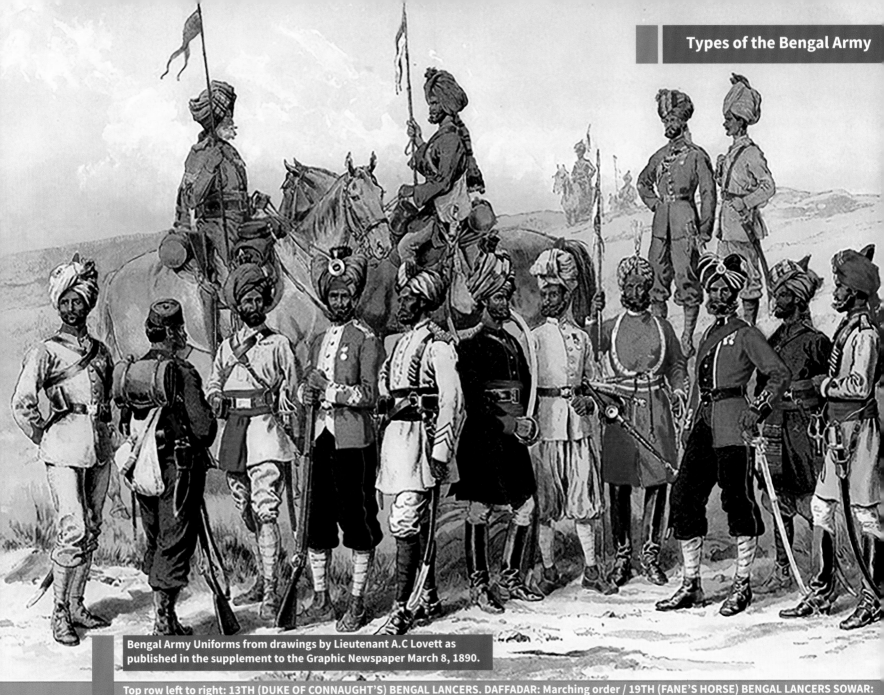

Bengal Army Uniforms from drawings by Lieutenant A.C Lovett as published in the supplement to the Graphic Newspaper March 8, 1890.

Top row left to right: 13TH (DUKE OF CONNAUGHT'S) BENGAL LANCERS. DAFFADAR: Marching order / 19TH (FANE'S HORSE) BENGAL LANCERS SOWAR: Marching Order / 1ST PUNJAUB INFANTRY (Coke's Rifles / 59th Frontier Force) NATIVE OFFICER: Full Dress / 4TH (HAZARA) MOUNTAIN BATTERY GUNNER: Field Service Dress / Bottom row left to right: QUEEN'S OWN CORPS OF GUIDES (Infantry), NATIVE OFFICER: Full Dress / 4TH GOORKHA REGIMENT SEPOY: Marching Order / QUEEN'S OWN CORPS OF GUIDES (Cavalry) NATIVE OFFICER: Field Service Dress / 45TH RATTRAY'S SIKHS SEPOY: Full Dress / 3RD BENGAL CAVALRY SOWAR: Field Service Dress / 1ST PUNJAUB CAVALRY SOWAR: (later 21st Cavalry Frontier Force) Full Dress / 1ST SIKH INFANTRY PIPER (later 51st Sikhs): Full Dress / H.E THE VICEROY'S BODYGUARD SOWAR: Full Dress / 18TH BENGAL INFANTRY: NATIVE OFFICER Full Dress / 15TH MOOLTANEE CAVALRY SOWAR(15th Lancers) : Full Dress / 1ST BENGAL CAVALRY SOWAR Full Dress

Indian Army Role & Campaigns

Within India the BIA had a dual role in preserving internal peace and defending the country's borders. This was a huge undertaking because prior to 1947, the notion of a single cohesive Indian nation did not exist. Instead, South Asia was a patchwork of independent princely states, disparate races, many languages, and a society divided along communal lines and fragmented allegiances. Banditry, guerrilla activities, peasant revolts, lockouts, labour unrest, and Hindu-Muslim communal riots were common scenarios in which the Indian Army had to be deployed.

During much of the 19th Century, Great Britain was focused on expanding and maintaining a global Empire that would be the largest in history. Much of this expansion was in Asia and Africa, which added to older possessions such as Canada, Australia, and New Zealand. When the need arose, the BIA was also tasked with a 3rd responsibility of being ready to mobilise rapidly for service overseas to play a role in these imperial campaigns. These operations included enforcing treaties, suppressing revolts, and launching punitive expeditions for acts against imperial authority. Punjab's soldiers distinguished themselves in many of these 'small wars' of the Empire, and they became much sought after recruits for the military administration of the Crown's new possessions. In Africa newly raised Imperial regiments such as the Central African Rifles would employ many Sikhs. In the Far East, Punjabis were also involved in the policing of Hong Kong, Shanghai and the new territories of Singapore and Malaysia's Straits settlements as part of the Malay State Guides. Service in the outposts of the Empire served to build a unique camaraderie between Indian Army British officers and their Indian soldiers.

The Malta Expeditionary Force

In 1878 the BIA saw its first deployment to Europe. Following a Russian victory over Turkey in the Russo -Turkish war of 1877, Turkey was forced to concede some Balkan territories to Russia. In April 1878, the British Government dispatched the Malta Expeditionary Force from India to support Turkey against further Russian encroachment. In Great Britain, there were grave concerns that Russian success in the Eastern Mediterranean could threaten British shipping and communication connections with India. Although the expected war with Russia did not break out, Turkey granted control of Cyprus to Great Britain in return for its support against Russia. When the Malta Expeditionary Force moved from Malta to Cyprus, Indian cavalry was deployed to quell any local opposition to the change in administration. A prestigious Indian cavalry unit, Hodson's Horse, provided armed escorts for officers and parties in mountainous areas of the island where bandits were a problem. This action showcased the calibre of the Indian soldier in a display of power designed to signal Britain's capability to deploy the Indian Army in any future wars in Europe.

Hodson's Horse

Hodson's Horse was raised in 1857 from experienced soldiers of the disbanded Khalsa army. During the Mutiny, it was tasked with the capture of the Mughal Emperor Bahadur Shah Zafar and his family. The regiment's founding British Officer, William Raikes Hodson, was a graduate of Cambridge University who had served with the Punjab Frontier Force. During the Mutiny, he would become infamous for the execution of the Mughal Emperors' son and grandchildren in retribution for the murders of British civilians in Delhi. This in effect ended the line of Mughal rule in India. Another British Officer that served with Hodson's horse during the Mutiny was Sir Charles MacGregor, who was a descendant of Rob Roy, the infamous Scottish folk hero of the Jacobite rebellion. MacGregor would go on to become a Major General in the Indian Army. The regiment's first Indian Officer, Man Singh Wariach, had been a cavalry officer in the Khalsa Army of Ranjit Singh and had fought against the British. After the Anglo-Sikh Wars, Man Singh joined the Indian Army to avenge the defeat of the Sikh Kingdom at the hands of the Purbiyas, and to plunder Delhi which was the Mughal capital of India. During the Mutiny, he served with distinction winning both an Indian Order of Merit and Order of British India 1st Class. He served as Risaldar-Major until his retirement in 1877 when he was made an Honourary Magistrate at Amritsar and then manager of the Darbar Sahib (Golden Temple).

In addition to the Malta Expedition, Hodson's Horse was the only cavalry regiment sent to join the Sudan expedition in 1885 where Indian troops would fight alongside Canadians in their first international campaign. During the Great War, Hodson's Horse would see action on the Western Front fighting alongside Canadians once again as part of the 2nd Indian Cavalry Division.

The Second Anglo-Afghan War 1878 - 1880

The despatch of the Indian Expedition to Malta forced Russia's attention from Europe to its Asian frontiers. When Russian authorities sent an uninvited military mission to Kabul, Great Britain despatched its own envoy from India to Afghanistan. The tribal border with Afghanistan had throughout history been a gateway for incursions into India by a host of foreign invaders, and during the latter half of the 19th century, it was the threat of a Russian invasion that loomed large. In 1878, with tensions mounting, Britain declared war on Afghanistan after the Afghan Amir agreed to see the Russian agent while refusing to see the British agent. In July 1880, in a key battle, a force of British and Indian troops was overwhelmed by Afghan soldiers and tribesmen and defeated at the Battle of Maiwand. After incurring heavy losses, the survivors retreated into Kandahar, where, within a few days, they were besieged by Afghan forces.

A rescue mission was then quickly formulated in which General Frederick Roberts took his crack regiments comprising Sikhs, Gurkhas and British Highlanders on a 300 mile march from Kabul to Kandahar to rescue the British garrison. After covering over 16 miles a day over harsh conditions, a force of 10,000 men defeated the Afghan Army at the Battle of Kandahar on 1 September. The delivery of a swift victory after a notorious disaster captured the hearts and minds of the British people and Roberts was celebrated as a national hero and became titled Lord Roberts of Kandahar.

The Battle of Maiwand was the first significant engagement of the war fought by the Bombay Army, and its defeat brought heavy criticism of those troops. The Indian troops that fought all the victorious battles of the Second Anglo-Afghan War were the Punjabi dominated regiments from the Bengal Army. Upon victory over the Afghans, Lord Roberts was advanced to command the Indian Army. In this role, working closely with future Viceroys, he influenced Indian defence policy on the North-West Frontier and endorsed Martial Race recruitment policies centred on the Punjabis, who had been critical in winning a war that had now successfully delivered control of Afghanistan's foreign policy to Britain.

The North West Frontier

After the annexation of the Punjab, the BIA had been forced to launch many punitive military campaigns to repel incursions by the warlike tribes of the frontier including the Waziris, Mahsuds, and Mohmands. To confront this ongoing threat the 'Punjab Frontier Force' was originally raised from disbanded regiments of the former Sikh Kingdom of Maharaja Ranjit Singh. The Khalsa army had earlier defeated the Afghans and driven them back beyond the Khyber Pass and captured Peshawar, the summer capital of the Afghans. Tensions along the border would continue after the 2nd Anglo-Afghan War requiring troops stationed on the frontier to be in a constant state of readiness in case of attack. In 1887, new single class regiments such as the 35th & 36th Sikhs were raised from the ranks of the original Frontier Forces and the 14th & 15th Sikhs. These new regiments enlisted more men from the Sikh heartlands of Amritsar, Jalandhar, Ludhiana and Patiala. In 1897 these new regiments quickly distinguished themselves when an uprising led by Orakzais & Afridis led to the largest military campaign in India since the 1857 rebellion. Following these border campaigns, further Martial Race recruitment continued from ranks of the Punjab's Sikhs with the 47th Sikhs being established in 1901 with drafts from 35th and 36th Sikhs. By the turn of the new century, the BIA stood ready to confront domestic and international threats with high-quality battle tested regiments adept in hill warfare capabilities - skills that would be brought to bear on entering the front lines in Flanders where trench warfare would limit open battle offensive manoeuvres.

Key BIA regiments and their Battle Honours in the 2nd Anglo-Afghan War 1878-80

Battle Honours: Ali Masjid Date 1878-11-21 , Afghanistan '78-80 Date 1878-11-22, Afghanistan '78-79 Date 1878-11-22, Peiwar Kotal Date: 1878-12-02, Kabul '79 Date: 1879-12-10, Ahmad Khel Date: 1880-04-19, Kandahar '80 Date 1880-05-19

Cavalry: Queen Victoria's Own Corps of Guides Cavalry (Frontier Force) (Lumsden's), 1st Duke of York's Lancers (Skinner's Horse), 3rd Lancers (Skinner's Horse), 4th Indian Cavalry, 5th Indian Cavalry, 8th Indian Cavalry, 10th Duke of Cambridge's Own Lancers (Hodson's Horse), 11th King Edward's Own Lancers (Probyn's Horse), 12th Indian Cavalry, 13th Duke of Connaught's Own Lancers (Watson's Horse), 14th Murrey Jat Lancers , 15th Lancers (Cureton's Multani's), 17th Indian Cavalry, 18th King George's Own Lancers, 19th Lancers (Fane's Horse), 21st Prince Albert Victor's Own Cavalry (Frontier Force) (Daly's Horse), 22nd Sam Browne's Cavalry (Frontier Force), 23rd Indian Cavalry (Frontier Force), 25th Indian Cavalry (Frontier Force), 26th King George's Own Light Cavalry, 31st Duke of Connaught's Own Lancers, 32nd Lancers, 33rd Queen Victoria's Own Light Cavalry, 34th Prince Albert Victor's Own Poona Horse, 35th Scinde Horse, 36th Jacob's Horse, 38th King George's Own Central India Horse

Infantry/Sappers/Pioneers: Queen Victoria's Own Corps of Guides Infantry (Frontier Force) (Lumsden's), 3rd Sappers and Miners, 9th Bhopal Infantry, 14th King George's Own Ferozepore Sikhs, 15th Ludhiana Sikhs, 19th Punjabis, 20th Duke of Cambridge's Own Infantry (Brownlow's Punjabis), 21st Punjabis, 22nd Punjabis, 23rd Sikh Pioneers, 24th Punjabis, 25th Punjabis, 26th Punjabis, 27th Punjabis, 28th Punjabis, 29th Punjabis, 30th Punjabis, 31st Punjabis, 32nd Sikh Pioneers, 34th Sikh Pioneers, 45th Rattray's Sikhs, 51st Sikhs (Frontier Force), 52nd Sikhs (Frontier Force), 53rd Sikhs (Frontier Force), 55th Coke's Rifles (Frontier Force), 56th Punjabi Rifles (Frontier Force), 57th Wilde's Rifles (Frontier Force), 58th Vaughan's Rifles (Frontier Force), 90th Punjabis

In WW1 the Indian Army would become the most widely deployed army of the Allies, its battle honours across the globe included:

France & Belgium: La Bassee, 1914 / Messines, 1914 / Festubert, 1914 Neuve Chapelle, 1915 / Ypres, 1915 / St Julien, 1915 Aubers, 1915 / Loos, 1915 / Defence of Givenchy 1915 Winter Bazentin, 1916 / Delville Wood, 1916 / Morval, 1916 Cambrai, 1917 **Mesopotamia:** Mesopotamia 1914-1918 / Basra, 1914 / Shaiba, 1915 Ctesiphon, 1915 / Defence of Kut-al-Amara, 1915-1916 /17 Tigris, 1916 / Baghdad, 1917 / Khan Baghdadi, 1918 Sharqat, 1918 **Sinai & Palestine:** Gaza, 1917 / Megiddo 1918 / Nablus 1918 Sharon 1918 / Damascus 1918 **Gallipoli:** Gallipoli, 1915-1916 / Krithia, 1915 **German East Africa** East Africa 1914-1918 / Kilimanjaro 1916 / Narugombe 1917 **Egypt:** Egypt, 1915-1917 / Suez Canal, 1915 **Salonika:** Macedonia, 1915-1918 **Persia:** Persia, 1915-1919 **Arabia** : Aden, 1915-1918 **Afghanistan /North-West Frontier Province:** India 1914-1915, 1916-1917 / Baluchistan, 1915-16 & 1918 Afghanistan

See map overleaf for more on WW1 campaigns

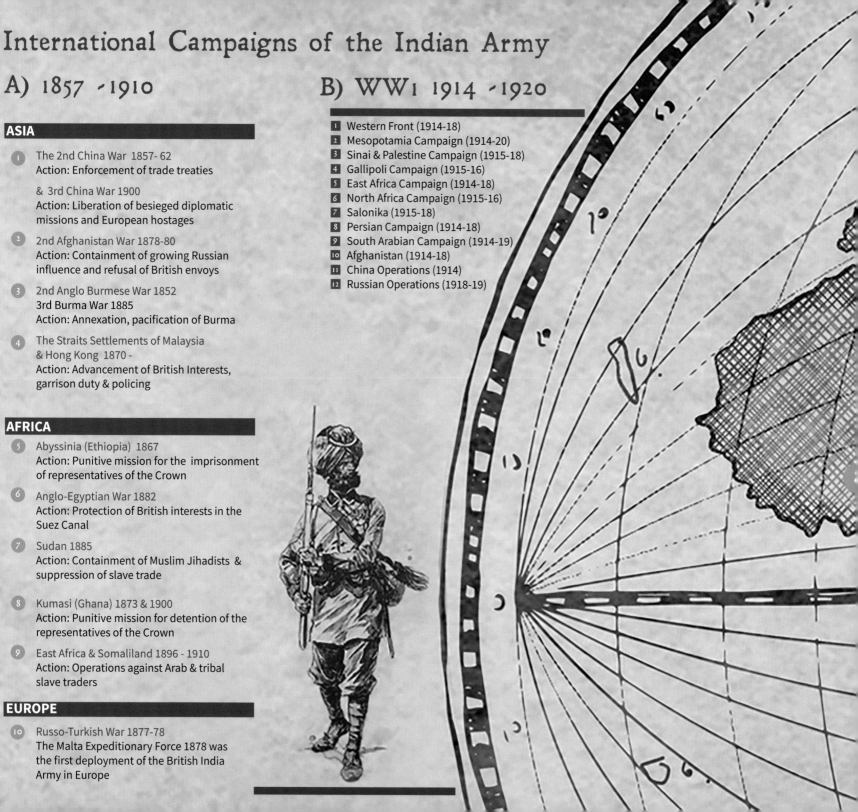

International Campaigns of the Indian Army

A) 1857 - 1910

ASIA

1. The 2nd China War 1857- 62
   Action: Enforcement of trade treaties

   & 3rd China War 1900
   Action: Liberation of besieged diplomatic missions and European hostages

2. 2nd Afghanistan War 1878-80
   Action: Containment of growing Russian influence and refusal of British envoys

3. 2nd Anglo Burmese War 1852
   3rd Burma War 1885
   Action: Annexation, pacification of Burma

4. The Straits Settlements of Malaysia & Hong Kong 1870 -
   Action: Advancement of British Interests, garrison duty & policing

AFRICA

5. Abyssinia (Ethiopia) 1867
   Action: Punitive mission for the imprisonment of representatives of the Crown

6. Anglo-Egyptian War 1882
   Action: Protection of British interests in the Suez Canal

7. Sudan 1885
   Action: Containment of Muslim Jihadists & suppression of slave trade

8. Kumasi (Ghana) 1873 & 1900
   Action: Punitive mission for detention of the representatives of the Crown

9. East Africa & Somaliland 1896 - 1910
   Action: Operations against Arab & tribal slave traders

EUROPE

10. Russo-Turkish War 1877-78
    The Malta Expeditionary Force 1878 was the first deployment of the British India Army in Europe

B) WW1 1914 - 1920

1. Western Front (1914-18)
2. Mesopotamia Campaign (1914-20)
3. Sinai & Palestine Campaign (1915-18)
4. Gallipoli Campaign (1915-16)
5. East Africa Campaign (1914-18)
6. North Africa Campaign (1915-16)
7. Salonika (1915-18)
8. Persian Campaign (1914-18)
9. South Arabian Campaign (1914-19)
10. Afghanistan (1914-18)
11. China Operations (1914)
12. Russian Operations (1918-19)

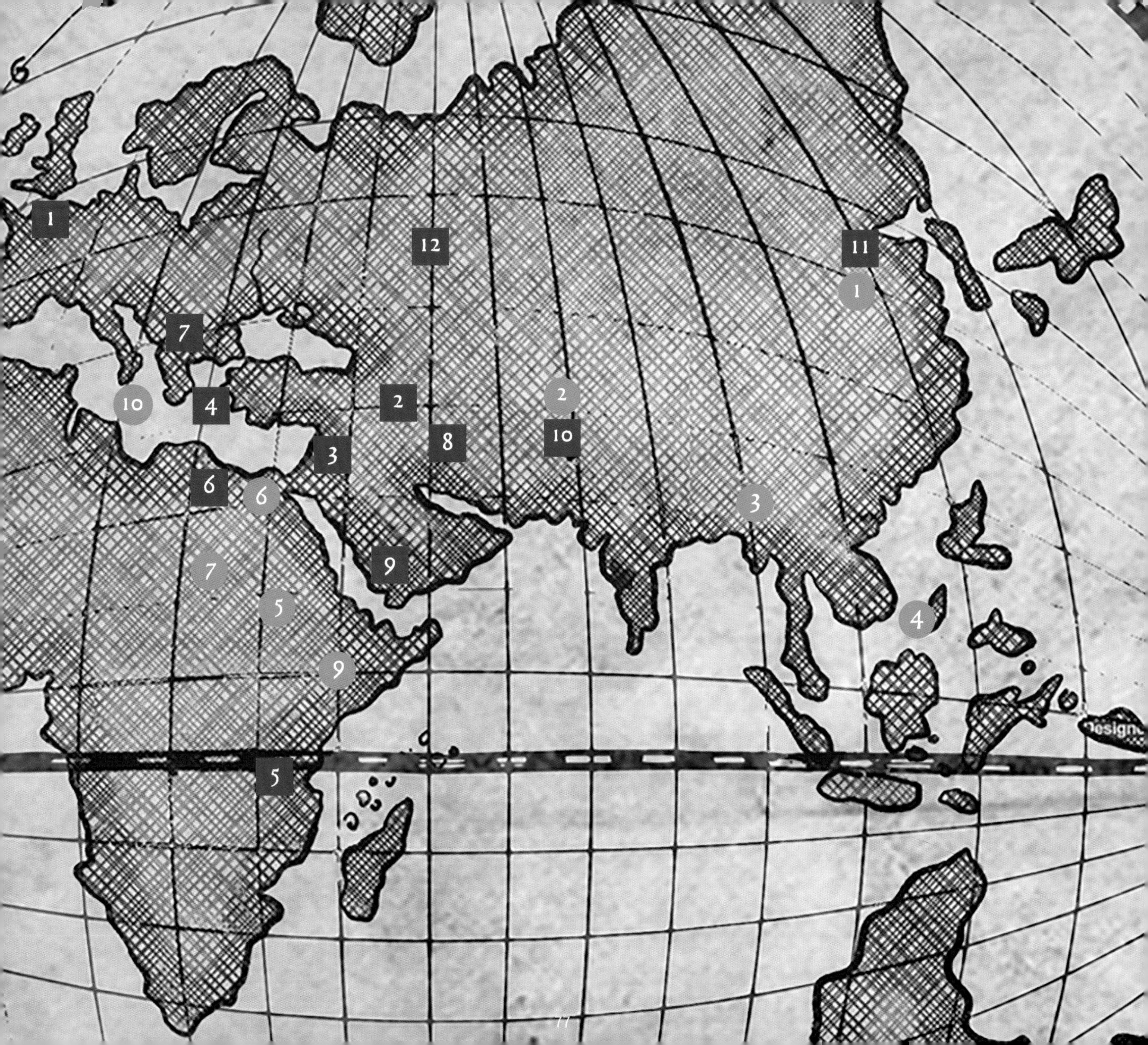
6
1
12
11
1
7
10
4
2
2
8
10
3
6
6
3
7
9
5
4
9
5

The Sahib

Ruling a vast and diverse country like India presented British rulers with significant challenges in governing with so few personnel. Locally raised native troops were essential because it was uneconomic to relocate British soldiers en masse to defend and police the whole of the subcontinent. The Mutiny, however, proved that the use of local manpower was a tough balancing act. The Mutiny also triggered widespread anxiety amongst the British about their safety in a country in which they were outnumbered so significantly. These concerns pushed the military to the forefront in the governance of India. Unlike the British Army in Europe, the BIA was not subordinate to civilian masters, and this enabled the army, the single largest community of British expatriates, to wield considerable political, economic and cultural power in India.

For many Britons, the first half of the 19th Century represented a period in which work ethic and professionalism proved an avenue to respectability in lieu of an aristocratic pedigree. The Indian Army offered an attractive opportunity to those amongst the upper classes of British society who could not afford to support a career in the British Army. Higher wages and lower living costs combined to offer a lifestyle that attracted many Britons to choose India. Men also joined the Indian Army because their fathers had served in the Indian Civil Service or as Army officers and in many instances, they had been born in India. Amongst these were a great many Scots and Irish, who were offered opportunities to enter the HEIC by English politicians wanting to encourage a Scottish interest in the political and economic cohesion of the United Kingdom.

British Indian Army officers had to be carefully selected to ensure they had the right qualities to lead troops and command remote outposts. As with their counterparts in the British Army, BIA officers had to pass through either the Royal Military College (RMC) Sandhurst or Woolwich. Officers were also expected to study the languages of their troops, and take time to develop an understanding of native cultures and religions. This was done to cultivate mutual feelings of respect and trust in order to engender loyalty within the inherent notions of honour prevalent amongst the peasantry of North West of India.

British officers were also expected to be avid sportsmen. Within the military, sports were considered to imbue teamwork, discipline, bravery, commitment, aggression, and fitness, skills and values intrinsic to warfare. Friendly matches between regimental teams helped to break down barriers and build camaraderie and also served to impart 'manly' British values to the sepoys, such as fair play and gentlemanly conduct. Many officers also spent their free time in India hunting. Both sports and hunting were deemed to portray potency. Those who did not participate were seen as outcasts lacking the masculinity to be successful on the battlefield.

After the Mutiny, the mantra of the Martial Races pushed masculinity into everyday army life because men from different regions were now designated as either being masculine or effeminate. Naturally, regiments comprising those who were perceived as the most 'manly', such as the Sikhs or Pathans (Pashtuns), became sought-after appointments for up and coming British officers. However, the Mutiny had proven control of even 'non-martial races' could not be taken for granted. A regiment of hardy 'martial race' soldiers was then a double-edged sword offering great opportunity, but failure to placate and control those soldiers presented the possibility of more dangerous insubordination. Accordingly, officers who could inspire the loyalty of their Martial Race troops and who could balance all the demands of efficient training and put on a strong display in battle were celebrated. As one British publication (the Foreign and Quarterly Review) put it in 1844: "nowhere, within the wide circle of civilised society, will we meet with individuals more mild, more unassuming, more refined, more intellectual, in one word, more completely gentlemen, than the officers of the Indian Army."

The Regiment

When British India inherited Punjab's border with Afghanistan, this North West Frontier of the subcontinent gained notoriety as the most turbulent of postings throughout the Crown's realms. Thus those Officers that were up for the challenge of leading martial race regiments in this the most hostile of environments tended to be higher calibre men, which ensured higher standards of leadership and greater achievements for the Punjabi regiments while other regiments stagnated. This, in turn, compelled Punjabi soldiers to maintain the hard-won 'Izzat' (reputation) of their regiments and fostered unity across religious lines amongst the Punjabis themselves. Within the secular forces of Maharaja Ranjit's Kingdom, nationalist Punjabi Muslim forces had fought alongside Khalsa forces against the enemies of Punjab - Afghan and Briton alike. Under the British mixed class regiment system, each company within a regiment comprised a 'class unit' of a distinct caste or creed. Punjabis would continue to vie for glory as one cohesive force, in which the prestige (Izzat) of the regiment or 'Paltan' superseded that of any individual creed. An outstanding example of this unity occurred in the second Afghan War of 1878 when a Punjab Frontier Force regiment faced an army of Afghans in Kabul, surrounded and with all British officers dead. The outnumbered Punjabis were given a chance to lay down their arms, but to a man, they elected to stand their ground. Led by a Sikh officer, Jemadar Jewand Singh, even the Muslim Punjabi sepoys chose to die defending the Izzat of their regiment rather than join their co-religionists.

Regimental pride also spurred single class regiments to heroic actions on the North West Frontier as in the case of the defence of Saragarhi, a remote, windswept signalling post on the Samana Range. Here on

September 12 1897, an invading force of over 10,000 Pashtun Afridi and Orakazai tribesmen zeroed in on the post, which provided the line of sight communications between two adjoining British forts. Not wanting to lose time in a skirmish, and seeing that no British officer was present, the attacking Pushtun force offered the detachment of 21 Sikh soldiers of the 36th Sikhs a chance to surrender. When the defenders elected to stand their ground, a seven-hour battle ensued in which the Sikhs, having expended all ammunition, resorted to hand-to-hand fighting. Every defender was killed, but they inflicted over a thousand casualties on the Afghans, with over 600 killed according to enemy records. All 21 Sikh non-commissioned officers and soldiers were posthumously awarded the 1st Class Indian Order of Merit (IOM), the highest gallantry award an Indian soldier of the Queen could receive from the Crown. Later, in 1911 when King George V made Indian soldiers eligible for the Victoria Cross (VC), the IOM 1st Class was then deemed the equivalent of the VC. Had the award been made retroactive the last stand at Saragarhi would have eclipsed the defence of Rorke's Drift in 1879 as the conflict with the most awards of the Crown's highest decoration for bravery.

The Sepoy

On enlisting with the BIA, the Sikhs tended to look upon the British as a neutral power, neither Hindu nor Muslim, in the hope that the British would become a powerful partner for a minority group such as theirs who had been betrayed by their own leadership. For the British, the Sikhs represented a potential ally against the scourge of the Afghans who, in 1842, had inflicted upon them an embarrassing defeat in the 1st Anglo-Afghan War. The Sikhs were a power that had once defeated the Afghans, pushing them out of the Punjab, extending their borders to include the Trans-Indus territories of Afghanistan. Along with sharing an enemy, other factors aligned the interests of the ruler and the ruled. As a result of the Mutiny the British had developed a disdain for Bengali soldiers as cowardly murderers of European women and children. In this, they now shared the Punjabis' longstanding distrust of easterners (Purbiyas) from the Ganges belt.

Soldiers to Imperial Citizens

Preferential treatment under the 'martial race' theory, enabled Punjabis to find status as allies of 'the ruling castes'that controlled the political and economic directions of their colonial state. Under British rule the authorities in Punjab had successfully enacted infrastructure development programs and paternalistic policies to establish peace, stability and prosperity. Religious freedom was proclaimed for all, but for the Sikhs, the British went a step further with specific measures to foster a strong religious identity. British authorities regarded Sikh religious doctrines to combine high moral and physical qualities with a strong work ethic and so feared a loss in orthodoxy would degrade the Sikhs' fighting value. Thus Sikhs were not permitted to enlist unless they strictly observed the outward distinctions of the Khalsa. Sikh regiments also employed priests and adopted religious ceremonies and practices such as the carrying of the Sri Guru Granth Sahib (the holy book of the Sikhs) at the head of their marching units while British officers were instructed to be respectful of the Sikh scriptures and would often attend ceremonies at gurdwaras (temples).

The rural Punjabis, both Muslim and Sikh, from which the rank and file of the army were primarily enlisted, then became the beneficiaries of a vast imperial enterprise that spanned the globe and were witness to the pomp & circumstance of Empire at its height. Many soldiers had visited London as part of ceremonial duties where expressions of regimental glory and the splendour of uniforms and regalia served to blur the boundaries between colonisers and colonised. Returning to India, soldiers brought back stories of European civilization and technological marvels that gave them improved social status and position of influence within the cloistered villages of the Punjab. Some were able to tour Canada (1897) and Australia (1901) and other possessions of the Crown, and still others saw service across the globe from China to Africa to the Middle East, helping them to conceive themselves as Imperial citizens. At home, the dominance of the Punjab within India was underscored by King George V in 1911 at his Coronation Durbar in Delhi. In another blow to Bengal's direct access to political power and privilege, Delhi, then a part of the Province of Punjab, was declared the new capital city of India, replacing Calcutta which had stood as the capital for 150 years.

Despite this progress, the hierarchy of 'race' still loomed large over military affairsand while the 1911 eligibility for the Victoria Cross afforded Indian soldiers parity with white soldiers for acts of bravery, Indian soldiers remained restricted from actually combating those belonging to the 'civilised' races, nor were they accepted as officer material for the King's commissions. This prevented Indian officers from leading European troops and subjected the most senior Indian ranks to the ignominy of having to answer to the whims of even the most junior British officer.

The 'Colour Bar' had been implemented in the South African Boer War of 1899-1902 in which Canadians, Australians and New Zealanders had fought for the Crown. In this conflict, the hitherto celebrated Indian Army was restricted to a supporting role in limited numbers. A desire to preserve racial superiority lay at the heart of this policy; if non-white soldiers were allowed to confront and defeat white men as equals in war, the prestige and dominance of Europeans would be undermined. However, on the outbreak of the Great War, the colour bar was lifted in the first weeks of the campaign when it became clear Britain's very survival was at stake. In 1917, in a small concession to recognise India's contribution to the war effort, ten King's commissions were offered to 'suitable Indians' drawn from conservative, aristocratic families.

By 1914, the Indian Army drew half of its recruits from the Punjab

The Martial Race policy had made the BIA dependent on a very narrow range of communities for its soldiers and amongst these, according to 1904 military caste-based returns, the Jat Sikh community constituted the single largest community in the army. By the 1880s regiments comprising single class-companies had come into favour with both the authorities and enlisted men. In Punjab, groups of neighbouring villages, often inhabited by related clans, sent their sons to the same regiments in which their relatives were usually dominant. This helped the young gain advancement and helped the community retain the lucrative 'martial race' status. The homogenous makeup of the men then fostered regimental cohesion and esprit de corps. By 1914 Sikhs who comprised only 1.5% of the Indian population constituted nearly 25% of the combatants of the BIA. Recruitment from across the Punjab had increased yearly, until, by the eve of the First World War, 66% of Indian cavalry, 87% of Indian artillery, and 45% of Indian infantry were Punjabi soldiers.

When Britain declared war against Germany on August 4 1914 the British Expeditionary Force, on landing in Europe, would suffer catastrophic losses in confronting German forces that outnumbered it 10:1. As a consequence, the initial resistance to call on the BIA, arising from an understanding on both sides to engage only white troops in a European conflict was dropped, and Indian troops were able to take to the field for the first time on equal footing with European soldiers. By war's end in 1918, India would contribute as much manpower (combatants & labour) to the war effort as all the other white Dominions put together. Nearly half of the one million Indian combatants who ultimately served in the Great War were Punjabi, despite Punjabis comprising no more than 10% of the Indian population.

Left : WW1 era Postcards. Post WW1 Kitchener remained Britain's most recognisable soldier and the 'pointing' recruitment poster would go onto become one the most enduring images of the Great War although at the time of WW1 it was never officially used for recruitment.

Punjabis settled in the Dominions also enlisted with Expeditionary Forces. The following are known to have served in the Canadian Expeditionary Force: JOHN BABOO, SUNTA GOUGERSINGH(KIA 1915), BUCKAM SINGH (BURIED MOUNT HOPE CEMETERY KITCHENER, ONTARIO CANADA), HARI SINGH, HARNOM SINGH, JOHN SINGH, LASHMAN SINGH(KIA 1918), RAM SINGH, SEWA SINGH, WARYMAN SINGH (WWW.CANADIANSOLDIERSIKHS.CA). Enlistments with the Australian Imperial Force (AIF) and the New Zealand Expeditionary Force (NZEF) included: AMAH SINGH , BIRGINH SINGH, DESANDA SINGH, GOODGER SINGH, HARDA SINGH, JAGT SINGH, JUWAN SINGH, NARAIN SINGH, SARN SINGH, SIRDAR SINGH, WEER SINGH, BASANT SINGH, DAVY SINGH, GANESSA SINGH, GURBACHAN SINGH, HAZARA SINGH, JOHAR SINGH, LINNA SINGH, NUNDAH SINGH, SHAM SINGH, SUNDA SINGH, YAHARRA SINGH (WWW.AUSTRALIANSIKHHERITAGE.COM/WORLD-WAR-1/)

Photo: The Illustrated London News June 1911
Lord Kitchener with the Indian Contingent at
Hampton Court for the Coronation of King George V

WW1 Manpower contribution of the British Empire:
India 1,401,350 / Canada: 640,000 / Australia 416,000 / New Zealand 220,000
Union of South Africa 136,000 / Labrador Newfoundland 11, 922

NO FEAR OF DEATH.

YOUNG OFFICER'S VALOUR.

LEADS ELEVEN INDIAN HEROES.

HOW ANOTHER V.C. WAS WON.

Nobody will be able to read unmoved the wonderful story of the winning of the V.C. by Lieutenant J. G. Smyth, of the 15th Ludhiana Sikhs, a young hero of 21. This narrative—one of the most inspiring which the war has produced—has been communicated from the front by an officer in touch with the head-quarters of the Indian Army Corps.

On the night of May 17, writes the officer, a company of the 15th Sikhs, under Captain K. Hyde-Cates, relieved a portion of the 1st Battalion Highland Light Infantry in a section of a trench known as the "Glory Hole," near the Fermo Du Bois, near Ypres, on the right of the Indian Army Corps front.

Furious fighting had been in progress here for some time, the position at the moment of relief being that we had taken and occupied a section of the German trench, a portion of the same trench on our left being still held by the enemy, who had succeeded in erecting a barri-cade between themselves and our men.

Necessity for Relief.

In the early morning Captain Cates observed that attempts were being made to reinforce the enemy in the trench. Numbers of Germans were seen rushing towards the further extremity of the enemy's trench. Rapid fire was brought to bear on them as they crossed the open, but in the dim light the effect could not be judged. When day broke it was ascer-tained that the German trench was packed with men with the evident intention of attacking us.

A short time afterwards the attack began by heavy bombing, to which the 15th replied vigorously, and succeeded in holding their own until noon, when the position became critical, as all our dry bombs had been expended, and those that had become wet from rain were found to be useless. It was then resolved to at-tempt to relieve the situation by sending up a bombing party from the reserve trenches.

The desperate nature of this undertaking may be gauged from the fact that two previous attempts had been made by the Highland Light Infantry. On both occa-sions they failed, the officers in command being killed and the parties having suf-fered very severely.

A Desperate Venture.

However, the position was desperate, and Lieutenant Smyth, a young officer, who, in spite of his years—only numbering 21—had already been brought to notice for his gallantry, was ordered to take command of the party.

Volunteers were called for, and were immediately forthcoming. The alacrity with which the demand was responded to speaks volumes for the spirit of the regi-ment, for each man felt sure that he was proceeding to almost certain death. Lieutenant Smyth and his little party of ten men started at 2 p.m. to cover the 250yds which intervened between them and our trench, taking with them two boxes of 96 bombs. The ground to be covered was absolutely open, devoid of all natural cover.

The only possible shelter from the frightful fire which met the party as soon as they were over our parapet was an old, broken-down trench which, at the best of times, was hardly knee-deep, but now in places was filled almost to the top with the dead bodies of High-land Light Infantry, Worcesters, Indians, and Germans.

Truly it was an undertaking to appal the stoutest heart. Dropping over our parapet, they wriggled their way through the mud, pulling and pushing the boxes with them, until they reached the scanty shelter of the old trench, where they commenced a progress which for sheer horror can seldom have been surpassed.

A Deluge of Fire.

Pagris—or pugrees, the turbans worn by Indians—had been attached to the front of the boxes. By means of these the men in front pulled the boxes along over and through the dead bodies, while those in rear pushed with all their might, the whole party lying flat. At any moment the bombs might have exploded.

The whole ground was hissing with the deluge of rifle and machine-gun fire, while the air above them was white with the puffs of shrapnel. To the anxious watchers in the rear it seemed impossible that a single man should win through.

After they had accomplished a mere 20yds of their deadly journey, Sepoy Fatteh Singh rolled over wounded, followed in the next 80yds by Sepoys Sucha Singh, Ujagar Singh, and Sunder Singh.

A Desperate Venture.

However, the position was desperate, and Lieutenant Smyth, a young officer, who, in spite of his years—only numbering 21—had already been brought to notice for his gallantry, was ordered to take command of the party.

Volunteers were called for, and were immediately forthcoming. The alacrity with which the demand was responded to speaks volumes for the spirit of the regiment, for each man felt sure that he was proceeding to almost certain death. Lieutenant Smyth and his little party of ten men started at 2 p.m. to cover the 250yds which intervened between them and our trench, taking with them two boxes of 96 bombs. The ground to be covered was absolutely open, devoid of all natural cover.

The only possible shelter from the frightful fire which met the party as soon as they were over our parapet was an old, broken-down trench which, at the best of times, was hardly knee-deep,

but now in places was filled almost to the top with the dead bodies of Highland Light Infantry, Worcesters, Indians, and Germans.

Truly it was an undertaking to appal the stoutest heart. Dropping over our parapet, they wriggled their way through the mud, pulling and pushing the boxes with them, until they reached the scanty shelter of the old trench, where they commenced a progress which for sheer horror can seldom have been surpassed.

A Deluge of Fire.

Pagris—or pugrees, the turbans worn by Indians—had been attached to the front of the boxes. By means of these the men in front pulled the boxes along over and through the dead bodies, while those in rear pushed with all their might, the whole party lying flat. At any moment the bombs might have exploded.

The whole ground was hissing with the deluge of rifle and machine-gun fire, while the air above them was white with the puffs of shrapnel. To the anxious watchers in the rear it seemed impossible that a single man should win through.

After they had accomplished a mere 20yds of their deadly journey, Sepoy Fatteh Singh rolled over wounded, followed in the next 80yds by Sepoys Sucha Singh, Ujagar Singh, and Sunder Singh.

Part of the allure of the BIA was that the bond between the British officer and his men was known to be stronger than that within the British Army. In India, paternalistic approaches worked to engender more intimate knowledge of the rank and file; British officers would often visit the villages and parents of the troops to maintain close links between the regiment and its recruitment sources. In turn, the Indian troops admired the courage of the British officers, who were traditionally tasked to lead from the front. This well-established relationship would be critical to the successful deployment of the Indian Army on the Western Front. However, British officers in these frontline roles incurred staggeringly high casualty rates; it was even said German snipers specifically targeted the white officers within Indian regiments. When replacement officers were drafted in, they often lacked the shared history, experiences, values and language that the original officers had laboriously acquired and, given this, it seems likely that in some instances trust and communication would have deteriorated on the battlefield.

Of the seven British officers who sailed with the 47th Sikhs to France, four were killed, and another forced to retire due to wounds. Likewise, of the 22 Indian Officers with the 47th Sikhs in 1914, seven were killed, one died on service, and three were forced to retire early due to wounds, of which two would die before the end of the war. Amongst the officers of Ferozepore Brigade's 57th Wilde's Rifles regiment, six of the seven British officers were killed within four days of entering the frontline on October 29, 1914 when the regiment suffered 314 casualties in its first action at Wystschaete and Messines. Despite these losses, any British officer desiring to lead Punjabis into battle had to spur his men on to glory by holding regimental Izzat above all else. In the 1915 Battle of Festubert, one young officer did survive to tell a tale about leading the valiant 15th Sikhs on such a quest.

Brothers-In-Arms

On the outbreak of the Great War, General Sir James Willcocks was appointed commander of the Indian Army in France, making him the senior-most officer in the British Expeditionary Force after Generals French and Smith-Dorrien. His tenure, however, was cut short when he clashed with General Haig, commander of the British Expeditionary Force, over the treatment of Indian troops. Haig would later be nicknamed 'Butcher Haig' for the two million British casualties sustained under his command. General Willcocks' devotion to the welfare of his men was typical of many Indian Army officers who had fought alongside Indian troops prior to WW1.

Indian Corps Order #1
General Willcocks - Western Front, October 10, 1914

On the eve of going into the field to join our British comrades, who have covered themselves with glory in this great war, it is our firm resolve to prove ourselves worthy of the honour which has been conferred on us as representatives of the army of India. In a few days we shall be fighting as has never been our good fortune to fight before, and against enemies who have a long history. But is their history as long as yours? You are the descendants of men who have been mighty rulers and great warriors for many centuries. You will never forget this. You will recall the glories of your Indian race. Hindu and Mohammedan will be fighting side by side with British soldiers and our gallant French Allies. You will be helping to make history.

You will be the first Indian soldiers of the King-Emperor who will have the honour of showing in Europe that the sons of India have lost none of their ancient martial instincts and are worthy of the confidence reposed in them. In battle, you will remember that your religions enjoin on you that to give your life doing your duty is your highest reward. The eyes of your co-religionists and your fellow countrymen are on you. From the Himalayan mountains, the banks of the Ganges and Indus, and the plains of Hindustan, they are eagerly waiting for the news of how their brethren conduct themselves when they meet the foe. From mosques and temples their prayers are ascending to the God of all, and you will answer their hopes by the proofs of your valour. You will fight for your King-Emperor and your faith so that history will record the doings of India's sons and your children will proudly tell of the deeds of their fathers.

Above: WW1 era patriotic postcard
Below: Colonial shoulder badge for a royal regime
Below left: Service badge issued to Indian soldiers the end of WW1

General Willcocks - London, August 2, 1919

In 1919 I was home on short leave, and it happened that the Indian contingent was in London for the peace celebrations. I was a spectator when they marched to Buckingham Palace to be reviewed by their beloved King-Emperor, and as they passed on their return from the palace, although I was in plain clothes, some of the Indian officers and men recognised me amongst the crowd. One of them shouted the Sikh war cry of "Fateh," and a number ran out of the marching ranks, saying, "Here is our General." It was a very short greeting, but it was nonetheless both moving and splendid. A few days later I visited their camp at Hampton Court. I will not attempt to describe what took place, but when I left in my motor car, this at least I clearly knew, that those faithful comrades would never forget their old Commander. It is my final and highest reward.

SOLDIERS OF THE KING

Members of a Sikh contingent march in the Victory parade, London August, 1919

Imperial Citizens - 2nd Class

By the turn of the 20th century, the many 'small wars' of the Victorian era had helped India establish a realm of influence along its borders and the Indian Ocean arena, and Punjab to acquire a strategic and influential position within the administration of the Empire. When the First World War began, many important and wealthy Indians expressed their support for Empire and the war effort and made generous donations of supplies and money. The Independent Princely States across India such as Mysore in the south and Patiala in the north also offered their soldiers for war. Even Mohandas Gandhi, a rising leader of the Indian people, endorsed the war effort, believing that it would bring India parity with other Dominions such as Canada and Australia. The white settler colonies of the Crown had been constituted as Dominions, which gave their parliaments control over domestic affairs, whereas India, despite its prominent position within the Empire, remained a colony, with Westminster dictating both domestic and foreign policy.

For the common soldier within the BIA, the professional esprit de corps between the races had instilled a sense of loyalty to the Sirkar (ruler), and pride in the Army's accomplishments abroad helped strengthen his ties to the British Crown. Over time, Punjabi peasants, soldiers, and farmers began to conceive of themselves as imperial citizens rather than colonial subjects, and this encouraged a culture of mobility as they looked towards the British Empire for new opportunities. 'Follow the flag' communities of Punjabis sprang up during the late 19th Century in far off lands such as Africa, Malaya, Burma and China. With the dawning of the new century, the Punjabi diaspora made the voyage across the Pacific to the Dominion of Canada.

Canada

By 1906, spurred on by glowing reports of life in the new land and the money sent back by early settlers, a community of over 5,000 Punjabis, predominantly male Sikhs, had settled in British Columbia. Many of these South Asian pioneers were veterans of the Indian Army and from their ranks leaders emerged to establish key community organisations. Amongst them were the founders of the Khalsa Diwan Society, who operated the first Sikh Gurdwara (temple) in Canada, which would become a centre for spiritual, political, social, and economic life for Indian immigrants of all faiths. The society's president, Bhag Singh, had served as a cavalryman in Hodson's Horse, and Balwant Singh, the high priest of the temple, had served in the 36th Sikhs. Another early community leader, Hakim Singh, had served in the 19th Bengal Lancers and became a Director of the Guru Nanak Mining and Trust Company, an organisation established to secure the economic welfare of the Sikh community. For the most part, the hard-drilled soldiers of the BIA were welcomed as labourers by many private employers and also at many of the sawmills operated by ex-British officers of the Indian Army. Colonel Davidson of Fraser Mills in New Westminister B.C., one of the biggest employers in the area, employed 350 Sikhs and considered them to be the most efficient workforce they used.

In 1907, anti-Asian sentiments had been growing with the influx of Chinese, Japanese and now East Indian workers and turned violent at a rally organised by the Asiatic Exclusion League in Vancouver. Although South Asians were not assaulted during the anti-Asian race riots, they were by now equally resented as cheap labour by local working-class whites. The B.C. government responded to this growing hostility with sweeping restrictions on Asian immigrants and their rights. New legislation was introduced to deny non-whites the right to vote, hold professional positions or to be employed in government, military or public works. In addition, restrictions were placed on serving on juries, access to public facilities and services, housing types and education. The restrictions served to shut off the traditional avenues of opportunity for Punjabis soldiers and farmers within the Empire.

The Canadian Militia department objected to a potential Sikh regiment, citing that Indian regiments had never been used in "white men's" countries, while a special Sikh constabulary to deal with Asians and perhaps First Nations people was contemplated on the proviso that "the Sikh police would have no jurisdiction over the white population". However, it too was scrapped when it became clear Canadians would oppose giving guns to non-whites. For Indo-Canadians, the prospects within the agricultural sector were just as bleak. At the turn of the 20th century, a key goal of Canadian immigration policy was to populate empty spaces with people who could turn vast open regions into fertile agricultural lands, a task for which authorities rated applicants according to their race, perceived hardiness and farming ability. While a long line of Punjabi agriculturalists came endowed with the boon of Imperial Martial Race credentials, their skin colour would prove an immutable barrier in Canada. To add insult to injury, Vancouver newspapers also characterised the once-loyal defenders of the Crown as filthy, sick and hungry undesirables who posed a deviant menace to women and children.

Then, in 1908, the Immigration Act was amended with the Continuous Voyage Regulation to circumvent the rights of Indians as British subjects to settle Canada. In the absence of any direct shipping lines to Canada from India, the regulation effectively shut down Indian immigration - as was its intent. Ensuing legal challenges to the new legislation strenuously appealed for protection of the British flag to be afforded equally to non-European British subjects, but the calls for fair play proved ineffective. Meanwhile, those sympathetic to the Punjabi soldiers, such as Colonel Falkland Warren, a retired officer of the Royal Artillery who lived in Vancouver, and who had spent much of his career in India, protested the unfair treatment of the Sikhs with imperial authorities. Writing to the Colonial office, he asserted that a great many of the aggrieved community were ex-soldiers that had served the Queen and were ideal immigrants looking to pursue a livelihood under the Union Jack and in that regard the Canadian government was being too subservient of the labour unions.

The 'colour bar' put in place to exclude South Asians from the country not only shattered their dreams of Imperial citizenship but left Punjabis fractured amongst themselves. Some reacted to the government's openly discriminatory policies by rebelling and aligning themselves with the Ghadar party, an organisation established in California in 1913 to oust the British from India. Others, in contrast, worked with sympathetic Canadians towards equal treatment for all citizens of the British Empire and Dominion status for India. One such activist, Sunder Singh, a son of a Subedar in the Indian Army, enlisted the help of the Presbyterian Church which had denounced the treatment of South Asians as unchristian. Other 'moderate' voices also appealed to the Viceroy in Delhi. In January 1913, the Khalsa Diwan Society lodged a petition with the Governor General of India, Viceroy Charles Hardinge, asserting that a majority of about 90% of the settlers were Sikhs, and amongst them were many retired soldiers who deserved the protection of the Crown. However, the letter, on failing to produce the desired results, only added to the voices advocating violence as the only remaining solution.

In April 1914, the arrival of the Komagata Maru, a ship carrying 376 Punjabi would-be immigrants brought the immigration issue to a head. Immigration officials firstly isolated the boat in Vancouver's harbour and then prevented passengers from disembarking, effectively imprisoning them without adequate food, water and sanitation for two months. When the case for the passengers' rights to settle Canada as British subjects was rejected by the British Columbia Court of Appeal, a Canadian warship was tasked in July 1914 to escort the ship out of Canadian waters. The incident, in which a group of unarmed and disillusioned British subjects were forced at gunpoint to relinquish their claim on the Crown for protection in one colony of the Empire while being returned to another, galvanised many followers of the Ghadar Movement in Canada and the USA to also return to India to preach revolution. Their goal was to trigger an insurrection amongst the Punjabi soldiers and succeed where the mutiny of 1857 had failed. Two weeks later, Britain declared war on Germany and Punjabi soldiers would once again be called upon by the Crown to rally in defence of the Empire.

The Noble Savage

The painting overleaf, 'God Save the Queen' by John Charlton 1899, depicts the Indian Cavalry officers who were given pride of place as Queen Victoria's personal escort in a procession through London to mark her Diamond Jubilee.

The representatives of the Indian Cavalry included officers of The Punjab Frontier Force (5th Punjab Cavalry), 2nd Lancers (Gardner's Horse), 3rd Skinners Horse , 4th Cavalry, 5th Cavalry, 7th Harianna Lancers, 8th Cavalry, 9th Hodson's Horse, 12th Cavalry, 13th Duke of Connaught's Lancers (Watson's Horse), 16th Cavalry Probyn's Horse (later King Edward's Own Lancers), 17th Bengal Cavalry and Central India Horse (later King George's Own).

The officer from the 5th Punjab Cavalry, Risaldar-Major Kesur Singh, was said to be one of the cavalry officers that visited Canada as part of a Jubilee entourage. His likeness was published on a Canada Post First Day cover in 1999 to mark the tri-centenary of the founding of the Khalsa. A memorial to these early visitors, in the form of a statue of cavalrymen, now stands on the grounds of the first Sikh temple to be built in Canada. The location in Abbotsford B.C. is now a National Heritage site.

The Jubilee procession also featured Punjabi soldiers parading in the colonial escort as part of the Hong Kong and Straits Settlements contingents and within the delegation of cavalry officers of the Indian Imperial Service Forces sent by the Princely States of India.

Canada was represented in the procession by Prime Minister Wilfrid Laurier, with Dominion troops from the Canadian Hussars, the 2nd Canadian Dragoons, 48th Canadian Highlanders, the 8th Battalion of Active Militia and The North-West Mounted Police, the forerunner of Canada's Royal Canadian Mounted Police.

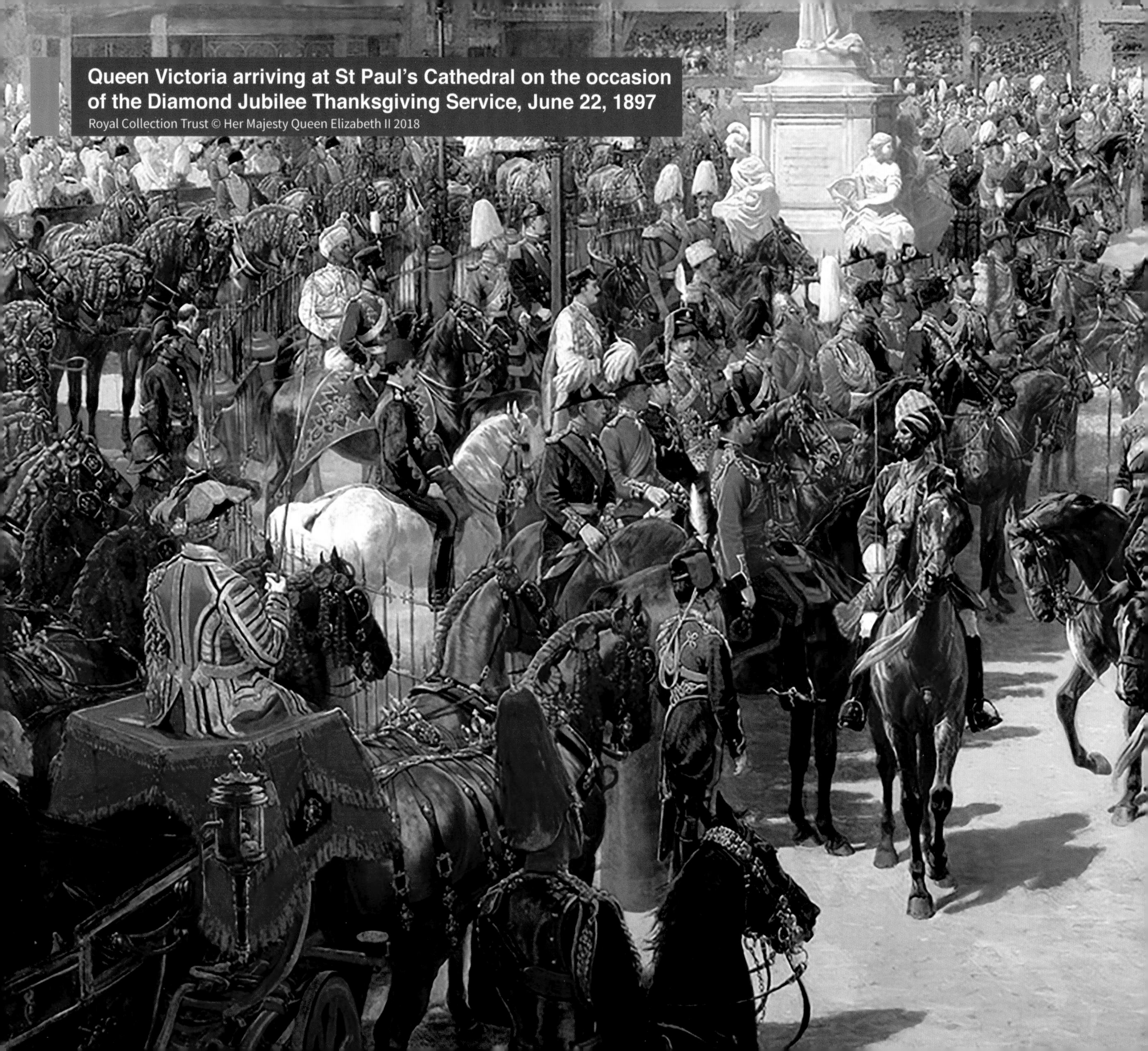

Queen Victoria arriving at St Paul's Cathedral on the occasion of the Diamond Jubilee Thanksgiving Service, June 22, 1897

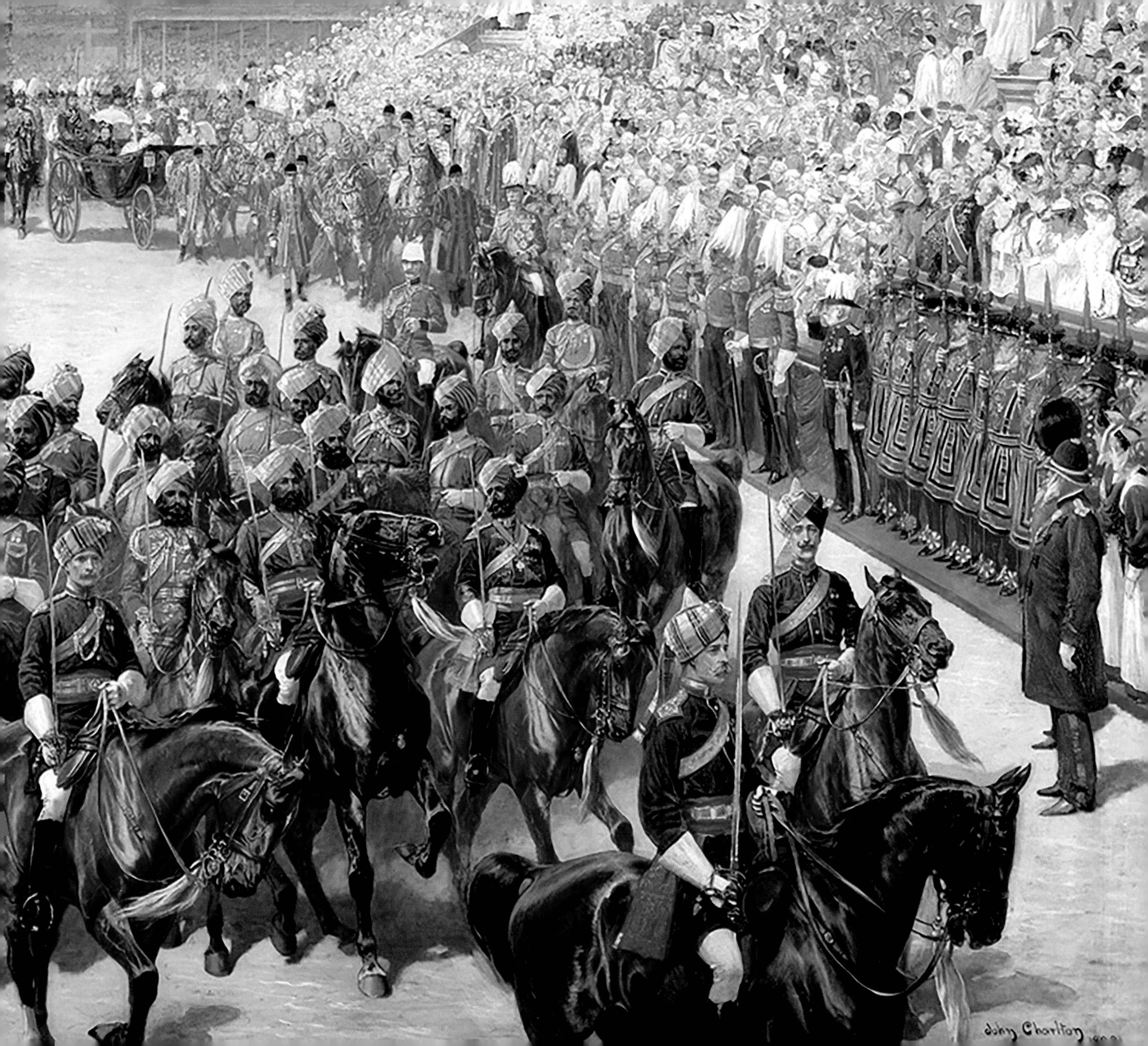
John Charlton

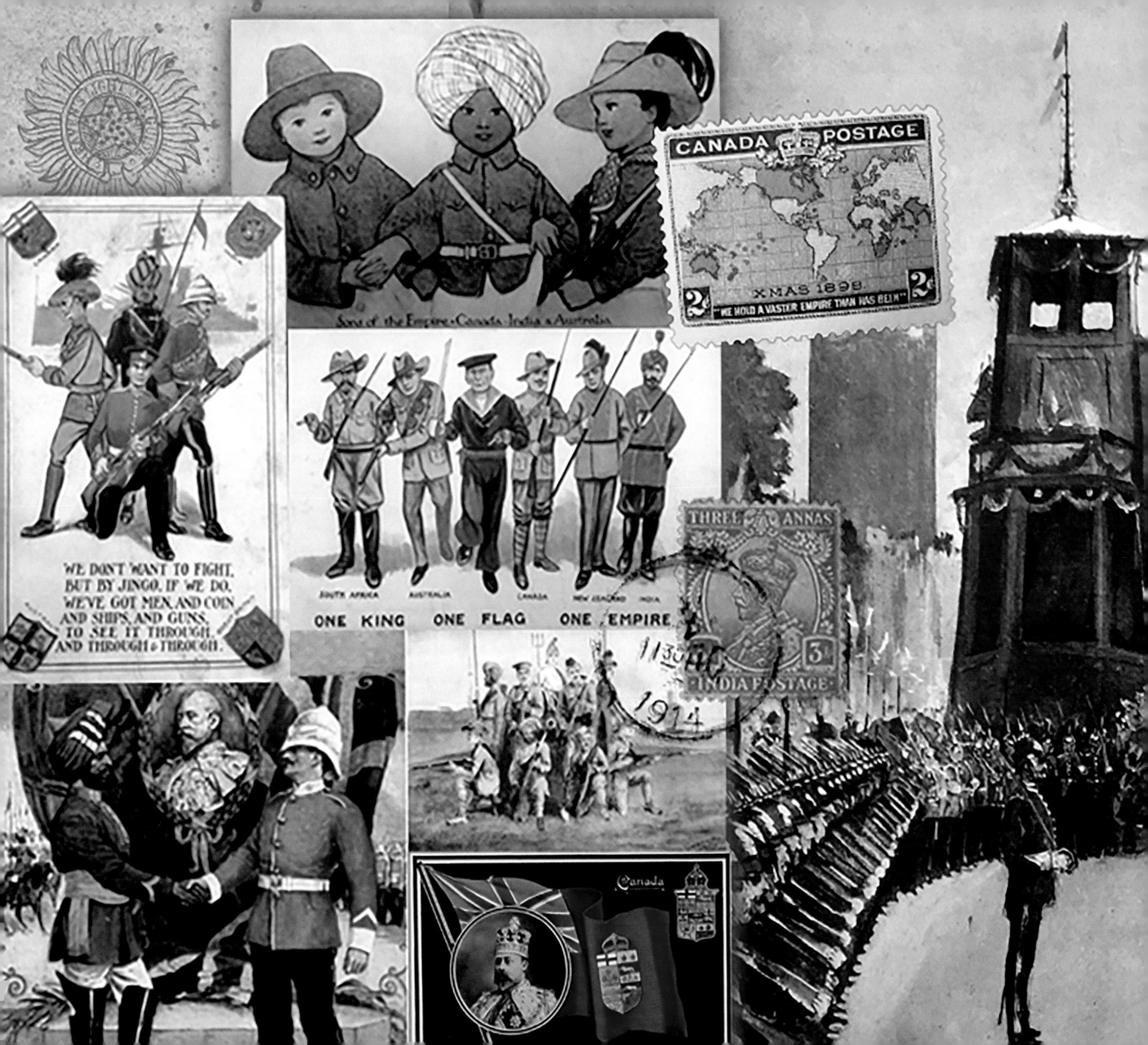
Sons of the Empire - Canada, India & Australia
CANADA POSTAGE
XMAS 1898
"WE HOLD A VASTER EMPIRE THAN HAS BEEN"
2¢
WE DON'T WANT TO FIGHT,
BUT BY JINGO, IF WE DO,
WE'VE GOT MEN, AND COIN
AND SHIPS, AND GUNS,
TO SEE IT THROUGH,
AND THROUGH & THROUGH.
SOUTH AFRICA
AUSTRALIA
CANADA
NEW ZEALAND
INDIA
ONE KING ONE FLAG ONE EMPIRE
THREE ANNAS
3a
INDIA POSTAGE
1914
Canada

A Tradition of Valour & Loyalty

Within a few short decades of the Punjab becoming a realm of the Crown, Punjabi soldiers were lauded across the Empire for their fighting skills. In 1867, at the time of Canadian Confederation, John A. MacDonald, Canada's first Prime Minister, convinced that war with the United States was inevitable, wrote in a private letter to a friend that India could do Canada a yeoman's service by sending an army of Sikhs to hold San Francisco "as security for Montreal and Canada."

After the First World War, speaking at Rawalpindi Punjab in 1921, the Duke of Connaught, who had served as Governor General of Canada, praised the contribution of the Punjabis to the Empire saying, "The achievements of Punjab were remarkable. Even before the war the Punjab had a name familiar in the military annals of the Empire. During the war, the name became a household word, and not only on account of the number of men who joined the colours but also on account of the splendid fighting qualities displayed".

Left: Victorian, Edwardian and Windsor era postcards and stamps.
Main: The Coronation of King Edward VII. Colonial and Indian troops passing under the Canadian Arch as specially chosen escorts of their King.
Special Number of The Illustrated London News, Aug 14, 1902

"That Canada should desire to restrict immigration from the Orient is regarded as natural, that Canada should remain a white man's country is believed to be not only desirable for economic and social reasons, but highly necessary on political and national grounds."

MacKenzie King Deputy Minister of Labour 1908
Prime Minister of Canada, 1921–1926, 1926–1930 & 1935–1948

Right: Photo Postcard a Sikh settler wearing a turban badge of the 45th Sikhs Regiment leads a religious procession in Vancouver 1908

HINDOO RELIGIOUS PROCESSION VANCOUVER B.C.

HINDOOS GO HOME

SEA LION

"We are subjects of the same Empire; we have fought, we have sacrificed. We have fought for the Empire, and we bear her medals; we have an interest in this country; we have bought about $2,006,000 of property in British Columbia; we have our church and pay our pastor, and we me to stay in this country,"

Dr Sunder Singh Speaking at Toronto's Empire Club on January 25, 1912

Photo Left: Vancouver 1906. Sikh settlers display their British Indian Army Campaign Medals

" His Majesty's Government share the hope of the Government of India that your Ministers will find it possible to avoid express discrimination against British Indian Subjects in any steps which it may be found necessary to take in the direction of restricting immigration.."

The Colonial Office, London 1908

"I challenge any man living to bring out a single instance in the whole history of the Indian nation to show their civilisation has done anything at all to uplift the other races of the world.. I say their civilisation is unproductive to the good of the human race as a whole."

Vancouver MP H.H. Stevens 1913

"Our fellow British subjects of the Asiatic race are of different racial instincts to those of the European race, ... In their own interest their proper place of residence is within the confines of their respective countries, not Canada where their customs are not in vogue and their adhesion to them here only gives rise to disturbances destructive to the well-being of society."

Supreme Court of BC July 6 1914

"The people of Canada want to have a white country, and certain of our fellow subjects who are not of the white race want to come to Canada and be admitted to all the rights of Canadian citizenship. They say: We are British Subjects, as you are; we were born under the British flag; some of us have worn British uniforms; some of us have fought under the British flag; you should open the gates to us... These men have been taught by a certain school of politics that they are equals of British subjects; unfortunately they are brought face to face with the hard facts when it's too late."

Wilfred Laurier, speaking before the House of Commons, June 1914
Former Prime Minister of Canada July 1896 to October 1911

Komagata Maru Departs Vancouver
July 23, 1914

The whole world is awake and alert
Why is India in deep slumber?
Why is your spirit slack O Indians? glory
Your body weak and clothes in tatters!
Black thieves is what the world calls us
Our children live a life of misery.
Where is that pride, that glory,
That splendour, that grandeur that
brilliance?
Where is your great exalted culture
The knowledge of the spirit and of matter?
We yearn for those men of past
With great minds and great bodies
Arjuna, Bhima, Kali Das Pandit
And just kings like Raja Bhoj.
O India! Where are your brave Hindus?
Where are the valiant Muslims?

"WANTED
Brave soldiers to stir up Ghadr in India.
Pay – Death
Prize – Martyrdom
Pension – Liberty
Field of Battle – India.
Hindustan Ghadr, November 1913

Divided we stray and suffer
Why don't we unite and strike together?
The oppression the tyranny we face daily,
What stops us from hitting back?
The world derides us and calls us coolie
No wonder our flag flutters no more
We face troubles from all quarters
Yet we lack the courage to fight back

We believe we are good for nothing
Why would the world honour us?
We carry the burden of slavery
And never do we dream of being free.
How long can we survive as slaves?
Let's now learn to rule
Kicked and humiliated we are everywhere
Treated with favour by none"

Sikhs Must Now Unsheathe Their Swords

> **Khalsa Akhbar Lyallpur, August 14, 1914**
>
> Germany may be proud of her superior land forces, but the Imperial and Indian governments are proud of their loyal Sikh subjects. Sikhs are ready to fight and shed their blood for the King-Emperor. The gravity of the present crisis forbids our thoughts turning towards the ill-treatment of Sikhs in Canada and the unpleasant speeches made by His Honour the Lieutenant-Governor about the Sikh community.

> **Loyal Gazette - Lahore August 16, 1914**
>
> Enemies of Government denounce Sikhs for serving in the army on a paltry pay of ten rupees and attempt to dissuade them from doing so. Sikhs turn a deaf ear to these scoundrels and should request Government to send them to the front. Moreover, they should desist from agitation of every description, for such action cannot but damn them as traitors to their country and Government.

King George V address to the Indian Army
August 23, 1914

SS AKBAR Departs Bombay August 28, 1914

> "I look to all my Indian soldiers to uphold the Izzat of the British Raj against an aggressive and relentless enemy. I know with what readiness my brave and loyal Indian soldiers are prepared to fulfil this sacred trust on the field of battle shoulder to shoulder with their comrades from all parts of the empire. Rest assured that you will always be in my thoughts and prayers. I bid you to go forward and add fresh lustre to the glorious achievements and noble traditions of courage and chivalry of my Indian Army, whose honour and fame are in your hands."

King George V
In the ceremonial uniform of the Colonel-in-Chief of the 18th Bengal Lancers a Punjabi Cavalry Regiment.

The Indian Army in France

The arrival of the Indian Corps at Marseilles was a landmark in history. No episode in this extraordinary war was more remarkable or, for Britons, more inspiring than the presence of Indian troops on the Continent of Europe. To India, the event was, if possible, of even greater significance. The march of her sons through the streets of Marseilles was a kind of initiation. A phantom had been laid that shadowed her prestige. Invisible barriers had been broken down. New vistas of honour were opened out before her. That hot September morning when the interminable line of transports was seen through telescopes at dawn creeping along by the Chateau dTf and the Islands of Pomique and Ratonneau, will long be remembered in Marseilles. No more romantic landing can have been witnessed by the old sea-city in all its varied past. Daily for a couple of months the streets had echoed to the tread of a medley of races_Zouaves and Turcos from Algeria, whiteturbanned swarthy Moors from Morocco, coalblack negroes from Senegal, and a score of different units from the South of France, but the welcome the Marseillais gave the Indians transcended all other demonstrations in spontaneity and warmth. Throughout the forenoon while the troops were landing excitement had been steadily rising in the city, and the dispatching of the British and Indian soldiers through the streets in the afternoon en route to their camps was a signal for the whole of Marseilles to turn out en fete.

From the Cannebiere to the Prado the gaily-dressed streets were packed with a seething mass of humanity. First came a detachment of Sikhs, for the greater part head and shoulders above the spectators. They received the plaudits of the crowd with the imperturbable smiling composure of the Oriental. The police guarding the road were swept aside, the ranks were rushed, men and women shook the sepoys by the hand, and young girls showered flowers upon them, pinning roses in their tunics and in their turbans. Tricolours were distributed with prodigal favour, old ladies with bitter memories of '70 pressed forward the better to admire these handsome, bearded men, and it would be difficult to conjure up anything more touching than the sight of those frail women patting the bronzed giants on the back and calling down blessings on their heads. So it proceeded for hours.

When it was dusk and the last troops had gone by, the crowd followed them to their camps at St. Marcel and La Barrasse and Borely, and watched them cook their evening meal while the camp fires twinkled in the dark, and the smell of wood smoke rose in the air. It was a historic camp this, pitched by the men of Ind on the soil of France between the landlo'ked harbour and the stately garden of the Borely.

The Times History of the War Volume 2 April 1915

On September 26th 1914, the Jullundur and Ferozepore Brigades of the Lahore Division Indian Expeditionary Force A (IEF A) landed in France to become the first of all the King's Colonial soldiers to be deployed on the Western Front.

Commdt. 15e Sikhs le Col

Lent à Allemagne. 15e Sikhs.

P. Sarrut

DUTY

DEFENDERS OF THE CROWN

War Declared!

The causes of the First World War were complex. Colonial and economic competition between the Great Powers combined with nationalism and distrust to catalyse an aggressive arms race between major European nations. Peace was finally shattered on June 28, 1914 when Archduke Franz Ferdinand of Austria-Hungary was assassinated in Sarajevo. One by one, the Great European Powers declared war upon each other, plunging Europe and then the world into the most devastating war yet seen.

On one side of this conflict stood the Triple Entente powers of Great Britain, France, and Russia. Opposing them were the Central Powers of Germany, Austria-Hungary, and the Ottoman Empire. Many other countries were also involved, often against their will, while others such as the United States entered into the fray much later. To win the war quickly, the German plan was to rapidly crush their traditional rival, France. To do this, Germany invaded neutral Belgium on August 4, 1914 to bypass the spearhead of the French Army and destroy it from the rear.

In response to this invasion of 'gallant little Belgium', and bound by an 1839 treaty to guard Belgium's neutrality, Great Britain declared war on Germany and at once despatched the British Expeditionary Force (BEF) to the European mainland. Reports of violent German atrocities against innocent Belgians added fuel to Britain's motivation for war. Unfortunately, while its Royal Navy maintained supremacy on the seas, Germany had now amassed the largest and most advanced army in the world. Facing the 120,000 troops of the BEF and the French were nearly one million German soldiers with the very latest artillery and weapons of war. Although the BEF was made up of proud, well-trained professional soldiers happy to wear the German leader's contempt for them as a badge of honour, they could do only so much when outnumbered nearly 10 to 1. At home, the British scrambled to train a much larger army to supplement the BEF, now known as the 'Old Contemptibles', but it would take time to transform civilians into soldiers.

In this most desperate hour, Great Britain also declared war against Germany on behalf of the entire British Empire. Unfortunately, the armies of Canada, Australia, and New Zealand were pitifully small. The regular Canadian Army, for example, was only 3110 strong when the war began. It was clear the Dominions would need time to train more soldiers, leaving only the colony of India capable of providing a large and well-trained army for battle.

The Call to Flanders Fields

On August 8, 1914, the call came to mobilise the BIA for war overseas. In line with the colour bar policy, Indian Expeditionary Force A (IEF-A), comprising two cavalry divisions and two infantry divisions, was initially sent to relieve British regiments in Egypt. However, with the Allied position in France deteriorating rapidly, calls for reinforcements became increasingly urgent. In response, Britain was compelled to lift the colour bar and reroute most of IEF-A to France itself. On arrival, the BIA was deployed to the front line on the British sector of the Western Front in northern France and Belgium. The BEF and the French army had halted Germany's invasion of France at the Battle of the Marne in early September 1914. Although stopped, the Germans remained in control of much of northern France with well-prepared trenches to hold their gains. Both sides attempted to outflank the other by pressing their attacks north, what would be known as the 'Race to the Sea'. By the third week of October, the last uncontested area was Flanders, a low-lying area of scattered villages and windmills straddling the French and Belgian border, with the ancient town of Ypres at its heart.

To the east of Ypres, the Germans had gathered a large force to take the northern French coast and the port of Calais, which would effectively cut off reinforcements from Britain. To oppose the Germans, the Allies dug a thin line of trenches running southwards from the Belgian coast, hinging on Ypres. The battle, known as 1st Ypres, began on 19th October 1914. According to General French, the commander of the BEF, the situation was dire. Intense German artillery bombardments battered the BEF day and night. Desperate for reinforcements after losing the majority of their force in their retreat from Mons in August, the BEF dug in along hedge lines, canals, and village outskirts.

First Blood - The First Battle of Ypres

On deployment to the front line, two Indian Divisions (the 7th Meerut Division had followed the Lahore Division to France in mid-October), numbering approximately 24,000 Indian and British soldiers, were immediately plunged into defensive actions along a 12-mile stretch of the 35-mile long British front line. Towards the end of October, pressed forward by the German Kaiser himself, the Germans stepped up their assaults with the intention of breaking through the critical Arras-La Bassee-Armentieres front, now manned by the BIA. The stage was now set for the Indians to prove themselves in Europe.

German command had strategised that with the coast in their possession they could mount big guns, with ranges capable of gaining command of half the width of the English Channel, between Britain and France. Then, under cover of these guns, mines would be laid to prevent the landing of new troops, including the Canadians, and a base would be prepared for the future invasion of England. For the advancing Germans, the shortest route to Calais was along the Belgian coast via Nieuport, but the deliberate flooding of the countryside by the Belgians blocked this path.

SS. "Akbar". Sept. 1914.

German command then looked to pierce the British front further south where a breach at Arras or La Bassee would have opened up a passage for all German troops released after the fall of Antwerp, the largest city in Belgian Flanders. This route would also cut off two of the Allied armies, pinning them between the enemy and the coast. When, on 27th October, the Germans took Neuve Chapelle, the Indians were tasked to recapture it to prevent an advance through the centre of the British line. The defence of the La Bassee gateway now fell into Indian hands. In the battles that ensued, acts of courage, selfless gallantry, and comradeship were performed in the best traditions of the Indian Army.

Amongst the many decorations for bravery won by the Lahore Division, Sepoy Khudadad Khan of the 129th Baluchis won the very first Victoria Cross awarded to the Indian Army. The Battle of Ypres lasted until November 22, 1914, when the Germans called off their offensive after repeatedly failing to break the allied line. Outnumbered, outgunned, and without the grenades that the Germans possessed in abundance, the Indian Corps held its ground and denied Germany's last chance to end the war quickly, and had saved the BEF from certain destruction. During the Battle of Ypres, IEF A suffered over 8500 casualties, British and French casualties numbered nearly 100,000. The Germans suffered over 200,000 killed and wounded.

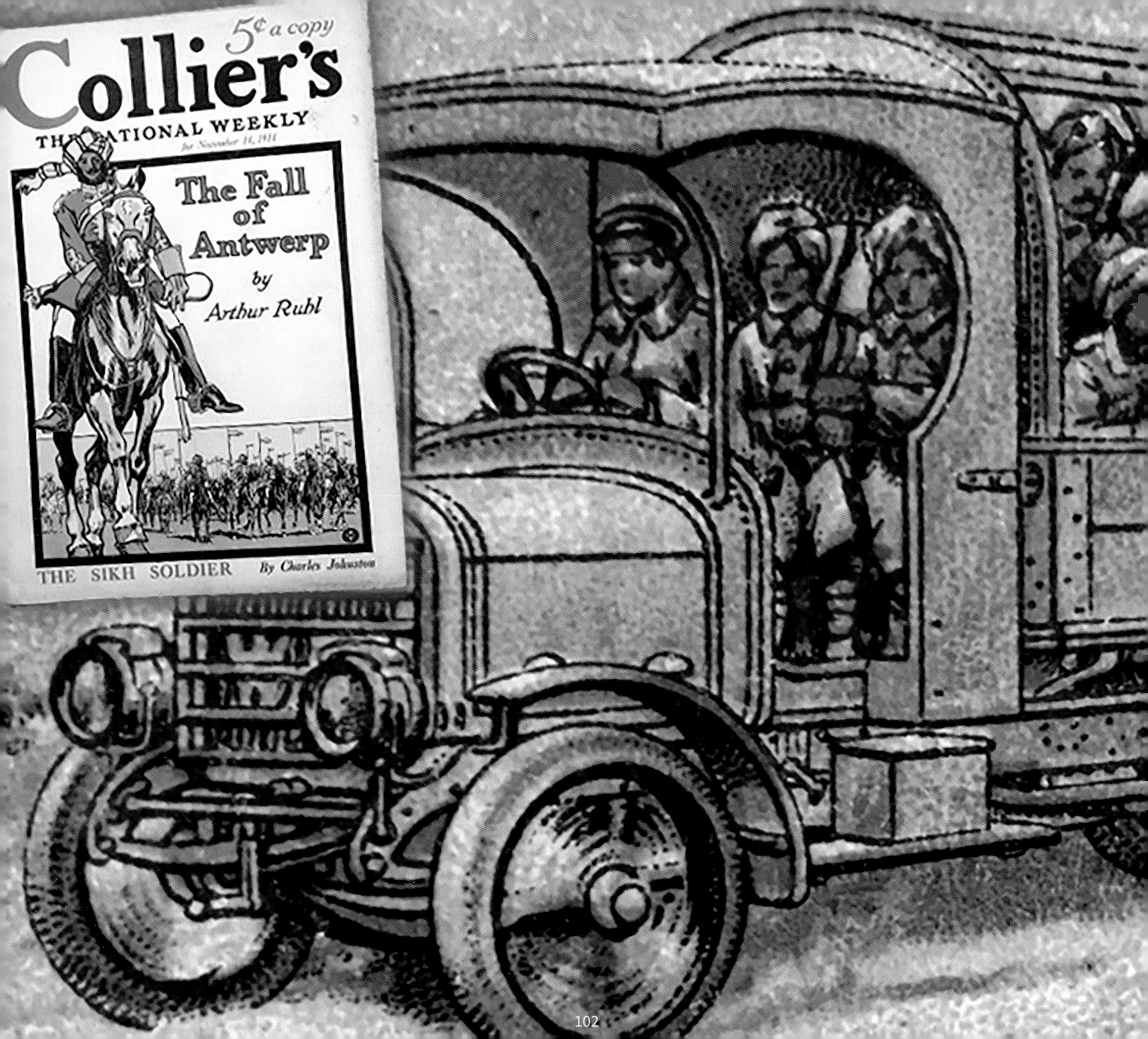
5¢ a copy
Collier's
TH ATIONAL WEEKLY
The Fall of Antwerp
by
Arthur Ruhl
THE SIKH SOLDIER
By Charles Johnston

All the King's Men: By October 1914, over half a million men had been recruited in Britain, but they needed to be trained and equipped before being deployed to France. The Canadian and Australian Expeditionary forces were bound for Europe but they were nowhere near the battlefields. The Canadian Expeditionary Force (CEF) arrived in England on October 14, 1914 and then began six months of additional training on the Salisbury Plain. The ANZACS (Australian and New Zealand Army Corps) were still in Western Australia waiting for naval protection from the German cruiser Emden which was hunting for Allied ships in the Indian Ocean.

"The Germans pressed forward to encounter, not retiring Belgians, but oncoming, swarthy figures. Before they could recover from their surprise, those dusky soldiers were amongst them. There was a short, sharp encounter, and then a rapid German retreat. Fright and the deadly Indian bayonets turned that retreat into nothing more dignified than a scamper to cover. Yet on came the soldiery which, till then, the German had regarded as a myth. The retiring troops were simply dug out of the trenches in which they had taken shelter and driven backwards farther still by the well-aimed bullets and the relentless steel of the East's finest fighters. When the Germans had hoped to break the line, the Indians turned the tide of the battle, and behind them followed the Belgians..." New Zealand Herald, December 11, 1914

INDIAN TROOPS MEET THE GERMANS.

Indian troops were in action against the Germans in France last week, & fought splendidly.

Our photo, taken in France a few days ago, shows Indian infantry carrying maxims into action after having taken them from the mules which had brought them up into a suitable point

TO NEWSAGENTS

The Daily Mirror

LATEST CERTIFIED CIRCULATION MORE THAN 1,000,000 COPIES PER DAY

GLORIOUS CHARGE BY THE INDIANS: GERMANS DRIVEN FROM CAPTURED TRENCHES AT THE POINT OF THE BAYONET.

.. "To Exterminate First the Treacherous English and to Walk Over General Foch's Contemptible Litte Army"

Kaiser Wilhelm II, Headquarters Aix-la-Chapelle, 19 August 19.

Right WW1 era postcard: German Chancellor Theobald von Bethmann Hollweg caused worldwide outrage when he dismissed the 1839 Treaty of London a mere "scrap of paper"

For a "LITTLE SCRAP OF PAPER"
Countless Thousands fought and died,
To prove the Allies' Honour
Was their Glory and their Pride,
Whilst the Gallant Fearless Navies,
Have swept clear the mighty sea,
Of those foes, who were a menace
To their PEACE and LIBERTY

> " In combat they are wild and undaunted by death, just like the Gurkhas, they are masters of knife fighting. As their officers make them believe that the Germans will not take them prisoner, they often fight to the death. There is no denying that the Sikh, and the Indians in general, are noble in combat and display a certain kind of gallantry, especially towards our wounded."
>
> Leutnant Karl Strölin, Infanterie-Regiment Nr. 121 - 1916

"OUTWHISKERED!"

THE WAR PICTURES
LONDON ILLUSTRATED WEEKLY

BRITAIN'S TRUE FRIEND INDIA

THE BRITISH STILL DRIVING BACK THE GERMANS.

The Daily Mirror

SEVENTY THOUSAND INDIAN SOLDIERS TO FIGHT FOR THE EMPIRE: PRINCES GOING TO THE FRONT.

Kaiser Rushes Men From All Fronts To Take Calais, Regardless of Cost

London, Oct 29- Telegraphing from Copenhagen the correspondent of the Times says

" It is learned in Berlin that from all parts of the east and west battle fronts soldiers are being rushed to Belgium in response to the order of emperor William to take Calais at all costs. It is semiofficially announced that the Germans will be able to control the southern part of the North Sea as soon as they possess Calais.

" All the entrances to Cuxhaven, by land and by sea, have been closed by imperial command. No civilians are allowed in the vicinity of the harbor, which is crowded with floating batteries, Zeppelins, and submarines.

Washington Post, Fri Oct 30th, 1914

BATTLE OF NEUVE CHAPELLE

For the Allies, the battles of 1914 had been fought to defend Belgium and to stop the German invasion of France. With the arrival of spring in March 1915, it was time to go on the offensive. A critical first move would be the recapture of Neuve Chapelle, which although having been briefly gained by Indian troops in October 1914, was lost when reinforcements were slow to arrive to support the small contingent of the Jullundur Brigade that had taken it after a brutal first encounter with the enemy. From Neuve Chapelle, British command planned to advance on to the strategic Aubers Ridge and push on to the town of Lille, located 21 miles behind the German front line. Lille was a vital transport hub in the rail network used to transfer German forces from north to south along the front. If successful, the capture of the village would breach the German front line, drawing attention away from a larger French assault further south. IEF-A, often referred to as the 'Indian Corps' by now, was to play a major role in the attack, and made up half of the British forces in the battle. After sustaining huge losses in the First Battle of Ypres, the Indian Corps had now been reinforced with new troops from India. The Canadian Expeditionary Force (CEF) had also just arrived in France; located north of the designated area of the main battle, they were assigned a diversionary role to draw enemy fire away from the main advance.

On March 10th, British and Indian troops attacked along a three-kilometre front after heavy artillery bombardment. The assault was a success, and Neuve Chapelle was taken in only four hours. Two days later, on March 12th, the Germans launched an intense counter-attack, but the Indian Corps managed to hold the village. Unfortunately, success at Neuve Chapelle could not be exploited, as it took too long to move British artillery up to support the further advance onto Aubers Ridge. However, the German front had been successfully breached by the British for the first time, with Germany sustaining 18,000 casualties during the three-day battle. The Allied cost was 7,000 British and 4,000 Indian casualties, but, by the standards of WWI, Neuve Chapelle was a success, and it was a clear demonstration that the Indian Army could take on Germany and come out on top.

Statement by Lord Kitchener at the House of Lords regarding the capture of Neuve Chapelle: "In these operations our Indian troops took a prominent part and displayed fine fighting qualities. I will in this connection read a telegram I have received from Sir John French: Please transmit following message to Viceroy of India: "I am glad to be able to inform your Excellency that the Indian troops under General Sir James Willcocks fought with great gallantry and marked success in the capture of Neuve Chapelle and subsequent fighting.... The fighting was very severe, and the losses heavy, but nothing daunted them. Their tenacity, courage, and endurance were admirable and worthy of the best traditions of the soldiers of India." Near La Bassee, for example, a mixed battalion made a gallant bayonet charge and captured a village. In a German counter attack they lost all their white officers, but retired in good order, and, rallied by others, retook the position. As usual with highly trained troops, the Indians are particularly good in attack, and when advancing against the Germans, they have shown wonderful dash."

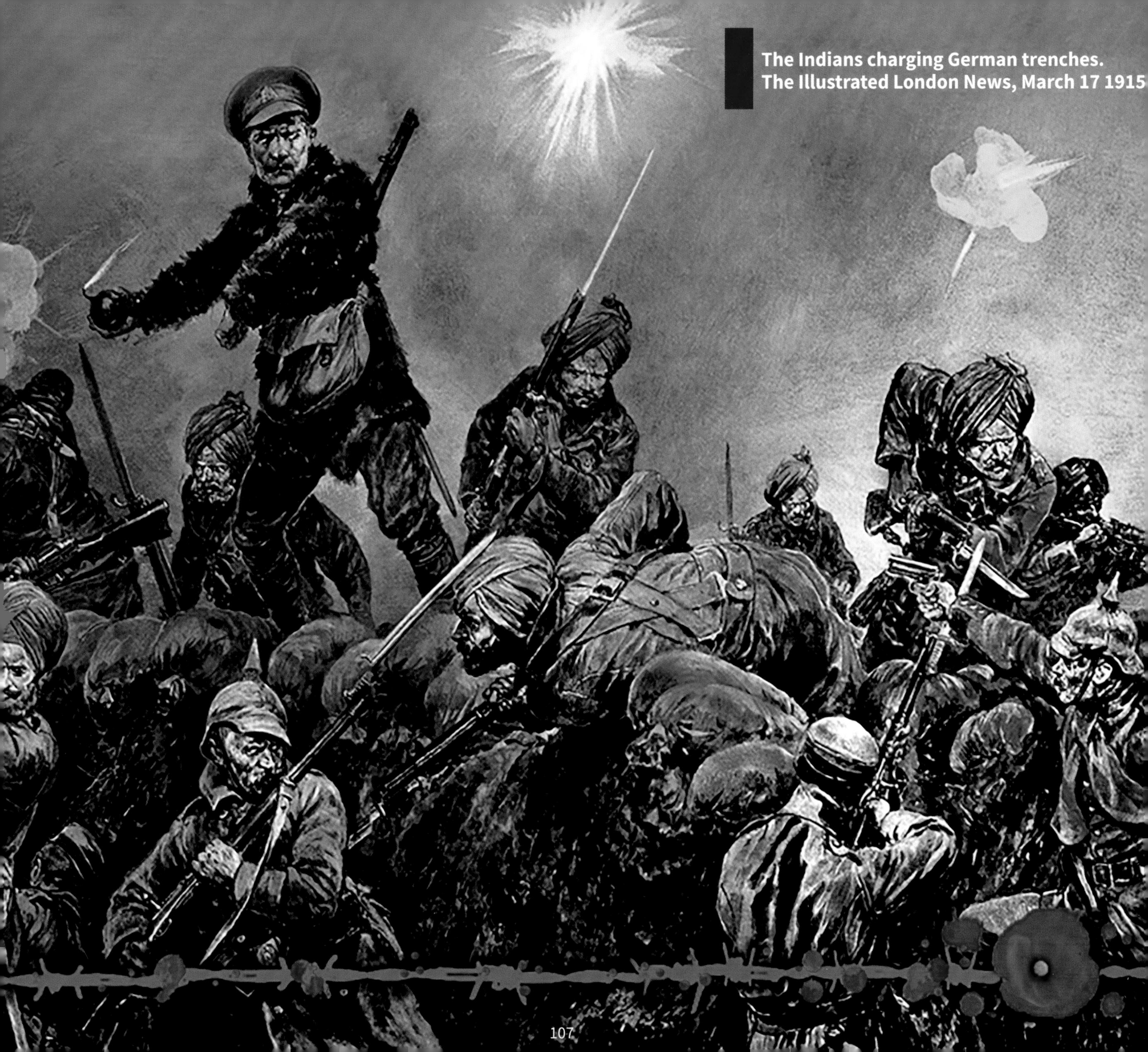

The Indians charging German trenches.
The Illustrated London News, March 17 1915

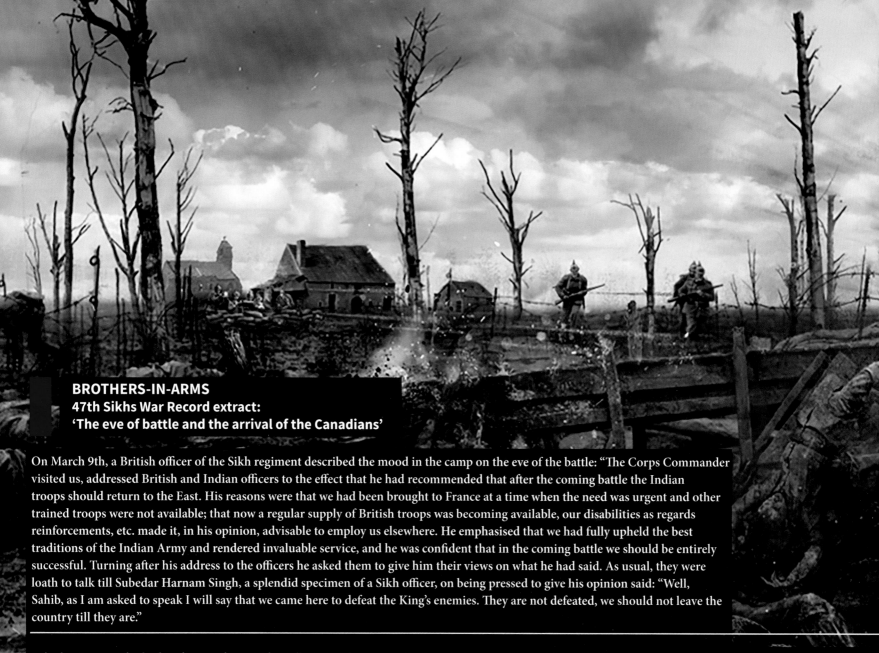

BROTHERS-IN-ARMS
47th Sikhs War Record extract:
'The eve of battle and the arrival of the Canadians'

On March 9th, a British officer of the Sikh regiment described the mood in the camp on the eve of the battle: "The Corps Commander visited us, addressed British and Indian officers to the effect that he had recommended that after the coming battle the Indian troops should return to the East. His reasons were that we had been brought to France at a time when the need was urgent and other trained troops were not available; that now a regular supply of British troops was becoming available, our disabilities as regards reinforcements, etc. made it, in his opinion, advisable to employ us elsewhere. He emphasised that we had fully upheld the best traditions of the Indian Army and rendered invaluable service, and he was confident that in the coming battle we should be entirely successful. Turning after his address to the officers he asked them to give him their views on what he had said. As usual, they were loath to talk till Subedar Harnam Singh, a splendid specimen of a Sikh officer, on being pressed to give his opinion said: "Well, Sahib, as I am asked to speak I will say that we came here to defeat the King's enemies. They are not defeated, we should not leave the country till they are."

Subedar Harnam Singh of Hari's story in part 1 is a tribute to this the real-life Subedar Harnam Singh of the 47th Sikhs from Nawanshahr, Jalandhar, who arrived in France in September 1914. Tragically, the real Harnam Singh having committed to performing his duty in the statement above is killed in battle the next day. There is no

March 11th, Subedar Manta Singh, having witnessed his friend, Captain George Henderson suffer a severe injury, picked him up to carry him to safety. Captain Henderson had been assigned to the 15th Sikhs after being awarded Sandhurst's coveted Sword of Honour as the top cadet in 1911. During the rescue, the Indian officer was hit in the leg while trying to navigate a hail of machine gun fire in no-man's land. Despite the injury, Manta Singh was able to find a wheelbarrow to help him carry his fellow officer to a nursing station.

Manta Singh's regiment, the 15th Sikhs, sustained many casualties during the Battle of Neuve Chapelle. The regimental diary entry for the battle describes the battlefield as being *"littered with German corpses, and the whole place showed signs of the heavy fighting that had been going on there. The stretcher bearers were at work all night picking up the wounded. About 60 other ranks were killed and wounded."'*

The injured Indians were moved across the English Channel to the coastal town of Brighton, where three newly converted buildings were set up as hospitals to care specifically for Indian troops wounded on the Western Front. Cheering crowds of well-wishers gathered in the town to greet the first arrivals in December 1914. By 1916, over 12,000 Indian soldiers had been admitted to these hospitals, many of whom would never recover from their critical injuries to see their homes again. Here, in Kitchener's Military Hospital, Manta Singh would tragically succumb to wounds that had become infected with gangrene. Manta's courageous act of duty would give rise to a century of friendship between the officers' families.

After the war, Captain Henderson travelled to Jalandhar in Punjab to assure Manta Singh's son, Assa Singh, that he would be taken care of, offering him a position in his father's regiment, the 15th Sikhs. Over time, Assa Singh Johal and Captain Henderson's son, Robert Henderson, would also become friends and would serve together in WW2. After the war, Assa Singh, with help from his British friend, settled in the UK where, to this day, the next generation of the Henderson and Johal families remain close friends.

Second Battle of Ypres (April-May 1915)

In April 1915, the 1st Canadian Division was assigned to the Ypres Salient, where the Allies had been entrenched since the 1st Battle of Ypres. With over 90% of Belgium occupied by German forces, Ypres had become an important symbol of resistance; the defence of Belgium had triggered Great Britain's entry into the war. If Ypres were to be abandoned, it would have handed the Germans both a symbolic and strategic victory. Recognising this, the Germans planned another major offensive to take Ypres, which included the use of a brand new weapon to break the deadlock. On the evening of April 22nd, chlorine gas was used for the first time on the Western Front. The heaviest cloud drifted into the French 45th (Algerian) Division. A French retreat ensued, exposing the Canadian left flank, and threatening the destruction of the whole Allied position in the Salient. In their first major engagement of the war, the Canadians fought bravely to hold the line in a series of chaotic engagements, including Mauser Ridge, Gravenstafel Ridge and Kitchener's Wood. Outnumbered, outgunned, and outflanked, on the 24th of April they faced a second, and this time direct, chlorine gas attack. Despite this, the Canadians successfully counter-attacked to stall the German advance, buying precious time for reinforcements to arrive. After four days of intense fighting, the Canadians were relieved on the 25th of April. As in 1914, the Lahore Division was again called on to defend Ypres. After an exhausting 35-mile overnight march from their own sector in Neuve Chapelle, the Jullundur and Ferozepore Brigades were immediately ordered to lead the attack on Mauser (Geddes) Ridge adjoining Kitchener's Wood, to regain lost ground around Langemarck and St Julien. On April 24, 1915, British and Indian infantry advanced across no man's land, only to be mowed down by devastating artillery and machine gun fire. Despite the futility of it, another attack was launched on the following morning. This time the Germans released chlorine gas in defence of their lines. The Lahore Division suffered nearly 4000 casualties, about one third of its deployed strength.

Battle of Festubert (May 1915)

Following the Second Battle of Ypres, the 1st Canadian Division marched south to join an Allied offensive already underway in French Flanders. The Battle of Festubert was the second major engagement fought by Canadian troops on the Western Front and was done again in conjunction with the Indian Corps. On May 15th, the Indian Corps launched a night attack which captured several German trenches. The displaced Germans then dug in along a new secondary line located directly in front of Festubert. A second assault undertaken by the Canadians was launched on May 18th but was eventually checked by heavy German artillery. The Allies regrouped under the control of the Indian Corps and launched a third set of attacks between May 20th-24th, which successfully captured the village of Festubert. In the course of the battle, the Canadians had managed to advance for five straight days to gain territory, but at the expense of over 2468 casualties.

Battle of Loos (25th September - 4th October 1915)

The Battle of Loos was to be the most significant British offensive yet in the war and the last in 1915. Like the Battle of Festubert, Canadian and Indian troops were deployed as part of an even larger French offensive, intended to force peace by winter. This battle would become notable for the first British use of gas against the Germans. The objective given to the Indian Corps was to act as a diversion before the main British assault. By attacking half an hour earlier, it was hoped that the Indians could tie down a larger German force so that the main British attack could succeed. On 25th September 1915, the Indians went 'over the top' under cover of a dense smoke screen and advanced on the Germans. Fighting was desperate, and the Indians suffered heavy casualties, but part of the India Corps did achieve its objective and occupied several German trenches. The main British assault fared far worse. The German defences were formidable and machine gunners proved deadly; 8,500 British troops were killed in a single day, the greatest single loss of life recorded since the beginning of the war. Such was the ferocity of the fighting that only 2,000 of these men have known graves. As the Germans began a serious counter-attack, the exposed Indians were ordered to give up their gains and return to their own trenches. During the single day, the Indians suffered 3,979 casualties, including 156 officers, and gained nothing other than the knowledge that they achieved their objectives while others had not and that again they had not faltered in doing their duty. By the end of September 1915, the Canadian Corps, comprising two infantry divisions, had reached a strength on the Western Front of 1,354 officers, and 36,522 other ranks. The Battle of Loos would be the last major operation of Indian Infantry in France.

IEF-A Infantry Departure (December 1915)

By Christmas 1915, after serving over a year on the Western Front, Indian infantry was withdrawn and sent to Mesopotamia (Iraq). The reasons for this withdrawal were numerous, although the most important factor was that the war in Mesopotamia was becoming a major conflict in its own right. On August 13, 1915, Sir John Nixon, commander of Indian Expeditionary Force D in Mesopotamia had requested one of the Indian infantry divisions in France as reinforcements for an advance on Baghdad. This timing of the request was opportune, as there were growing concerns over an under-strength Indian Corps spending another winter in France with limited prospects of reinforcements. Concentrating Indian soldiers closer to home made sound logistical sense. By early 1915, heavy casualties on the Western Front had left nearly all Indian Infantry battalions severely under-strength. The Indian Army's recruitment and reserve system had not been designed to handle losses on such a scale, and the distance between India and France only compounded the problem.

"

You leave France with a just pride in honourable deeds already achieved and with my assured confidence that your proved valour and experience will contribute to further victories in the new fields of action to which you go.

The message from the King-Emperor to the Indian Army Corps in France, delivered, before their departure, by the prince of Wales on behalf of his majesty.

The Illustrated War News, January 1916 FROM FRANCE TO NEW FIELDS OF ACTION:

A PUNJABI SOLDIER

It also became increasingly difficult to replace the British officers that held the longstanding trust of the Indian sepoys. Increasing numbers of troops from the Canadian Army and Kitchener's new British army were also now available to replace the battered Indian Corps on the continent. Although Lord Kitchener objected to the withdrawal of the Indian infantry, orders were issued on October 31st for the Lahore and Meerut Divisions to embark at Marseilles for Mesopotamia. Two Indian cavalry divisions and three Royal Field Artillery brigades of the Lahore Division would remain behind to continue to support British and Canadian forces on the Western Front.

Artillery

When the Lahore Division departed for Mesopotamia, its artillery remained behind to see further fighting in France. Although the artillery belonged to the British Royal Artillery, most of the drivers and some gunners were Indian. In December 1915, the Lahore Division's artillery was assigned to the 3rd Division of the Canadian Corps and saw action during all the phases of the battles of the Somme in 1916. In March 1917, further Indian artillerymen arrived from India for service on the Western Front. The Lahore artillery was subsequently attached to the 4th Canadian Division where it saw action supporting Canadian and British troops in April 1917 at the Battle of Vimy Ridge.

During this battle, Canadian and British artillery undertook the bombardment and the precision creeping barrages that were key to the capture of Vimy Ridge. The ridge, which overlooked the strategic Douai plain, had remained in German hands since its capture during the 'Race to the Sea' in 1914. The French Army had failed to dislodge the Germans in two attempts in 1915, suffering approximately 150,000 casualties. The Canadians, working together as one formation under Canadian command for the first time, captured the ridge in the most successful British advance of the Western Front to date. The Lahore Division's artillery supported the operation throughout.

SECOND BATTLE OF YPRES

Advance on Mauser Ridge April 26, 1915

The objectives of a hastily drawn plan required a frontal assault of a ridge well entrenched with the enemy; eyewitnesses described the carnage to follow as whole platoons being knocked out by shells, and men falling in heaps. As they crested the ridge, intense machine gun fire cut down the Indians as if a scythe was being drawn across their legs. After the battle, Lieutenant-General Sir James Willcocks would remember the heroic but doomed action at Mauser Ridge as a key battle

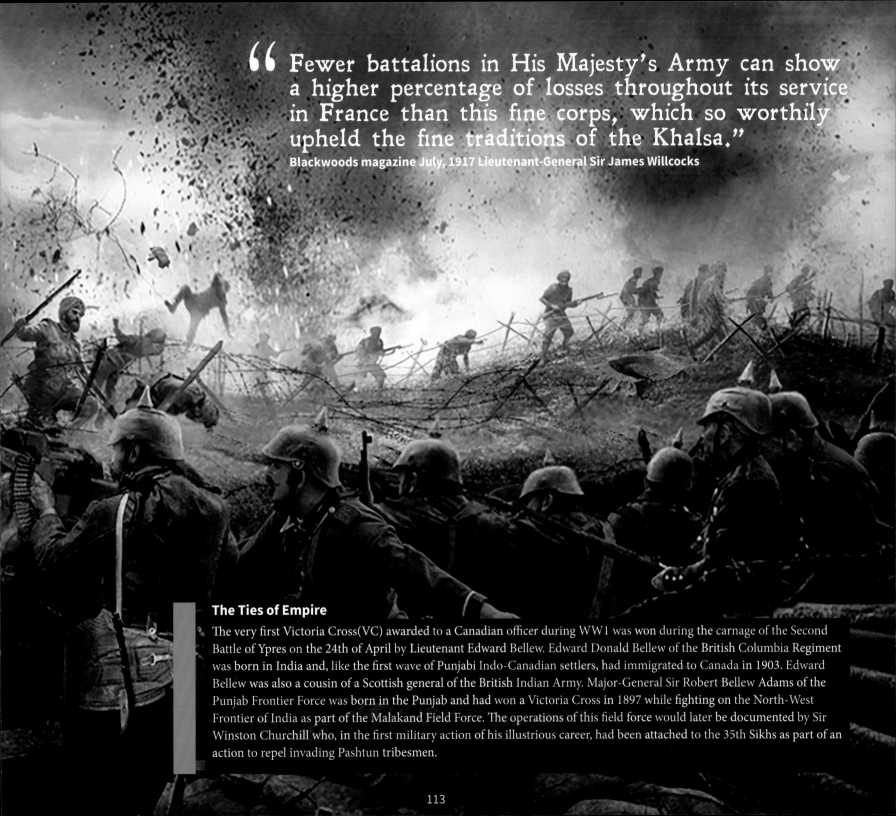

> " Fewer battalions in His Majesty's Army can show a higher percentage of losses throughout its service in France than this fine corps, which so worthily upheld the fine traditions of the Khalsa."
>
> **Blackwoods magazine July, 1917 Lieutenant-General Sir James Willcocks**

The Ties of Empire

The very first Victoria Cross(VC) awarded to a Canadian officer during WW1 was won during the carnage of the Second Battle of Ypres on the 24th of April by Lieutenant Edward Bellew. Edward Donald Bellew of the British Columbia Regiment was born in India and, like the first wave of Punjabi Indo-Canadian settlers, had immigrated to Canada in 1903. Edward Bellew was also a cousin of a Scottish general of the British Indian Army. Major-General Sir Robert Bellew Adams of the Punjab Frontier Force was born in the Punjab and had won a Victoria Cross in 1897 while fighting on the North-West Frontier of India as part of the Malakand Field Force. The operations of this field force would later be documented by Sir Winston Churchill who, in the first military action of his illustrious career, had been attached to the 35th Sikhs as part of an action to repel invading Pashtun tribesmen.

BATTLE OF VIMY RIDGE

The Road to Vimy

The Second Battle of Ypres had marked Canada's baptism of fire on the Western Front. The battle had cost the Canadians 6,035 casualties, but with Ypres saved the small force of militia members and newly joined, hastily trained civilians who had earned a reputation for being tough and effective soldiers. Desperate frontal assaults against enemy positions heavily defended by machine guns, would become a hallmark of the many battles that would ensue for the Canadians. By 1917, the growing Canadian Corps was lauded by many to be the finest shock troops of the Empire. The slopes of Vimy Ridge now awaited them. Here, a gradual incline would expose the Canadian's once again as the prime target for artillery and machine gun fire. Where previous British and French attempts to capture the heavily fortified ridge had failed disastrously, it would be the bitter lessons from past do-or-die assaults that would help carry Canada to victory.

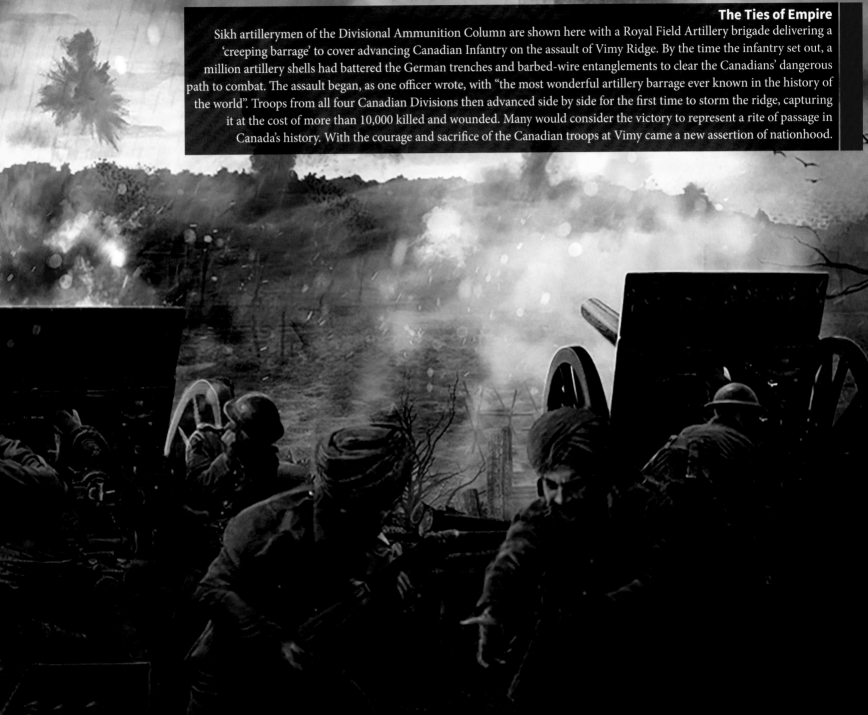

The Ties of Empire

Sikh artillerymen of the Divisional Ammunition Column are shown here with a Royal Field Artillery brigade delivering a 'creeping barrage' to cover advancing Canadian Infantry on the assault of Vimy Ridge. By the time the infantry set out, a million artillery shells had battered the German trenches and barbed-wire entanglements to clear the Canadians' dangerous path to combat. The assault began, as one officer wrote, with "the most wonderful artillery barrage ever known in the history of the world". Troops from all four Canadian Divisions then advanced side by side for the first time to storm the ridge, capturing it at the cost of more than 10,000 killed and wounded. Many would consider the victory to represent a rite of passage in Canada's history. With the courage and sacrifice of the Canadian troops at Vimy came a new assertion of nationhood.

The 1st and 2nd Indian Cavalry Divisions arrived in France, along with IEF-A in 1914. Over the following year and during both Battles of Ypres, they were used mainly to reinforce the front line and relieve weary infantry battalions. The Canadian Cavalry Brigade (CCB), which had been formed into a mounted brigade in 1915 in Britain, was initially sent to France on foot to reinforce the devastated Canadian infantry after losses in 2nd Ypres and Festubert. The nature of trench warfare combined with machine guns and artillery conspired to make the Western Front particularly unsuitable for large cavalry attacks. For the most part, cavalry were not engaged in open warfare but reconnoitring, patrolling and signalling. Despite this, British, Canadian, and Indian cavalry regiments still served on the Western Front with distinction.

The Battle of the Somme

In January 1916, the CCB was reconstituted as a mounted infantry unit and was transferred to the 2nd Indian Cavalry Division in June 1916. The Brigade, now comprised of the Royal Canadian Dragoons, Lord Strathcona's Horse and Fort Garry Horse saw its first action at the Battle of the Somme in July 1916. Two weeks into the battle, on July 14th, the British 7th Dragoon Guards and Indian 20th Deccan Horse launched one of the very few successful cavalry charges on the Western Front. Scattering enemy parties concealed in a cornfield while at full gallop, the Indian cavalry carried their objectives at the points of their lances. It was the first charge since trench warfare began and it would prove to become a unique event amongst the great exploits of courage in WW1, as the lance would rarely be used in a western theatre of war. British High Command, under General Haig, was encouraged by the cavalry's action at High Wood and, on visiting the 2nd Indian Cavalry Division the following day, Haig expressed his congratulations on the "well planned, carefully prepared and brilliantly carried out" operation. All were optimistic that the success of this small operation would mean future opportunities for mounted action on the Western Front. The cavalry had proved that it could still operate to some degree on the frontlines. A number of other similar small cavalry actions entailing small detachments of mounted cavalry charging at a gallop to an objective, then dismounting and holding the position with the support of mobile machine guns and artillery would follow through to the end of the war. While these tactics allowed cavalry to rush forward at great speed, the impact of these small actions was not substantial enough to be strategically significant on the Western Front. Indian cavalry would, however, find its stride in the desert expanses of the Middle East in the fight against Germany's ally the Ottoman Empire.

The Battle of Cambrai

In November 1916, the 1st and 2nd Indian Cavalry Divisions were renamed as the 4th and 5th British Cavalry Divisions. In February 1917, these Divisions were used to pursue the German withdrawal to their new defensive position known as the 'Hindenburg Line'. During this pursuit, Lt Frederick Harvey was awarded the CCB's first Victoria Cross for his actions in liberating a village. The Allies breached this line in the winter of 1917 when, on November 20th, cavalry, aircraft, artillery, and 381 tanks attacked German positions in front of the town of Cambrai. It was the first 'all arms' action of its type in history.

In the attack, the cavalry was deployed in both mounted and dismounted roles. Mounted cavalry was expected to use its superior mobility to pass through the gap created by the tanks and infantry and surround enemy positions, while the tanks were to break through enemy wire in a frontal assault. However, the Mark IV tanks employed at Cambrai could only advance at a maximum of 4 miles per hour and were also handicapped from covering large distances rapidly by high rates of fuel consumption. The tanks were also too large to advance through narrow streets or heavily wooded areas and were susceptible to breakdowns and getting stuck in muddy or broken ground. With the expectation that cavalry would advance where the tanks of a new 'mechanised cavalry' could not, it was the horsemen who, ironically, found an opportunity to shine. During the battle, both the Canadian and Indian cavalry each won a Victoria Cross. Lance-Daffadar Gobind Singh, 2nd Lancers, won the Victoria Cross for carrying messages under enemy fire, with three horses being killed under him.

Over the course of nine days, the Allies managed to advance up to five miles. Success was short-lived, however, as German counter-attacks regained most of the lost ground by 7th December. The failure of the Cambrai offensive brought about major changes to British strategy, and in March 1918 the British High Command decided to reduce the amount of cavalry on the Western Front. Despite serving with distinction and winning numerous battle honours, all the Indian cavalry regiments were withdrawn from France in March 1918 and sent to fight in Egypt and Palestine, where they played a major role in destroying the Turkish Army and forcing the Ottoman Empire to quit the war. Their victory would be critical to precipitating the German surrender just 11 days later.

L'ACTUALITÉ PAR LA CARTE POSTALE (1916). — UN 14 JUILLET HISTORIQUE
Nos Alliés des Indes place de l'Opéra   Visé Paris 957

" Le 14 Juillet à PARIS en 1916 " — Les Cipayes Indiens

Images above: WW1 period photo postcards of Indian Cavalry marching in July 1916 as part of a French Bastille Day parade.

Image Right: Detcahment of Indian cavalry on the march near the Franco-Belgium frontier 1914. French WW1 era preidocial.

Double Portrait 'Officers of the Indian Army'

Overleaf: Risaldar Jagat Singh, 12th Cavalry, and Risaldar Man Singh, 21st Cavalry by Philip de László, 1916.

Risaldar Jagat Singh joined the Indian Army February 26, 1905, as a Jemadar (junior Indian Officer) in the 12th Cavalry and was promoted to Risaldar 11 April 1916 in the 18th King George's Own Lancers.

Risaldar Man Singh joined the Indian Army 1 March 1890 as a Sowar (a cavalry trooper). He was promoted to Jemadar 1 May 1910 in the 21st Prince Albert Victor's Own Cavalry before being promoted to Risaldar 11 April 1916 in the 20th Deccan Horse.

Indian Cavalry Divisions on the Western Front Regiment Compositions (4 Squadrons)

1st Indian Cavalry Division:

The Ambala Cavalry Brigade (Lahore Division) was detached to form part of 1st Indian Cavalry Division November 1914. It was renamed as the 4th Cavalry Division in November 1916. Class Composition:

6th King Edward's Own Cavalry: 1 Sikhs, 1 Jats, 1 Jat Sikhs, 1 Hindustani Muslims
9th Horse Hodson's Horse: 1 1/2 Sikhs, 1 1/2 Punjabi Muslims, 1/2 Pathans, 1/2 Dogras
19th Lancers (Fane's Horse): 1.5 Sikhs, 1 Punjabi Muslims, 1 Pathans, 1/2 Dogras
30th Lancers (Gordon's Horse): 2 Sikhs, 1 Jats, 1 Hindustani Muslims
29th Lancers Deccan Horse: 1 Sikhs, 2 Jats, 1 Deccani Muslims
36th Horse Jacobs Horse: 1 Sikhs, 1 Pathans, 2 Derajat Muslims & Baluchis
Jodhpur Lancers: Rajasthani Rajputs

2nd Indian Cavalry Division:

The Meerut Cavalry Brigade (Meerut Division) was detached to form part of 2nd Indian Cavalry Division on arriving in France in December 1914. It was renamed as the 5th Cavalry Division in November 1916: Class Composition:

2nd Lancers (Gardner's Horse): 1 Sikh, 1 Rajputs, 1 Jats, 1 Hindustani Muslims
3rd Skinner's Horse: 1 Sikh, 1 Jat, 1 Rajputs, 1 Muslim Rajputs
18th King George's Own Lancers: 1 Sikhs, 3 Punjabi Muslims
20th Royal Deccan Horse: 1 Sikhs, 1 Jats, 2 Deccani Muslims
34th Prince Albert Victor's Own Poona Horse: 1 Punjabi Muslims, 2 Rajputs, 1 Kaim Khanis
38th King George's Own Central India Horse: 2 Sikhs, 1 Pathans, 1 Muslim Rajputs(Gakkars)

Canadian Cavalry Brigade (CCB):

The CCB was attached to the 2nd Indian Cavalry Division on 17/6/16 from the 3rd Cavalry Division: Composition - Royal Canadian Dragoons, Lord Strathcona's Horse, Fort Garry Horse Royal Canadian Field Artillery Brigade (A & B Batteries), Canadian Cavalry Machine Gun Section.

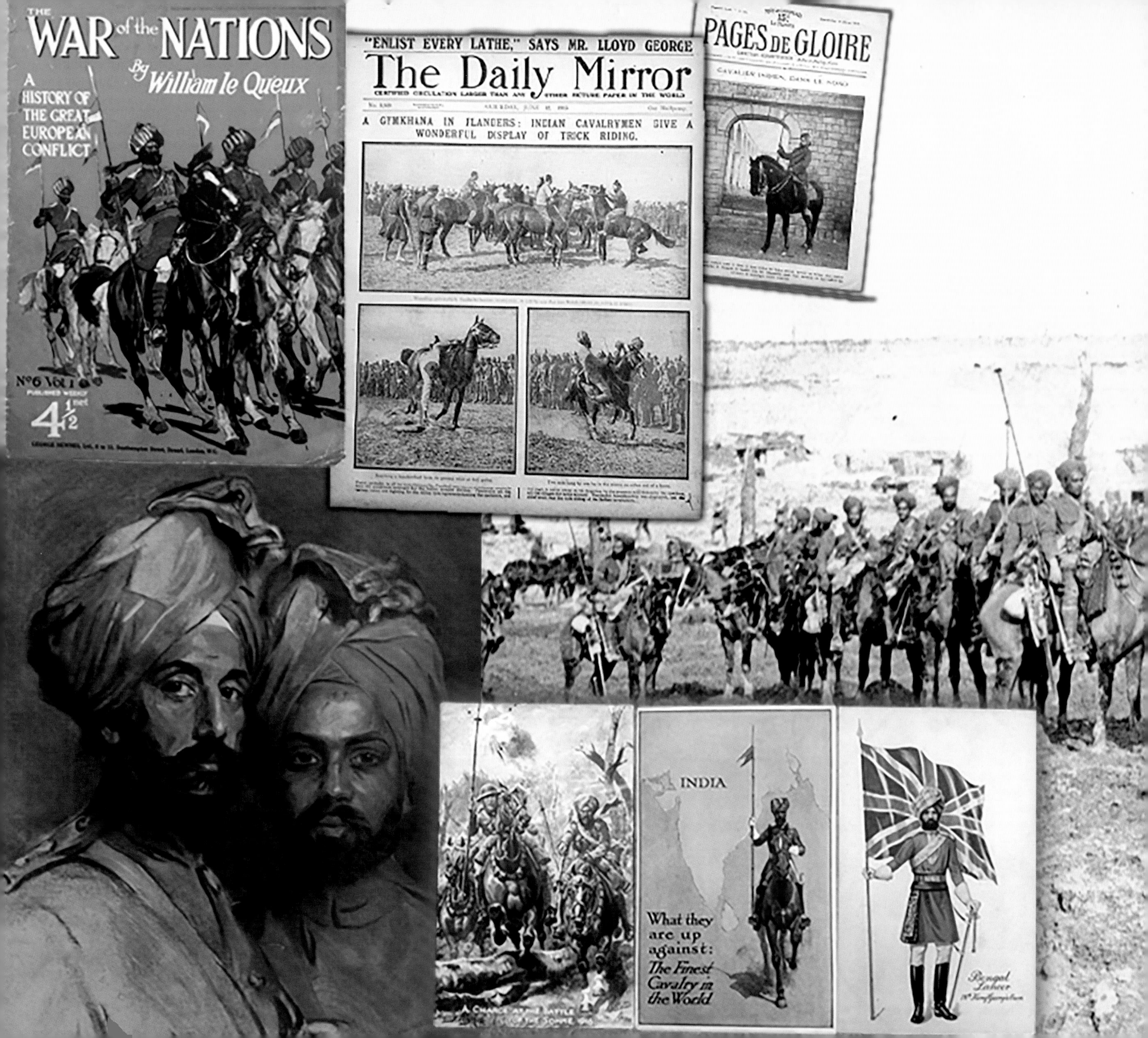
THE WAR of the NATIONS
By William le Queux
A HISTORY OF THE GREAT EUROPEAN CONFLICT
No 6 Vol 1
PUBLISHED WEEKLY
4½ net
"ENLIST EVERY LATHE," SAYS MR. LLOYD GEORGE
The Daily Mirror
A GYMKHANA IN FLANDERS: INDIAN CAVALRYMEN GIVE A WONDERFUL DISPLAY OF TRICK RIDING.
PAGES DE GLOIRE
INDIA
What they are up against: The Finest Cavalry in the World
Bengal Lancer

Sikh Squadron A.
29th Deccan Horse
Near Pys, Somme,
France
March 1917

Within the 1st and 2nd Indian Cavalry Divisions serving on the Western Front, Sikhs fielded the most number of Indian squadrons. Within the majority of the Indian cavalry regiments deployed in other WW1 theatres, Sikhs comprised at least one squadron as follows:

4th Cavalry 1, 7th Hariana Lancers 1, 10th Duke of Cambridge's Own Lancers (Hodson's Horse) 1.5, 11th King Edward's Own Lancers (Probyn's Horse) 2, 12th Cavalry 2, 13th Duke of Connaught's Lancers 1, 16th Cavalry 2, 21st Prince Albert Victor's Own Cavalry - Punjab Frontier Force (Daly's Horse) 1.5, 22nd Sam Browne's Cavalry- Punjab Frontier Force 1.5 , 23rd Cavalry - Punjab Frontier Force 1.5 , 25th Cavalry - Punjab Frontier Force 1, 31st Duke of Connaught's Own Lancers 1, 32nd Lancers 1, 33rd Queen Victoria's Own Light Cavalry 1, 37th Lancers (Baluch Horse) 1, 39th King George's Own Central India Horse 2, Queen Victoria's Own Corps of Guides (Frontier Force) Lumsden's Cavalry 1

BATTLE OF THE SOMME

An Indian Cavalry Squadron Charge at the Battle of the Somme July 1916.

Squadron 'A' (Sikh), 20th Deccan Horse of the 2nd Indian Cavalry Division leads the charge against the German 26th Infantry Regiment at High Wood.

BROTHERS-IN-ARMS

New trench bridges, an innovation of the Canadian Cavalry Brigade had been used to lay tracks to the front line to enable the attack on 14, 1916. A squadron of Fort Garry Horse, attached to the advancing cavalry, prepared the tracks under direct machine gun fire.

At the time, highly romanticised eye-witness accounts marvelled at the daring Indian horsemen, describing the scene as "cavalry riding into action through waving corn with bugles blaring and lances glittering, a glorious vision that crumbled into a slaughter as the German machine guns opened fire". Lieutenant-Colonel G. Seton Hutchinson of the 33rd Division Machine Gun Corps, a Distinguished Service Order, and Military Cross winner himself, who was trapped with his men in no man's land at the time recounted "a squadron of Indian Cavalry, dark faces under glistening helmets, galloping across the valley towards the slope. No troops could have presented a more inspiring sight than these natives of India with lance and sword, tearing in mad cavalcade on to the skyline. A few disappeared over it: they never came back. The remainder became the target of every gun and rifle turning their horses' heads with shrill cries, these masters of horsemanship galloped through a hell of fire, lifting their mounts lightly over yawning shell-holes, turning and twisting throughout the barrage of great shells: the ranks thinned, not a man escaped."

In reality, the casualties were relatively light for a force of approximately 1,500 troops in action in one of the bloodiest battles of the Western Front. The German position at High Wood was taken, and with 100 Germans killed or taken prisoner in the cornfields, at a loss to 20th Deccan Horse of two Indian officers wounded, and three other ranks killed, and fifty wounded. Eighteen horses were killed and fifty two wounded.

BATTLE OF CAMBRAI

At Cambrai, Indian cavalry along with the Canadian Cavalry Brigade featured prominently in the attack on Gauche Wood and the neighbouring village of Villiers-Guislain.

BROTHERS-IN-ARMS

When a mounted advance by the 2nd Lancers (Gardner's Horse), made in conjunction with dismounted cavalrymen of the 38th Central India Horse, was unable to recapture the village, mounted squadrons of Hodsons' Horse gallantly charged across open ground in the face of hostile fire to successfully check a German advance and prevent British troops from being overwhelmed. At Gauche Wood during an incident of indiscriminate shelling, trapped members of Strathcona Horse were attached to Squadron A of the 18th King George's Own (KGO) Lancers, and stranded companies of the Grenadier Guards, the elite regiment of the British Infantry, were taken over by officers of the Indian regiment. Later in 1918, a bugle was presented by the Grenadiers as a gift to the 18th KGO Lancers along with a letter affirming the gallant actions at Gauche Wood and that the "friendly relations between the two regiments should never fade". To commemorate the bonds of friendship between the British Guardsmen and the Indian Sowar, the 18th KGO Lancers reciprocated the honour of having fought alongside the senior-most infantry regiment of the Empire with a silver statuette of an Indian cavalryman

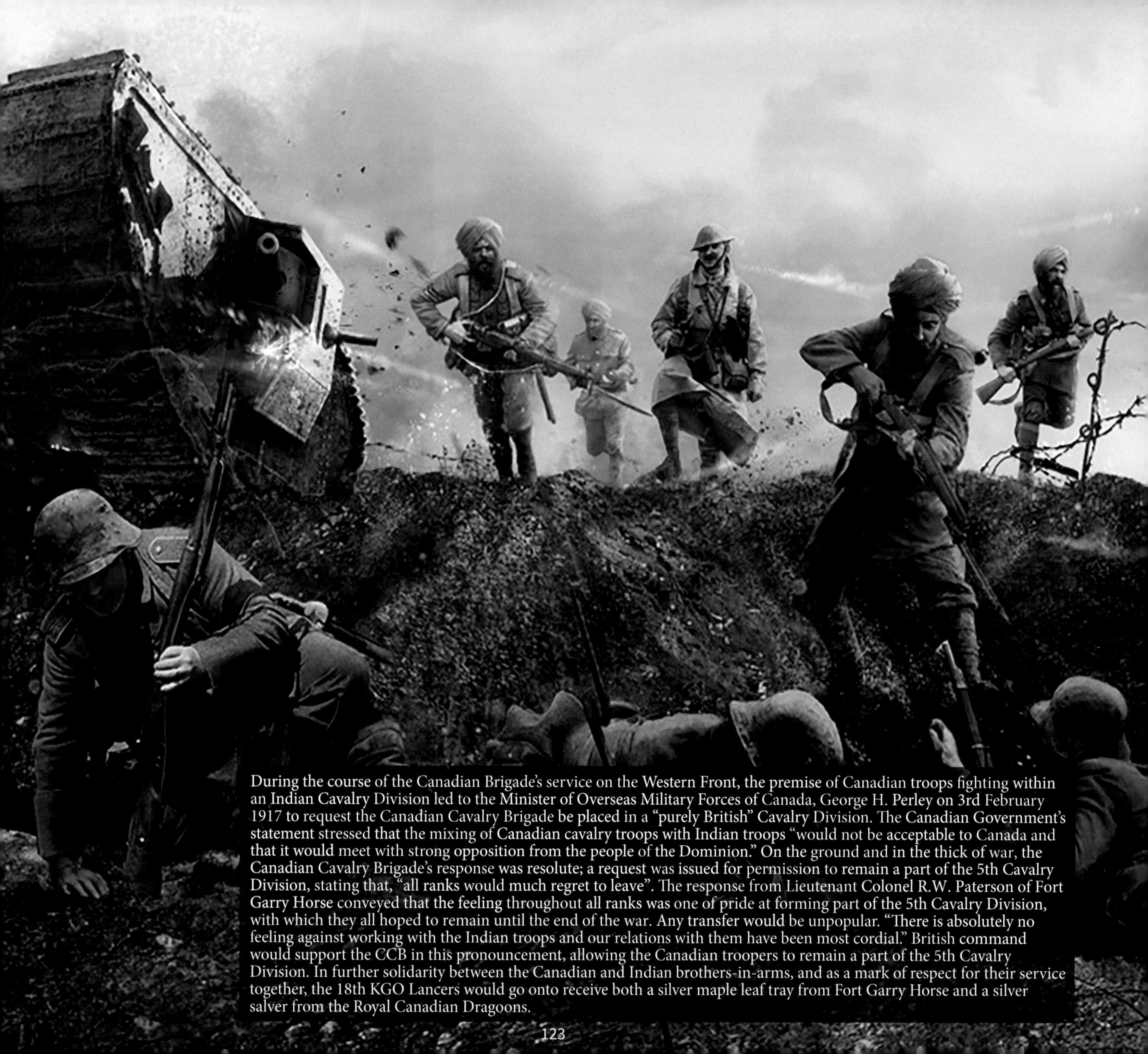

During the course of the Canadian Brigade's service on the Western Front, the premise of Canadian troops fighting within an Indian Cavalry Division led to the Minister of Overseas Military Forces of Canada, George H. Perley on 3rd February 1917 to request the Canadian Cavalry Brigade be placed in a "purely British" Cavalry Division. The Canadian Government's statement stressed that the mixing of Canadian cavalry troops with Indian troops "would not be acceptable to Canada and that it would meet with strong opposition from the people of the Dominion." On the ground and in the thick of war, the Canadian Cavalry Brigade's response was resolute; a request was issued for permission to remain a part of the 5th Cavalry Division, stating that, "all ranks would much regret to leave". The response from Lieutenant Colonel R.W. Paterson of Fort Garry Horse conveyed that the feeling throughout all ranks was one of pride at forming part of the 5th Cavalry Division, with which they all hoped to remain until the end of the war. Any transfer would be unpopular. "There is absolutely no feeling against working with the Indian troops and our relations with them have been most cordial." British command would support the CCB in this pronouncement, allowing the Canadian troopers to remain a part of the 5th Cavalry Division. In further solidarity between the Canadian and Indian brothers-in-arms, and as a mark of respect for their service together, the 18th KGO Lancers would go onto receive both a silver maple leaf tray from Fort Garry Horse and a silver salver from the Royal Canadian Dragoons.

"I am not afraid either to live or die. This is all in God's hands. 1 have escaped hitherto from a rain of shells and bombs, and 1 believe it will be the same in the future. If He has laid down that my work shall lie in the midst of such a blazing fire I shall go on doing it with His help. There are two points to note in this. The first is that God has ordained my career; and the second is that loyalty to the King compels me to serve him and to be true to my salt. I am sure victory is at hand, and we shall soon return to our native land. The enemy's condition is very bad and it is difficult for him to preserve his life. He is surrounded on every side, and you will soon hear of a glorious victory being won. He will soon be crushed under foot, for the condition of our Army and those of our allies is improving day by day. No one fears death. If a demand is made for a volunteer to go ahead, a thousand offer. The evil deeds of the German have excited universal indignation. He utterly destroyed all the towns and villages, and blew up the roads, and cut down the fruit trees, and has burnt everything. He has seized and taken away the civilian inhabitants. This is not a royal way of waging war. Our Government's behaviour is of a very different kind. It is that of a real King."

From Risaldar Dayal Singh 6th Cavalry, France to Chuni Lal Campbellpur, Attock District, Punjab (translated from Urdu)

July 14, 1917

"My son, you are indeed fortunate in that you have had the opportunity to discharge your debt of loyalty towards the Sirkar. You are not far from us; you are the son of your country, and a ready sacrifice in her welfare. My hopes are fixed on you, and our King takes pride in being served by such as you. You are a hero of this great age. May the Guru keep you well and happy. You are under the protection of God. You are a hero, and the security of my life. Our Government relies on you. When Aurangzeb ruled over the land, he desired to root out our race [the Sikhs] root and branch. Today our King, ruler over the seven Kingdoms, is the protection of our race. His armies have subjugated Baghdad. To you and to your fellows is due the honour of this achievement, and of the fact that the heart's blood of the Germans is being consumed... We should send up unlimited thanks to Almighty God who has bestowed on us such honour and glory. Now I pray that God will speedily bring the day when your voice will be raised in the 'Hurrah' of victory, when you will feel the kisses of your mother, and be clasped in the arms of your wife, and when all of us, being filled with happiness, will raise our voices in praise to our Government."

Kishan Singh in Urdu from Nabha State Punjab to Veterinary Assistant Gajan Singh, 18th Lancers, France

November 2, 1917

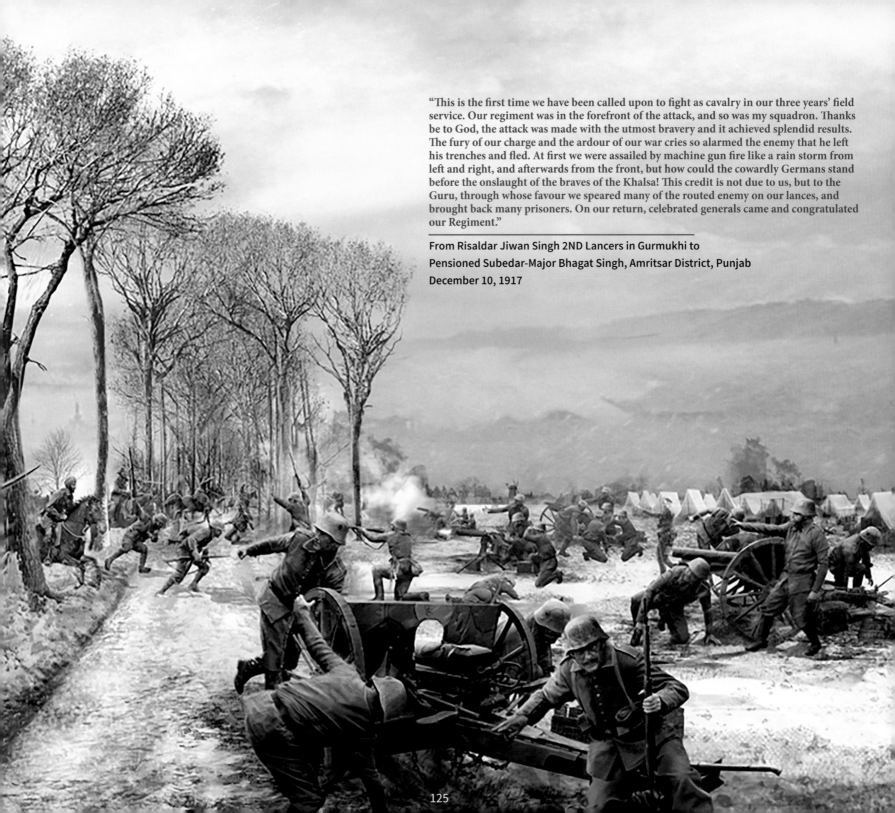

"This is the first time we have been called upon to fight as cavalry in our three years' field service. Our regiment was in the forefront of the attack, and so was my squadron. Thanks be to God, the attack was made with the utmost bravery and it achieved splendid results. The fury of our charge and the ardour of our war cries so alarmed the enemy that he left his trenches and fled. At first we were assailed by machine gun fire like a rain storm from left and right, and afterwards from the front, but how could the cowardly Germans stand before the onslaught of the braves of the Khalsa! This credit is not due to us, but to the Guru, through whose favour we speared many of the routed enemy on our lances, and brought back many prisoners. On our return, celebrated generals came and congratulated our Regiment."

From Risaldar Jiwan Singh 2ND Lancers in Gurmukhi to

Pensioned Subedar-Major Bhagat Singh, Amritsar District, Punjab

December 10, 1917

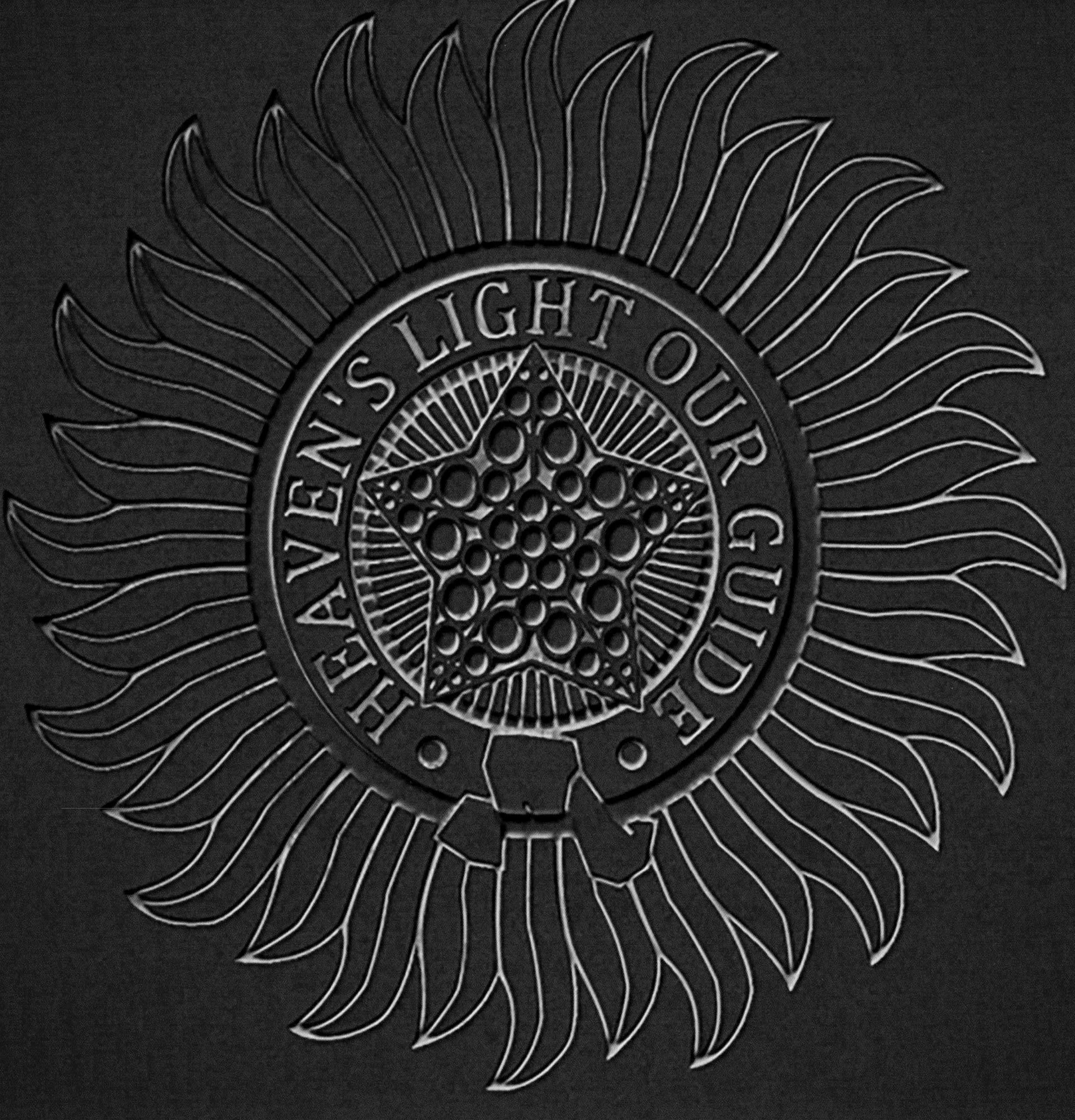
HEAVEN'S LIGHT OUR GUIDE

HONOUR

Going Above & Beyond
the Call of Duty

HONOUR ROLL: INFANTRY

Queen Victoria's Own Corps of Guides (Frontier Force) Lumsden's Infantry: IDSM: Lance Naik Alam Khan, 1016. Sepoy Bhan Singh, 5510. 3rd Sappers and Miners: IOM 2nd Class: Havildar Dalip Singh, 3795. Havildar Muhammad Khan, 2479. Jemadar Gurmukh Singh, 3108. Jemadar Liyakat Ali. Jemadar Muhammad Bakhsh, 3144. Jemadar Uttam Singh. Naik Shah Nawaz, 2584. Subadar Malla Singh. Military Cross: Subadar Malla Singh. OBI: Subadar Ganpat Mahadeo. Subadar Ismail Khan. IDSM: Havildar Ghulam Kadir, 4049. Jemadar Datadin Badhai. Jemadar Ganga Charan Dikshit. Jemadar Maroti Jodhao, 3348. Jemadar Muhammd Baksh, 3144. Jemadar Nur Alam. Lance Naik Bagga Singh, 4012. Lance Naik Indar Singh, 4052. Naik Salah Muhammad, 3450. Subadar Ali Bahadur. Subadar Ismail Khan. 9th Bhopal Infantry: IDSM: Jemadar Amar Singh, 2203. Naik Angad Pande, 2867. Naik Sheikh Abdul Latif, 2069. Subadar Major Bhure Singh. Ward Orderly Umrao Singh, 2747. 14th King George's Own Ferozepore Sikhs: IMSM: Havildar Sawan Singh, 2703. 15th Ludhiana Sikhs: IOM 2nd Class: Havildar Bishan Singh, 4011. Havildar Mahan Singh, 4727. Jemadar Bakshi Singh. Lance Naik Mangal Singh, 131. Sepoy Bakshi Singh, 698. Military Cross: Subadar Bir Singh. OBI: Subadar Bir Singh. IDSM: Havildar Bachan Singh, 4572. Havildar Bhagwan Singh, 4616. Havildar Bishan Singh, 4576. Havildar Bishan Singh, 3989. Havildar Budh Singh, 4429. Jemadar Bir Singh. Jemadar Wazir Singh. Naik Bhagwan Singh, 53. Sepoy Dan Singh, 435. Sepoy Dewan Singh, 219. Sepoy Lal Singh, 702. Sepoy Sapuran Singh, 962. Sepoy Sucha Singh, 638. Sepoy Tilok Singh, 529. Subadar Phuman Singh. IMSM: Havildar Dalbara Singh, 4369. Havildar Gajjan Singh, 4635. Havildar Kehar Singh, 4634. Havildar Mall Singh, 4348. Havildar Mangal Singh, 4362. Havildar Nagina Singh, 3897. Havildar Pancham, 4845. Havildar Thakur Singh, 3982. Havildar Waryam Singh, 4272. Naik Sham Singh, 4536. Sepoy Rattan Singh, 4434. Sepoy Sham Singh, 3946. 19th Punjabis: IDSM: Havildar Ganda Singh, 1339. Havildar Harnam Singh, 1360. Havildar Sundar Singh, 1249. Sepoy Sarian Singh, 1255. IMSM: Lance Naik Tulsa Singh, 51. Naik Dhera Singh, 36. 21st Punjabis: IDSM: Havildar Fateh Ali, 4287. Sepoy Muhammad Shah, 14. 26th Punjabis: IDSM: Ward Orderly Devi Dyal, 4484. 29th Punjabis: IDSM: Sepoy Albel Singh, 4902. IMSM: Packstore Havildar Saiyid Ahmed Shah, 2252. Sepoy Sher Singh, 4829. 30th Punjabis: IOM 2nd Class: Sepoy Bali Ram, 4423. OBI: Subadar Dewan Singh. IDSM: Sepoy Lal Singh, 4095. 32nd Sikh Pioneers: IOM 2nd Class: Havildar Mangal Singh, 3623. Jemadar Kharak Singh. IDSM: Subadar Wasawa Singh. 33rd Punjabis: IOM 2nd Class: Subadar Attar Khan. Subadar Major Bahadur Khan. Subadar Major Maluk Singh. IDSM: Naik Farman Ali, 1635. Sepoy Chowdre Khan, 1029. Sepoy Lachman Singh, 2209. Sepoy Mowaz , 2260. Subadar Muzarab Shah. 34th Sikh Pioneers: IOM 2nd Class: Havildar Nikka Singh, 1871. Havildar Pala Singh, 1148. Lance Naik Tota Singh, 2775. Naik Bir Singh, 2071. Naik Gujar Singh, 1907. Sepoy Mastan Singh, 4563. Subadar Natha Singh. Subadar Major Jawala Singh (Sardar Bahadur). Subadar Natha Singh. Military Cross: Subadar Sant Singh. IDSM: Havildar Narayan Singh, 1452. Havildar Prem Singh, 1576. Havildar Sundar Singh, 1862. Sepoy Gopal Singh, 3013. Sepoy Ishar Singh, 2578. Sepoy Ishar Singh, 2709. Sepoy Katha Singh, 2398. Sepoy Sant Singh, 3036. Subadar Maghar Singh. Subadar Sher Singh . 35th Sikhs: IOM 2nd Class: Havildar Bir Singh, 2103. Havildar Lal Singh, 2479. IDSM: Havildar Mula Singh, 2882. Jemadar Fauja Singh, 2242. Sepoy Asa Singh, 3201. 36th Sikhs: IOM 2nd Class: Sepoy Bhagwan Singh, 2277. 45th Rattray's Sikhs: IDSM: Lance Naik Kesar Singh, 4474. Sepoy Fateh Singh, 1036. Sepoy Ujagar Singh, 1001. IMSM: Colour Havildar Sundar Singh, 2929. Lance Naik Santa Singh, 183. Lance Naik Ujagar Singh, 1001. 47th Sikhs: IOM 2nd Class: Havildar Gajjan Singh, 514. Havildar Lachman Singh, 337. Havildar Narain Singh, 231. Jemadar Sucha Singh. Sepoy Rur Singh, 2270. Subadar Bakshi Singh. Subadar Harnam Singh. Subadar Mota Singh. Military Cross: Subadar Thakur Singh. OBI: Subadar Saudagar Singh. IDSM: Havildar Bhagat Singh, 482. Havildar Bhola Singh, 228. Havildar Lachman Singh, 337. Naik Jagat Singh, 355. Naik Kishen Singh, 2116. Naik Mit Singh, 1189. Naik Mota Singh, 1336. Sepoy Bhuta Singh, 2266. Sepoy Kehr Singh, 1308. Sepoy Kesar Singh, 1410. Sepoy Wariam Singh, 1791. 54th Sikhs (Frontier Force): IDSM: Sepoy Delavara Singh, 3577. 55th Coke's Rifles (Frontier Force): Victoria Cross: Jemadar Mir Dast. IOM 2nd Class: Sepoy Usman Khan, 1695. IDSM: Sepoy Mehr Khan, 2625. Sepoy Mir Badshah, 2108. 56th Punjabi Rifles (Frontier Force): IDSM: Havildar Madar Khan, 1723. 57th Wilde's Rifles (Frontier Force): IOM 2nd Class: Havildar Gagna, 2630. Havildar Yakub Khan, 2584. Jemadar Mangal Singh. Lance Naik Said Akbar, 2718. Naik Lalak Khan, 2544. Sepoy Atma Singh, 2609. Sepoy Diwan Singh, 3402. Sepoy Daulat Khan, 3576. Sepoy Pala Ram, 2632. Military Cross: Subadar Major Arsla Khan (Bahadur). OBI: Subadar Imam Ali. Subadar Major Arsla Khan. IDSM: Havildar Karim Khan, 2595. Havildar Narayan , 2583. Havildar Sahib Sher, 2760. Havildar Sar Mast, 2540. Jemadar Bur Singh, 991. Naik Sohan Singh, 2063. Sepoy Alvas Khan, 3484. Sepoy Bahadur Khan, 2589. Sepoy Mir Badshah, 3119. Sepoy Mir Baz, 3223. Sepoy Ram Saran, 2702. Subadar Fateh Jang. 58th Vaughan's Rifles (Frontier Force): IOM 1st Class: Subadar Suhel Singh. IOM 2nd Class: Havildar Karam Singh, 1811. Havildar Kashmir Singh, 2830. Havildar Roshan Khan, 1848. Havildar Saidak, 3572. Havildar Santa Singh, 1925. Jemadar Harchand Singh. Jemadar Muhammad Arbi. Lance Naik Phangan Singh, 3131. Lance Naik Sher Khan, 2834. Naik Lal Badshah, 3032. Sepoy Isar Singh, 2742. Military Cross: Jemadar Hawinda. Jemadar Indar Singh. OBI: Subadar Abdul Ali. Subadar Raj Talab. IDSM: Havildar Arjun, 2763. Havildar Baidullah, 3404. Havildar Fazal Dad, 2198. Havildar Hawindah, 2008. Havildar Lashkar, 3212. Havildar Sardar, 3066. Havildar Sarfaraz, 3136. Havildar Sundar Singh, 2164. Lance Naik Muhammad Amin, 2934. Lance Naik Said Asghar, 3567. Naik Dewa Singh, 2758. Naik Sergun Shah, 2634. Naik Zar Baz, 3083. Sepoy Dewa Singh, 3374. Sepoy Maluk Singh, 3133. Subadar Hamid Khan. Subadar Indar Singh. Subadar Phuman Singh. Subadar Raj Talab. IMSM: Havildar Makhmad Ali, 2412. 59th Scinde Rifles (Frontier Force): IOM 1st Class: Sepoy Zarif Khan, 27. IOM 2nd Class: Havildar Dost Muhammad, 3191. Havildar Muhammad Jan, 3638. Jemadar Abdul Wahab, 3063. Lance Naik Baiz Gul, 3907. Lance Naik Buta Singh, 3705. Subadar Muzaffar Khan. Subadar Major Nasir Khan (Sardar Bahadur). Military Cross: Subadar Major Parbat Chand. OBI 1st Class: Subadar Major Nasir Khan (Bahadur).IDSM: Havildar Amir Ali, 3529. Havildar Niyaz Ali, 4264. Havildar Nur Ali, 4016. Jemadar Ghamai Khan, 3581. Jemadar Zaman Ali. Sepoy Akbar Khan, 4845. Sepoy Lal Khan, 4731. Subadar Bishan Singh. Subadar Major Muhammad Khan. 62nd Punjabis: IOM 2nd Class: Sepoy Nihal Singh, 1434. IDSM: Jemadar Baldeo Singh. Naik Bari Sher, 13. Naik Imam Shah, 1209. 69th Punjabis: IOM 2nd Class: Jemadar Sardar Khan. Lance Naik Nidhan Singh, 440. Sepoy Kirpa Ram, 649. Subadar Major Jagindar Singh (Bahadur). Subadar Major Muhammad Khan. IDSM: Havildar Bhulla Singh, 1734. Havildar Ghulam Ali, 862. Havildar Gurdit Singh, 466. Jemadar Gheba Khan. Naik Punna Singh, 433. 74th Punjabis: IOM 2nd Class: Subadar Dost Muhammad Khan. 82nd Punjabis: IMSM: Havildar Fateh Khan, 163. Lance Naik Gouhar Din, 2146. Sepoy Rukham Din, 245. 84th Punjabis: IDSM: Acting Naik Burhan Ali, 1172. 89th Punjabis: IOM 2nd Class: Havildar Hira Tiwari, 1088. Sepoy Indar Singh, 2316. IDSM: Havildar Harnam Singh, 1528. Havildar Muhammad Sadiq, 2352. Havildar Narayan Singh, 1998. Jemadar Bagga Singh. Jemadar Ramji Misra, 2029. Naik Karam Dad, 1485. Sepoy Muhammad Khan, 2102. IMSM: Havildar Chirag Din, 2254. Havildar Harnam Singh, 1654. Havildar Kishun Singh, 2129. Havildar Sakhi Muhammad, 1535. Havildar Sheorattan Singh, 1816. Havildar Teja Singh, 2378. Lance Naik Mutsaddi

Singh, 2518. Lance Naik Saudagar Khan, 2720. Lance Naik Sirinewas Misr, 2079. Naik Isser Singh, 2079. Sepoy Nawab Khan, 2824. 90th Punjabis: IDSM: Sepoy Bhagat Singh, 1776. IMSM: Lance Naik Sawaya Singh, 2081. Sepoy Bishen Nath Singh, 1722. 91st Punjabis (Light Infantry): IOM 2nd Class: Naik Suleman Khan, 3275. IMSM: Sepoy Durga, 3137. 92nd Punjabis: IDSM: Lance Naik Sucha Singh, 2636. 129th Duke Of Connaught's Own Baluchis: Victoria Cross: Sepoy Khudadad Khan, 4050. IOM 2nd Class: Colour Havildar Sar Mir, 4280. Colour Havildar Ghulam Muhammad, 2524. Lance Naik Habib Gul, 3814. Sepoy Redi Gul, 4333. Subadar Mir Badshah. Naik Sahib Jan, 453. Subadar Makhmad Azam. Naik Nek Amal, 118. Sepoy Saida Khan, 250. Sepoy Raje Khan, 471. Jemadar Fateh Haidet, 3836. Military Cross: Subadar Zaman Khan, OBI: Subadar Zaman Khan. Subadar Makhmad Azam. IDSM: Sepoy Kassib, 105. Sepoy Lal Sher, 2813. Sepoy Afsar Khan, 3600. Sepoy Said Ahmed, 4182. Jemadar Nur Khan, 2268. Sepoy Auliya Khan, 2012. Sepoy Mehrab Gul, 4267. Jemadar Ghulam Jilani.

HONOUR ROLL: CAVALRY

Queen Victoria's Own Corps of Guides (Frontier Force) Lumsden's Cavalry: OBI 2nd Class: Risaldar Khwaja Muhammad Khan (Bahadur). 1st Duke of York's Own Lancers (Skinner's Horse): OBI: Risaldar Mardan Khan. IDSM: Lance Dafadar Ali Hussain, 1763. IMSM: Sowar Abdul Shakoor Khan, 1873. Sowar Sabr Ali Khan, 1775. 2nd Lancers (Gardner's Horse): IOM 2nd Class: Lance Dafadar Anokh Singh, 1725. Lance Dafadar Sahib Singh, 1417. Lance Dafadar Udey Singh, 2266. Risaldar Suraj Singh. Sowar Liakat Hussain, 2136. Military Cross: Risaldar Mukand Singh (Bahadur). OBI: Risaldar Mukand Singh. Risaldar Suraj Singh. Risaldar Major Ganga Dat. IDSM: Dafadar Atta Muhammad Khan, 2051. Dafadar Jiwan Singh, 1396. Dafadar Ram Singh, 1861. Jemadar Dhara Singh. Kot Dafadar Dharam Singh, 1515. Kot Dafadar Ram Pershad, 1329. Lance Dafadar Gordham, 1950. Lance Dafadar Sobha Singh, 2026. Lance Dafadar (Armourer) Bishan Singh, 989. Ressaidar Abdul Latif Khan. Risaldar Het Ram. Risaldar Krishna Chandra Singh. Sowar Amar Singh, 2049. Sowar Assa Singh, 2318. Sowar Kehar Singh, 2152. Sowar Lohara Singh, 1917. Sowar Mohan Singh, 1705. Sowar Rati Ram, 2296. IMSM: Dafadar Basti Singh, 1621. Dafadar Bhagwan Das, 1188. Dafadar Mehbub Ali, 1502. Dafadar Muhammad Zaman Khan, 1409. Dafadar Ram Pershad Singh, 1260. Dafadar Sham Singh, 1336. Dafadar (Salutri) Abdul Rahman Khan, 1318. Dafadar (Salutri) Ahmed Ullah Khan, 1313. Farrier Major Nizam-ud-Din, 1090. Kot Dafadar Ali Raza Khan, 1184. Kot Dafadar Molar, 1706. Kot Dafadar Natha Singh, 1298. Kot Dafadar Ram Pershad, 1329. Kot Dafadar Sarjit Singh, 1608. Kot Dafadar Udey Singh, 1179. Sowar Chandrapal Singh, 1775. Sowar Lachman Singh, 1564. Trumpet Major Ganga Ram, 1443. 3rd Skinner's Horse: OBI: Risaldar Major Balwant Singh. 4th Cavalry: OBI: Risaldar Major Awal Khan. Risaldar Major Saddha Singh. IDSM: Dafadar Karam Singh, 333. Dafadar Sheo Ram, 2100. Risaldar Udmi Ram. 5th Cavalry: IDSM: Dafadar Mazar Ali Shah, 1919. Risaldar Khurshed Muhammad Khan. Sowar Gokal, 2321. Sowar Yakub Khan, 1916. 6th King Edward's Own Cavalry: IOM 2nd Class: Lance Dafadar Karam Singh, 2386. Military Cross: Risaldar Jai Singh. OBI: Risaldar Major Fateh Singh. Risaldar Dayal Singh. IDSM: Dafadar Jot Ram, 2475. Dafadar Parbhu Dayal, 2813. Dafadar Siri Ram, 2632. Dafadar (Honoraray Jemadar) Arjan Singh, 1436. Jemadar Amir Singh. Jemadar Amir Singh. Jemadar Bachittar Singh. Lance Dafadar Gurmukh Singh, 2339. Lance Dafadar Mul Singh, 2621. Quartermaster Dafadar Udey Chand, 821. Risaldar Jai Singh. Sowar Raja Singh, 2943. Sowar (Ward Orderly) Jaimal Singh, 2738. Ward Orderly Abdul Wahab Khan, 2671. IMSM: Dafadar Jowala Singh, 1936. Dafadar Maksud Ali, 2111. Dafadar Tek Chand, 2921. Farrier Yakub Khan, 2259. Kot Dafadar Ghulam Hussain, 1898. Kot Dafadar Kartar Singh, 2098. Kot Dafadar Kehar Singh, 1609. Kot Dafadar Sheo Karan, 2191. Lance Dafadar Amar Singh, 2780. Lance Dafadar Amar Singh, 2823. Lance Dafadar Behari, 1774. Lance Dafadar Lehna Singh, 2000. Sowar Harnam Singh, 2758. Sowar Rahmat Khan, 2079. Sowar Ram Singh, 2566. Trumpet Major Mangal Singh, 2599. Trumpeter Tara Singh, 2459. 7th Hariana Lancers: IDSM: Lance Dafadar Niadar Singh, 3125. Risaldar Hazura Singh. 8th Cavalry: IDSM: Jemadar Kale Khan. 9th Hodson's Horse: IOM 1st Class: Risaldar Nur Ahmad Khan. IOM 2nd Class: Dafadar Hakim Singh, 2764. Jemadar Sardar Khan. Lance Dafadar Muhammad Azam, 2804. Risaldar Nur Ahmad Khan. Sowar Abdullah Khan, 3456. OBI: Risaldar Jai Ram. Risaldar Muhammad Akram Khan. Risaldar Ram Singh. Risaldar Major Malik Khan. IDSM: Dafadar Abdul Satar Khan, 2588. Dafadar Sikandar Khan, 2845. Farrier Wali Muhammad, 3367. Jemadar Habib Gul. Jemadar Sardar Khan. Lance Dafadar Dhir Singh, 2661. Lance Dafadar Nawab Ali Khan, 2762. Lance Dafadar Preetam Singh, 3150. Risaldar Harditt Singh. Risaldar Tek Singh. Sowar Baz Singh, 3189. Sowar Firoze Khan, 3086. Sowar Hashim Khan, 2929. Sowar Kapur Singh, 2965. Sowar Ramzan Khan, 3568. Sowar Sarain Singh, 2762. Sowar Shamsuddin Khan, 3341. Sowar Sujjan Singh, 3090. IMSM: Dafadar Fateh Singh. Dafadar Ghulam Rasul, 2701. Dafadar Hira Singh. Dafadar Labh Singh, 2657. Dafadar Malang Khan, 2688. Dafadar Muhummad Khan. Dafadar Sayed Habib, 2941. Dafadar (Head Clerk) Imam Din, 2596. Kot Dafadar Channan Singh, 2794. Kot Dafadar Mangal Singh, 2430. Kot Dafadar Tohid Gul, 2206. 10th Duke of Cambridge's Own Lancers (Hodson's Horse): IOM 2nd Class: Dafadar Sarfaraz Khan, 2967. Sowar Hayat Muhammad, 2793. IDSM: Lance Dafadar Rattan Singh, 2916. IMSM: Dafadar Foja Singh. 11th King Edward's Own Lancers (Probyn's Horse): IOM 2nd Class: Dafadar Amir Muhammad Khan, 2782. Dafadar Fateh Khan, 3095. Lance Dafadar Ganga Singh, 2614. Lance Dafadar Jit Singh, 2889. IDSM: Dafadar Fateh Khan, 3095. Sowar Mehain Singh, 298. Sowar Ram Saran, 302. Sowar Sita Ram, 175. IMSM: Kot Dafadar Fateh Khan, 3095. 12th Cavalry: IOM 2nd Class: Jemadar Zari Gul Khan. IDSM: Dafadar Sangar Khan. Sowar Fauja Singh, 873. IMSM: Sowar Shiv Ram, 367. 13th Duke of Connaught's Lancers (Watson's Horse): Military Cross: Risaldar Jai Singh. 15th Lancers (Cureton's Multanis): IOM 2nd Class: Jemadar Malik Mehr Khan. IDSM: Dafadar Ibrahim Khan, 346. Lance Dafadar Allahdad Khan, 2176. IMSM: Dafadar Choor Singh, 340. Dafadar Fatehullah Khan, 353. Lance Dafadar Dost Muhammad Khan, 2305. Lance Dafadar Ghulam Muhammad Khan, 2063. Lance Dafadar Gul Muhammad Khan, 1739. Lance Dafadar Khuda Bakhsh Khan, 363. Lance Dafadar Sarbuland Khan, 362. 17th Cavalry: IOM 2nd Class: Sowar Muhammad Hussain, 2205. IDSM: Jemadar Malik Alam Sher Khan. IMSM: Dafadar Quadratullah Khan, 1511. Lance Dafadar Muhammad Azam, 1930. 18th King George's Own Lancers: IOM 2nd Class: Dafadar Mohamed Khan, 2094. Jemadar Adalat Khan. Jemadar Muhammad Khan. Lance Dafadar Mobara Khan, 1995. Risaldar Dhuman Khan. Risaldar Major Haji Gul Nawaz Khan (Bahadur). OBI: Risaldar Dost Muhammad Khan. Risaldar Muhammad Inayat Khan. Risaldar Lakha Singh. Risaldar Malik Ahmadyar Khan. Risaldar Sundar Singh. Risaldar Major Gul Mawaz Khan. IDSM: Dafadar Allah Ditta Khan, 1937. Dafadar Bhagwan Singh, 1941. Dafadar Zahid Khan, 2147. Driver Fateh Khan, 13196. Farrier Major Hashim Ali Khan, 1866. Jemadar Adalat Khan. Jemadar Khuda Baksh Khan. Kot Dafadar Khuda Baksh, 1575. Lance Dafadar Baz Khan, 2135. Lance Dafadar Ghulam Muhammad, 2293. Lance Dafadar Hyat Khan, 2002. Risaldar Malik Sultan Khan. Sowar Channan Singh, 2480. Sowar Hidayat Khan, 2466. Sowar Lall Singh, 1595. Sowar Makan Khan, 2400. Sowar Muhammad Sharif Khan, 2686. Sowar Talib Hussain, 2533. Sowar Sultan Khan, 2385. IMSM: Dafadar Ali Mardan Khan,

1759. Dafadar Falak Sher, 2200. Dafadar Hazara Singh, 1778. Dafadar Kehar Singh, 1625. Dafadar Muhammad Khan, 1801. Dafadar Muhammad Khan, 394. Dafadar Nur Khan, 2059. Kot Dafadar Allah Yar Khan, 1710. Kot Dafadar Kishen Singh, 1696. Kot Dafadar Mirza Khan, 1648. Kot Dafadar Muhammad Ashraf Khan, 1963. Kot Dafadar Sher Ali Khan, 1779. Sowar Dilawar Khan, 2403. Sowar Muhammad Ibrahim, 2578. Sowar (Ward Orderly) Makkan Khan, 2400. 19th Lancers (Fane's Horse): IOM 2nd Class: Dafadar Mehar Singh, 2810. Dafadar Sarbuland Khan. Jemadar Bishen Singh. Kot Dafadar Hashim Khan, 2939. Sowar Alla Ditta, 3600. OBI: Risaldar Khwaja Muhammad. Risaldar Khushal Khan. Risaldar Major Abdul Aziz Khan. Risaldar Major Hira Singh. IDSM: Dafadar Ghazni Khan, 2914. Dafadar Gulbar Khan, 2947. Dafadar Sant Singh, 3067. Dafadar Sham Singh, 2788. Jemadar Mahan Singh, 2780. Lance Dafadar Bhagat Singh, 3576. Lance Dafadar Hussain Ali, 2986. Lance Dafadar Musali Khan, 3260. Risaldar Ghulam Hussain. Risaldar Moti Singh. Risaldar Major Hira Singh (Bahadur). Sowar Bishan Singh, 2077. Sowar Kishen Singh, 3534. Sowar Nadir Khan, 3761. Sowar Sundar Singh, 3485. IMSM: Dafadar Arjan Singh, 2668. Dafadar Gul Din, 2821. Dafadar Hari Singh, 2627. Dafadar Maula Dad, 2906. Dafadar Mehr Singh, 2810. Dafadar Sher Bahadur, 2418. Dafadar Shiv Charan Singh, 3504. Dafadar Sundar Singh, 2736. Dafadar Walayat Khan, 2877. Farrier Major Niaz Muhammad, 2461. Kot Dafadar Abdul Ghani, 3035. Kot Dafadar Fateh Baz, 2566. Kot Dafadar Mal Singh, 2277. Lance Dafadar Attar Singh, 3307. Lance Dafadar Jagat Singh, 2814. Quartermaster Dafadar Man Singh, 2307. Sowar (Clerk) Amar Singh, 3889. Trumpet Major Lehna Singh, 2493. 20th Deccan Horse: IOM 2nd Class: Dafadar Sardar Singh, 295. Dafadar Shankar Rao, 255. OBI: Risaldar Konsal Singh. Risaldar Prem Singh. Risaldar Major Nigahia Ram. IDSM: Dafadar Kasim Khan, 540. Dafadar Mirza Muhammad Ali Beg, 441. Dafadar Muhammad Ali Khan, 3702. Dafadar Muhammad Zaman Khan, 653. Dafadar Rai Singh, 134. Dafadar Ram Sarup, 670. Dafadar Shaikh Ahmad Hussain, 1095. Farrier Major Tika Ram, 13. Jemadar Dalip Singh. Jemadar Yusuf Ali Khan. Kot Dafadar Hira Singh, 294. Kot Dafadar Lehri, 226. Lance Dafadar Mir Ronuk Ali, 1108. Risaldar Dalip Singh. Risaldar Shaik Faiz-ud-din. Risaldar Ali Sher. Risaldar Khurshed Muhammad Khan. Risaldar Konsal Singh. Salutri Sayed Ghulam Mahbub, 340. Sowar Gokal Singh, 830. Sowar Mam Chand, 1228. Sowar Saiyad Abdul Majid, 1156. Sowar (Ward Orderly) Ali Muhammad Khan. Sowar (Ward Orderly) Sirdar Singh, 991. IMSM: Dafadar Bhim Singh, 292. Dafadar Jhanda Singh, 210. Dafadar Mahabali Singh, 301. Dafadar Siddi Nur Muhammad, 1015. Kot Dafadar Abdul Razak Khan, 425. Kot Dafadar Bharat Singh, 221. Kot Dafadar Mirza Ahmad Beg, 904. Lance Dafadar Ahmad Khan, 450. Lance Dafadar Gopal Singh, 837. Lance Dafadar Lehri, 927. Lance Dafadar Tamizzudin Khan, 373. Quartermaster Dafadar Muhammad Ibrahim, 528. Sowar Sawai Singh, 1192. Sowar (Ward Orderly) Damodar Rao, 73. Trumpet Major Zahur Muhammad, 388. 21st Prince Albert Victor's Own Cavalry (Frontier Force) (Daly's Horse): IOM 2nd Class: Lance Dafadar Mutthra Singh, 3192. IDSM: Dafadar Santokh Singh, 3080. Sowar Avtar Singh, 3461. Ward Orderly Mahmud Ali Khan, 3242. IMSM: Dafadar Kala Khan, 2780. Lance Dafadar Santa Singh, 3274. Sowar Hasan Khan, 3241. Sowar Muzaffar Khan, 3041. 22nd Sam Browne's Cavalry (Frontier Force): IDSM: Dafadar Santokh Singh, 3080. Sowar Avtar Singh, 3461. Ward Orderly Mahmud Ali Khan, 3242. IMSM: Dafadar Jetha Singh, 600. 23rd Cavalry (Frontier Force): OBI: Risaldar Major Habib-ur-Rahman Khan. IDSM: Dafadar Sher Singh, 964. Sowar Asta Buddin, 1734. IMSM: Farrier Abdulla Khan, 1706. Kot Dafadar Adalat Khan, 1126. Kot Dafadar Mustafa Khan, 1304. 26th King George's Own Light Cavalry: IDSM: Kot Dafadar Khadir Nawaz, 590. 27th Light Cavalry: IOM 2nd Class: Risaldar Balwant Singh. IDSM: Risaldar Bulwant Singh. IMSM: Havildar Major Mitha Khan, 819. Havildar Major Sheikh Nizam-ud-din, 1547. Kot Dafadar Jog Singh, 1129. Lance Dafadar Feroze Khan, 828. Lance Dafadar Shaikh Chand, 740. Sowar (Ward Orderly) Muhammad Yunus, 1562. 28th Light Cavalry: Victoria Cross: Lance Dafadar Gobind Singh, 2008. IDSM: Lance Dafadar Karam Chand, 1863. 29th Lancers (Deccan Horse): IOM 2nd Class: Dafadar Puran Singh, 2221. Jemadar Abdul Rahim Khan. Risaldar Hayat Ali Beg. Sowar Chandan Singh, 3107. Sowar Indar Singh, 2581. OBI 1st Class: Risaldar Major Chandar Singh. Risaldar Major Ghulam Dastaghir Khan. OBI 2nd Class: Risaldar Hayat Ali Beg. IDSM: Dafadar Abdur Rahim Khan, 2139. Dafadar Darayo Singh, 2334. Dafadar Pirthi Singh, 2098. Dafadar Quasim Ali, 638. Jemadar Mahan Singh. Jemadar Natha Singh. Kot Dafadar Dale Ram, 2516. Kot Dafadar Imdad Ali, 2193. Kot Dafadar Lall Singh, 1405. Lance Dafadar Muhammad Hafiz, 2673. Naik Bhim Singh, 3072. Risaldar Chanda Singh. Sowar Hira Singh, 3094. Sowar Ram Chander, 2328. IMSM: Dafadar Basti Singh, 1586. Dafadar Jaswant Singh, 2369. Dafadar Kadir Muhammad, 2381. Dafadar Nihal Singh, 2533. Dafadar Ramcharan, 2258. Kot Dafadar Abdul Rahman Khan, 1611. Kot Dafadar Bakhtawar Singh, 2102. Kot Dafadar Kahan Singh, 1932. Kot Dafadar Mangal Singh, 1396. Kot Dafadar Molar Singh, 1722. Kot Dafadar Sita Ram, 2367. Lance Dafadar Balkishen, 1664. Lance Dafadar Muhammad Hussain, 2694. Lance Dafadar Ram Bilas, 2136. Lance Dafadar Shiam Singh, 2374. Sowar Hafizullah Beg, 2180. 30th Lancers (Gordon's Horse): OBI: Risaldar Partab Singh. Risaldar Major Hira Singh. IDSM: Jemadar Kapur Singh. IMSM: Dafadar Chandgi Ram, 1866. Dafadar Jind Singh, 1667. Dafadar Kehar Singh, 1766. Dafadar Mangal Singh, 2218. Dafadar Muhammad Yasin Khan, 2578. Dafadar Neeka Singh, 1962. Kot Dafadar Ajmer Singh, 2733. Lance Dafadar Des Ram, 2601. 31st Duke of Connaught's Own Lancers: IOM 2nd Class: Risaldar Kabul Singh. IDSM: Jemadar Arjun Singh. Lance Dafadar Joth Ram, 2207. Risaldar Kabul Singh. Sowar Karam Singh, 482. IMSM: Dafadar Indar Singh, 637. Dafadar Khwaja Muhammad Khan, 8446. 32nd Lancers: IDSM: Jemadar Jatan Singh. IMSM: Dafadar Gomman Singh, 1992. Lance Dafadar Santok Singh, 3488. 33rd Queen Victoria's Own Light Cavalry: IOM 2nd Class: Dafadar Nihal Singh, 2923. IDSM: Dafadar Mangal Singh, 2952. IMSM: Sowar Kirpa Singh, 3769. 34th Prince Albert Victor's Own Poona Horse: IOM 2nd Class: Sowar Madhu, 2743. OBI: Risaldar Hamir Singh. Risaldar Major Husain Bakhsh Khan. IDSM: Dafadar Fateh Muhammad Shah, 3177. Dafadar Ghulam Muhi-ud-din Khan, 2162. Dafadar Kan Singh, 3070. Dafadar Nadir Ali Khan, 3216. Dafadar Safdar Khan, 1766. Dafadar Sher Baz Khan, 3079. Dafadar Sugan Singh, 3354. Jemadar Annoo Khan. Lance Dafadar Allah-ud-din Khan, 3074. Lance Dafadar Budha Khan, 3323. Lance Dafadar Ganpat Singh, 3680. Lance Dafadar Jait Singh, 3212. Risaldar Amir Khan. Risaldar Badan Singh. Risaldar Rewat Singh. Risaldar Rawat Singh. Risaldar Sattar Khan. Salutri Abdullah Khan, 2146. Sowar Abdulla Khan, 3027. Sowar Fateh Khan, 3250. Sowar Firman Shah, 3154. Sowar Kalyan Singh, 3811. Sowar Qasim Ali Khan, 3689. IMSM: Dafadar Bahadur Singh, 2533. Dafadar Hukam Singh, 2215. Farrier Major Abdul Jabbar, 3353. Kot Dafadar Bhawal Bux Khan, 2099. Kot Dafadar Ghulam Shah, 2904. Lance Dafadar Alim Ali Khan, 2547. Lance Dafadar Balwant Singh, 3424. Lance Dafadar Devi Singh, 2531. Lance Dafadar Firoz Khan, 2072. Sowar Ghulam Ali Khan, 2400. Sowar Ghulam Haider Khan, 2382. Sowar Ugam Singh, 1967. Trumpet Major Narayan Singh, 2289. 35th Scinde Horse: IDSM: Jemadar Dalip Singh. IMSM: Dafadar Sobat Khan, 3070. Havildar Major Mir Muhammad, 3123. Lance Dafadar Ahmad Khan, 3573. Lance Dafadar Fazal Shah, 3189. Lance Dafadar Firoz Khan, 3866. Lance Dafadar Isher Singh, 3121. Sowar Arjan Singh, 3849. 36th Jacob's Horse: IOM 1st Class: Jemadar Wazir Singh. IOM 2nd Class: Dafadar Hajee Ahmed, 2786. Dafadar Harditt Singh, 3636. Jemadar Wazir Singh. Risaldar Muhammad Nur. OBI 1st Class: Risaldar Major Bagga Singh. OBI 2nd Class: Risaldar Sadik Muhammad Khan. IDSM: Dafadar Inzar Gul, 2727. Dafadar Jehan Khan, 2453. Jemadar Bahadur Singh. Jemadar Maqbul Shah. Kot Dafadar Abdul Khatel, 2143. Kot Dafadar Sahik Singh, 615. Lance Dafadar Akram Khan, 3046. Lance Dafadar Saleh Muhammad, 2767. Sowar Fakir Khan, 3414. Sowar Hazrat Singh, 2896. Sowar Lalla Jan, 3150. IMSM: Dafadar Ghulam

Muhammad, 2291. Dafadar Haq Nawaz Khan, 2715. Dafadar Hazara Singh, 2504. Dafadar Inzar Gul, 2729. Dafadar Latif Shah, 2890. Dafadar Mall Singh, 2057. Dafadar Nawab Khan, 2312. Dafadar Shahbaz Khan, 2274. Farrier Bashir Khan, 2136. Kot Dafadar Allahdad Khan, 2581. Kot Dafadar Ghulam Sarwar Khan, 2293. Kot Dafadar Gurmukh Singh, 1296. Kot Dafadar Mehar Khan, 1961. Kot Dafadar Mukand Singh, 1845. Kot Dafadar Sarfaraz Khan, 2169. Lance Dafadar Ghulam Sawar Khan, 2807. Lance Dafadar Isher Singh, 3368. Lance Dafadar Latif Ahmed, 2472. Naik Hussain Muhammad, 1293. Khan. Risaldar Sadik Muhammad Khan. 37th Lancers (Baluch Horse): IOM 2nd Class: Jemadar Alam Sher Khan. IDSM: Dafadar Fazal Karim, 2744. Dafadar Muhammad Amin Khan, 111. Lance Dafadar Dan Singh, 3115. Lance Dafadar Sajawal Khan, 114. 38th King George's Own Central India Horse: IOM 2nd Class: Lance Dafadar Faiz Muhammad Khan, 3116. Risaldar Jawand Singh. Risaldar Lihaz Gul Khan. Risaldar Dilawar Khan. OBI: Risaldar Dilawar Khan. Risaldar Major Amar Singh. IDSM: Dafadar Arjan Singh, 2783. Dafadar Khandara Singh, 2227. Dafadar Labh Singh, 2477. Dafadar Lal Khan, 2613. Dafadar Pertab Singh, 2562. Dafadar Sher Singh, 2183. Dafadar Sherjam Khan, 2421. Jemadar Juma Khan. Jemadar Ram Singh. Kot Dafadar Ghilzai Khan, 2143. Lance Dafadar Fateh Muhammad Khan, 2595. Lance Dafadar Mehr Singh, 2749. Lance Dafadar Nur Muhammad Khan, 2486. Lance Dafadar Shah Nawaz Khan, 2673. Lance Dafadar Tara Singh, 2788. Lance Dafadar Ujaggar Singh, 3187. Lance Dafadar Hastam Khan, 2896. Risaldar Bostan Khan. Risaldar Natha Singh. Sowar Aslam Khan, 2950. Sowar Durbara Singh, 2448. Sowar Nand Singh, 2499. Sowar Dost Muhammad Khan, 2637. IMSM: Dafadar Ali Mardan Khan, 2588. Dafadar Azad Gul Khan, 2329. Dafadar Balwant Singh, 2489. Dafadar Hari Singh, 2301. Dafadar Kapur Singh, 2381. Dafadar Natha Singh, 2170. Dafadar Shah Wali Khan, 2265. Dafadar Yakub Khan, 2324. Kot Dafadar Bhagat Singh, 2350. Kot Dafadar Kehri Singh, 2666. Kot Dafadar Khem Singh, 2650. Kot Dafadar Kishan Singh, 2158. Kot Dafadar Mal Singh, 2403. Kot Dafadar Mangal Singh, 2095. Kot Dafadar Mir Zaman Khan, 2560. Kot Dafadar Mirzaman Khan, 2669. Kot Dafadar Shahmadar Khan, 2202. Trumpet Major Abdul Rahman Khan, 2162. Lance Dafadar Teja Singh, 2509.

This Honour Roll presents gallantry medals awarded to the native officers and men of the Lahore Division and the Indian Cavalry Divisions that served on the Western Front between 1914 -15 and 1914 -1918, respectively. It lists regiments in the initial order of battle (1914) and regiments that would arrive later in 1915 together with the regiments of those servicemen who were attached as drafts during the Indian Corps service in this theatre. The awards were made for specific acts of bravery usually in the face of the enemy; as such, they were separate from the campaign medals given to soldiers for taking part in a particular battle, campaign, or war. In WW1, Indian combatants were issued three different campaign medals for their service during the war: the 1914 Star, 1914-15 Star, the British War Medal and the Victory Medal. These campaign medals were identical to those awarded to Canadians, Australians and New Zealanders, and British troops.

By far the most prestigious gallantry decoration in the British Empire was the Victoria Cross (VC), which was rarely awarded. Indian officers and other ranks became eligible for the VC in 1911, and a total of 19 VCs (including British officers) were awarded to the Indian Army during the Great War across all theatres of war. Today, the VC remains the highest decoration for bravery in Canada and Great Britain. After the Victoria Cross, the second highest honour in the Indian Corps was the Indian Order of Merit (IOM), which was both a military and civilian award. The Military Cross (MC) was instituted in December 1914 as an award for gallantry by junior officers (Captains and Lieutenants) and warrant officers. Indian officers were also eligible, and Subedar Major Thakur Singh of the 47th Sikhs was amongst the first to win this decoration. The Indian Distinguished Service Medal (IDSM), instituted in 1907, was awarded exclusively to Indian officers and other ranks for distinguished service in the field. Indian soldiers were also awarded other prestigious decorations based on their seniority and length of service including the Order of British India (OBI) and the Indian Meritorious Service Medal (IMSM). The Order of British India was instituted in 1837 as a reward for long and faithful service. Recipients of the 1st Class received the title 'Sardar Bahadur' while recipients of the 2nd Class received the title 'Bahadur'. It was a prestigious order often awarded to senior Indian officers upon retirement. The IMSM medal was usually awarded to senior non-commissioned officers for 18 years of exemplary service. During the Great War, however, the medal was also awarded for acts of meritorious service not directly in the face of the enemy. For an Indian soldier to be awarded a gallantry decoration required a British officer to witness and recommend the act for an award. Given the high casualty rates sustained by officers of British Indian Army, many commendations would have been missed. One such example would be Subedar Manta Singh's courageous act of valour. The names of other Indian soldiers included in this book are highlighted in red in the honour roll.

Gallantry on the Western Front:
In total, the Indian Corps won over 900 gallantry decorations in France and Belgium: Victoria Cross 9 (including British Officers), Military Cross 25 (excluding Indian Army British Officers), Indian Order of Merit (IOM) 242, Indian Distinguished Service Medal (IDSM) 625.

Gallantry across the Globe:
During the period 1914-1920, the Indian Army was awarded over 9,000 gallantry awards for actions across all theatres of war. In addition to the British awards, this number includes awards extended to Indian soldiers by the French, Belgian and Russian armies.

VICTORY

LES ALLIÉS

L'INDE MYSTÉRIEUSE
est aux côtés de la loyale Angleterre
pour la défense de la civilisation

Illustration: India's Loyalty
The Graphic Christmas Number 1916

Top: The British War Medal
This silver medal was awarded
to all Commonwealth soldiers
who served in a theatre of war
between August 5, 1914 and
November 11, 1918

The Gre
War Fo
Civilisa

In August 1914, on the outbreak of the w
Prime Minister Herbert Asquith declare
Britain and its Empire would unsheathe
for justice and the defence of principles
civilisation of the world. Thus, the 1919
Medal bearing the figure of Nike, the Go
Victory of the ancient Greeks and proger
democracy, was issued to all the troops
Empire to mark the Allied victory over G
militarism's threat to democracy, liberal

BROTHERS-IN-ARMS

In 1914 the Indian Corps fought as the first of the colonials to defend Ypres, and in 1915, Canadian and Indian troops fought shoulder to shoulder during the second battle of Ypres. In 1917, after the departure of Indian infantry from the Western Front, Canada would go on to win a great victory in the third battle of Ypres.

Speaking after the war in 1929, in a new year's message to the Canadian people, Marshal Ferdinand Foch, supreme commander of the Allied forces, underscored Canada's valiant role in the third battle of Ypres: "Passchendaele is a place of sacred memories and there are other spots along the whole battlefront sacred to the memory of the valour of the men in your Dominion. But it is as the men who saved Ypres when it seemed at the mercy of the enemy that the Canadians will live in history. For days, the enemy rained on those devoted Canadians a weight of metal such as had never before been hurled at men in battle. Not content with that, the enemy let loose poison gas and liquid fire. One might have been pardoned for thinking that there was here a combination that human nature could not prevail against, but the Canadians were there to repeat the old lesson that the capacity of the human soul to endure for a great cause has not yet reached its limit."

THEY SHOWED US THE FIRST STEPS TO VICTORY

Earlier in 1927, at the unveiling of an Indian Army memorial at Neuve Chapelle, Marshall Foch, who had been credited with the final Allied victory, had also underscored the critical actions of the Indian Corps on the hallowed ground of Flanders. In an address to the gathered Indian dignitaries, Foch declared:

"Return to your homes in the distant, sun-bathed East and proclaim how your countrymen drenched with their blood the cold northern land of France and Flanders, how they delivered it by their ardent spirit from the firm grip of a determined enemy; tell all India that we shall watch over their graves with the devotion due to all our dead. We shall cherish above all the memory of their example. They showed us the way, they made the first steps towards the final victory."

"Their civilisation is unproductive to the good of the human race as a whole"
"THE GREATEST EVENT IN MANKIND'S HISTORY"

"The Indian Army Corp. was to be pitted against the most powerful military organisation in the globe, against a European enemy who had brought to the highest pitch of sinister perfection both the science and the practice of war, and who was about to plunge not Europe alone, but the entire civilised world, into such welter of continuous devilry and horror as the mind of man had never imagined and history had never known. The landing of the two Indian divisions, numbering 24,000 men on the quays of Marseilles in September and October 1914 was a great event, not merely in the annals of the Indian army but in the history of mankind"

Lord Curzon - Proceedings of the Imperial War Cabinet 191[?]

Vancouver 1914: They are destructive to society"
"WE OWE THEM A GREAT DEBT"

In proceedings of the War Cabinet the following year (1918) British Prime Minister Lloyd George would underscore India's critical role in the war

"At this point I think I ought to say how much we owe to India... had it not been for India which made special efforts to increase and strengthen our forces in Mesopotamia and Egypt, it would have been impossible to withdraw divisions as we did in Egypt in order to strengthen our forces in France"

He further added that he wished to add India to the Peace Talks alongside the other Dominions. India deserved to be represented. His proposal was accepted by the War Cabinet which included Robert Borden Prime Minister of Canada

Victory & Valour

V

100

Remembrance

Over the course of the war, India sent more than 140,000 men to the Western Front, of whom 90,000 served in the infantry and cavalry and another 50,000 served as non-combatant labourers. By war's end the Indian force had suffered nearly 60,000 casualties with more than 8,550 killed and over 50,000 wounded. The bodies of more than half of those killed were never recovered.

Indian & Canadian servicemen are buried or commemorated at 115 cemeteries and memorials across BELGIUM and FRANCE.

REMEMBRANCE

LEST WE FORGET

BELGIUM

Bedford House Cemetery; Belgian Battery Corner Cemetery; Belgrade Cemetery; Brandhoek New Military Cemetery; Charleroi Communal Cemetery; Duhallow A.d.s. Cemetery; Halle Communal Cemetery; Harlebeke New British Cemetery; La Brique Military Cemetery No.2; Lijssenthoek Military Cemetery; New Irish Farm Cemetery; Nieuwkerke (neuve-eglise) Churchyard; Nine Elms British Cemetery; Oosttaverne Wood Cemetery; Railway Dugouts Burial Ground (transport Farm); The Huts Cemetery; Tournai Communal Cemetery Allied Extension; Vlamertinghe Military Cemetery; Westouter Churchyard And Extension; White House Cemetery, St. Jean-les-ypres; Ypres (menin Gate) Memorial; Ypres Reservoir Cemetery; Ypres Town Cemetery Extension; Zantvoorde British Cemetery

FRANCE

Abbeville Communal Cemetery; Abbeville Communal Cemetery Extension; Aire Communal Cemetery; Albert Communal Cemetery Extension; Anzin-st. Aubin British Cemetery; Arras Flying Services Memorial; Ascq Communal Cemetery; Aveluy Communal Cemetery Extension; Bagneux British Cemetery, Gezaincourt; Bailleul Communal Cemetery Extension, Nord; Bailleul Communal Cemetery, Nord; Beaulencourt British Cemetery, Ligny-thilloy; Bethune Town Cemetery; Beuvry Communal Cemetery; Boulogne Eastern Cemetery; Bray Military Cemetery; Bruay Communal Cemetery Extension; Bucquoy Road Cemetery, Ficheux; Cabaret-rouge British Cemetery, Souchez; Canadian Cemetery No.2, Neuville-st. Vaast; Caudry British Cemetery; Charmes Military Cemetery, Essegney; Chocques Military Cemetery; Couin British Cemetery; Crouy British Cemetery, Crouy-sur-somme; Dantzig Alley British Cemetery, Mametz; Daours Communal Cemetery Extension; Dartmoor Cemetery, Becordel-becourt; Dernancourt Communal Cemetery Extension; Doullens Communal Cemetery Extension No.1; Duisans British Cemetery, Etrun; Dunkirk Town Cemetery; Esquelbecq Military Cemetery; Estaires Communal Cemetery And Extension; Etaples Military Cemetery; Euston Road Cemetery, Colincamps; Faubourg D'amiens Cemetery, Arras; Gezaincourt Communal Cemetery Extension; Godewaersvelde British Cemetery; Gordon Dump Cemetery, Ovillers-la Boisselle; Gouzeaucourt New British Cemetery; Grevillers British Cemetery; Guards Cemetery, Windy Corner, Cuinchy; Haute-avesnes British Cemetery; Hazebrouck Communal Cemetery; Heudicourt Communal Cemetery Extension; La Targette British Cemetery, Neuville-st. Vaast; Le Touret Military Cemetery, Richebourg-l'avoue; Le Treport Military Cemetery; Les Baraques Military Cemetery, Sangatte; Lillers Communal Cemetery; Lillers Communal Cemetery Extension; London Cemetery And Extension, Longueval; Longuenesse (st. Omer) Souvenir Cemetery; Maroeuil British Cemetery; Meaulte Military Cemetery; Merville Communal Cemetery; Meteren Military Cemetery; Mont Huon Military Cemetery, Le Treport; Noeux-les-mines Communal Cemetery; Norfolk Cemetery, Becordel-becourt; Orleans Main Cemetery; Pernes British Cemetery; Pont-du-hem Military Cemetery, La Gorgue; Post Office Rifles Cemetery, Festubert; Premont British Cemetery; Quatre-vents Military Cemetery, Estree-cauchy; Ribemont Communal Cemetery Extension, Somme; Rue-david Military Cemetery, Fleurbaix; Rue-petillon Military Cemetery, Fleurbaix; St. Hilaire Cemetery, Frevent; St. Pierre Cemetery, Amiens; St. Pol Communal Cemetery Extension; St. Riquier British Cemetery; St. Sever Cemetery Extension, Rouen; St. Sever Cemetery, Rouen; St. Souplet British Cemetery; St. Venant Communal Cemetery; Ste. Marie Cemetery, Le Havre; Sunken Road Cemetery, Boisleux-st. Marc; Templeux-le-guerard British Cemetery; Terlincthun British Cemetery, Wimille; Tincourt New British Cemetery; Trois Arbres Cemetery, Steenwerck; Vadencourt British Cemetery, Maissemy; Valenciennes (st. Roch) Communal Cemetery; Vermelles British Cemetery; Vieille-chapelle New Military Cemetery, Lacouture; Vignacourt British Cemetery; Vitry-le-francois French National Cemetery; Y Farm Military Cemetery, Bois-grenier

Memorials in Flanders

The main memorial honouring the fallen of the British Indian Army on the Western Front was built at Neuve Chapelle in French Flanders, the location where the Indian Corps fought its first major action as a single unit in March 1915. The memorial lists the names of 4,700 men who have no grave. The monument was unveiled in October 1927 by Frederick Edwin Smith the Earl of Birkenhead. Lord Birkenhead, then Secretary of State for India, had served with the Indian Corps during the Great War. In Belgian Flanders, the Menin Gate in Ypres was built between 1923 and 1927 and lists the names of over 400 Indian soldiers amongst the 54,000 commonwealth soldiers lost in the Ypres Salient who have no known grave.

■ Menin Gate (left) and Neuve Chapelle Memorial (right)

■ WW1 era photo of a Punjabi Mussalman (left) , Punjabi Sikhs (middle) , Hindu and Commonwealth soldiers in Europe (right)

Brothers In Arms

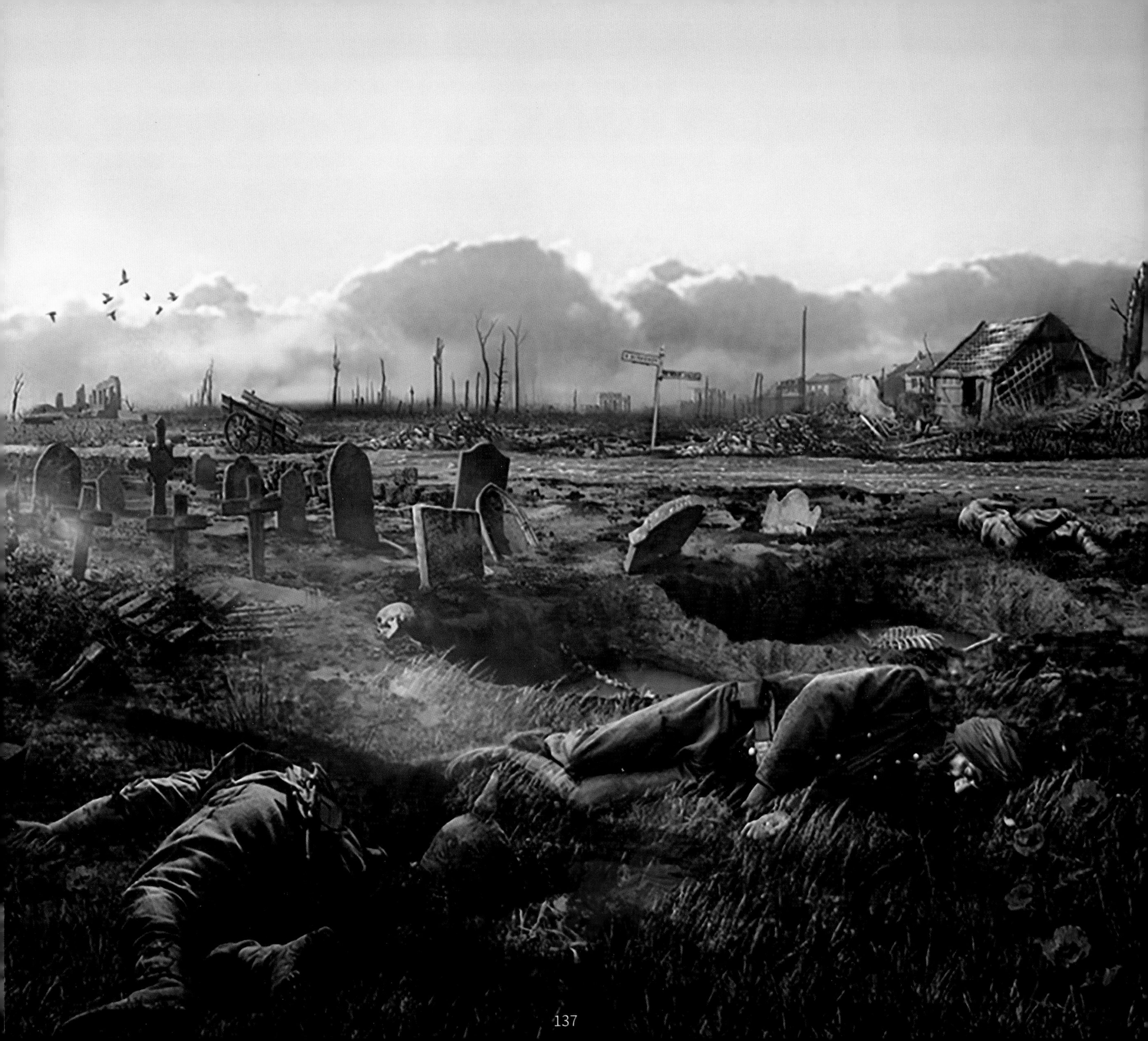

I Z

Part III

The Truth

Z A T

Izzat: The Way of the Punjab

Within the lands of the Indus, barricaded in by the soaring Himalayas in the north and the arid deserts in the south, the local population had dwelled for millennia within an inescapable cauldron of war. Throughout history, Punjab had been a thoroughfare for invaders seeking the riches of India and new settlers looking to homestead the fertile plains of the five rivers. Within this brutal playground of the sword, men forged deep-rooted martial traditions and personal codes of conduct from which a warrior culture arose. In shaping the Punjab, the nobility of personal honour was as elemental as the rivers and mountains themselves, for upon the honest man's word rested the friendships and alliances necessary to survive the turbulence of war. Dishonour then, as its corollary, invited disaster and the collapse of kingdoms, as was the case with the fall of the Sikh Kingdom in the Anglo-Sikh wars. Within this defeat, however, even as treacherous generals entrapped their troops to confront certain death, the British authorities were witness to the reckless courage of the Punjabi soldier, who preferred to desert life rather than desert his colours.

To these observers, the fiery spirit of the Punjabi remained seemingly untempered, even upon Punjab's annexation. A deep-rooted sense of personal honour yet prevailed upon the conduct of the warrior peasantry, a conviction remarked upon by Lord Canning, the Governor General of India, in a despatch written at the time of the 1857 mutiny: "*Amongst the native officers killed was Subedar Ruttun Singh, who fell mortally wounded in the glacis. He was a Patiala Sikh and had been invalidated (retired) from service at the onset of the mutiny. As the 1st Punjab neared Delhi, Major Coke saw the old man standing in the road with two swords on. He begged to be taken back into the service and when Coke demurred he said: "What! My old corps going to fight at Delhi without me! I hope you will let me lead my old Sikh company into action again. I will break these two swords in your cause." Coke acceded to the old man's wish, and throughout the siege of Delhi, he displayed the most splendid courage. At the great attack on the 'Sammy House' on 1st and 2nd August, when Lieutenant Travers of his Regiment was killed, Ruttun Singh, amidst a shower of bullets, jumped on to the parapet and shouted to the enemy, who were storming the piquet: "If any man wants to fight, let him come here and not stand firing like a coward! I am Ruttun Singh, of Patiala." He then sprang down amongst the enemy, followed by the men of his company, and drove them off with heavy loss. On the morning of the assault, the regiment had marched down to the rendezvous at Ludlow Castle, 'left in front'. While waiting for the Artillery to fire a few rounds at the breeches, the men sat down and, falling in again, were doing so 'right in front'. Ruttun Singh came up to Lieutenant Charles Nicholson, who was commanding the regiment, and said, "We ought to fall in 'left in front", thereby making his own company the leading one in the assault. In a few minutes more Ruttun Singh was mortally wounded."* *

* Forty-one years in India From Subaltern To Commander-In-Chief. London: Richard Bentley & Co, 1898.

Izzat Reconstructed

In battling the enemies of the Crown in the Mutiny, the Sikhs sought 'badla' (revenge) against a Mughal regime that had committed crimes against their people. In 1858, upon the installation of the Crown in India, for a foreign government to now stir the sentiments of loyalty required unravelling the Punjab's notion of Izzat, the Punjab's code of honour. Izzat could be won or lost in any context, fulfilling a sense of personal honesty and self-respect in matters of reputation, prestige, pride and justice. This multifaceted nature of honour also allowed the Punjabi to bear multiple external identities to gain Izzat for himself, his family, caste, clan, locality and religion. To gain Izzat as a soldier of the Queen, architects of the Martial Race policy elevated the profile of the Punjabi soldier from a position of lost Izzat to an identity that could gain Izzat. With the defeat in the Anglo-Sikh Wars, the Punjabis had lost royal patronage and a kingdom. As soldiers of the Crown, they were offered upward mobility within the military administration of the largest Empire the world had ever seen. In the case of the Sikh regiments, British authorities went further by tethering regimental esprit de corps to Sikh religious doctrines and values, mandating their Khalsa identity as a paragon of the ideal soldier and a prerequisite for employment. Such was the allure of the opportunities unlocked by the British uniform that a wave of enlistments reversed a trend in the decline of Sikh baptisms following the fall of the Sikh Empire. As defenders of the Crown, Punjabis would come to be lauded for their ancient and courageous abilities to bear arms, and would be paraded outside the hallowed halls of Westminster itself as the sovereign's honoured escorts at jubilees and coronations. The Izzat gained within such pomp and circumstance of Empire inspired Punjab's soldiers to cast themselves and their clans as the industrious, loyal sons of Great Britain and India, a colony whose stature had grown to that of the jewel in the Crown itself.

Izzat Tested

In the summer of 1897, mere weeks after Queen Victoria's Diamond Jubilee procession, 10,000 jihadi tribesmen would amass on Britannia's Afghan frontier to test the handiwork of the Martial Race architects and Punjabi fealty. On 12th September events unfolded in which 21 Sikhs of the 36th Sikhs regiment were tasked with defending the signalling post of Saragarhi without a British officer present. When the hordes of invading tribesmen attacked the post, the Sikhs refused to surrender and laid down their lives at the foot of the British banner, just as they had done for their sovereign kingdom 50 years earlier. Winston Churchill, seconded to the 35th Sikhs, a sister regiment to that of the Saragarhi defenders, was also stationed on the frontier that summer. He observed the temperament of the locality as one in which "i*n the clear light of the morning, when the mountainside is dotted with smoke puffs and every ridge sparkles with bright sword blades, the spectator may observe and accurately appreciate all grades of courage, the wild* *fanaticism of the Ghazi, the composed fatalism of the Sikh, the steadiness of the British soldier, and the jaunty daring of his officers."* Churchill's observations underscored the uncompromising nature of Punjabi Izzat. According to him, *"the Sikh needed no one to bear witness to his courage".*

The British understanding of just how deeply personal this innate sense of Izzat could run was also recounted by Lord Curzon in his memoirs of his time as Governor General of India, where he wrote of the Sikhs, *"The standards of personal or family honour and self-respect that prevail among the Sikh community in India are of a very rigid and uncompromising character. A Sikh will not only take life, but will freely give up his own life, sooner than an ineffaceable stain should rest upon his family escutcheon. I came across several instances of this remarkable trait while in India, of which I will relate the following. There were four brothers, Sikhs, who were small landowners in a village in the Native State of Patiala in the Punjab. The two elder were soldiers in the Indian Army, where they both bore exemplary characters as quiet and well-behaved men. The two younger brothers stayed at home, and cultivated the family land, which was not inconsiderable in extent. They were, however, continually harassed by their maternal relatives, who turned beasts into their crops when green, or went in and cut them when ripe, in the hope of driving the brothers out of their holding, and forcing them to leave the village, in which case the land would have devolved upon the usurpers as nearest kin. The two soldier brothers were being constantly obliged to take leave in order to protect their interests. But endless makadmas (lawsuits) brought them no relief, the maternal relatives forming an overwhelmingly strong faction against the brothers, who had no local following. At length the soldier brothers decided to bring matters to a head; but before doing so they made a final appeal to their persecutors. Attar Singh, one of the two soldiers, laid his turban at the feet of his principal enemies and implored them to desist from further hostility; but in reply he only met with abuse. He then returned to his military station, sent for his brother, obtained four days' leave for both, and collected a revolver and sword and as much ammunition as he could procure. The brothers arrived at the village, and announced that they had come to fight it out. They then opened fire upon the opposite faction, and in the course of the conflict that ensued, killed seventeen persons and wounded ten, the result being that the entire clique of maternal relatives, women as well as men, were wiped out.*

It remained only to complete the work of combined murder and self-sacrifice. The four brothers then mounted to their house~top, whence they sent word to the police station that they wanted to die fighting and would not be taken alive; and accordingly that they were waiting for afar to come and finish them off. The police having declined the hazardous invitation, the second brother, Attar Singh, saying that his work was done, did public shinan (purification), and then sat down and made his elder brother, Ruttan Singh, shoot him through the head The latter then remembered that he had a private enemy in the same native regiment, against whom he had to pay off some old score. He accordingly descended, sought out his enemy, and inflicted upon him a severe sword cut and two bullet wounds. He would have killed him if he could. Having thus satisfied his honour to the full, he returned to the housetop and resumed his seat with his two surviving brothers, the other villagers continuing to supply them with food and water, though not permitted to come near. After two more days Ruttan Singh then did shinan for himself, and made one of the two surviving brothers shoot him dead. The latter, who were not soldiers, and perhaps were allowed to have a less sensitive feeling of honour, then came down and disappeared. The remarkable feature of the story was that though these men had completely annihilated the whole of their maternal relatives, their conduct was in no sense reprobated by their fellow-countrymen. On the contrary, the entire community looked upon the tragedy as having been conducted in a most seemly manner, Coram publico. Justice had in fact been satisfied all round." **

That Izzat courted absolute honesty in personal affairs was apparent to all such commentators. While this assured those in command of the brutal honesty demanded of a soldier, it also put British authorities on guard to tread carefully in Punjab, lest they aroused such truculent spirits.

By the turn of the 20th century, paternalistic policies had cemented the military's position as the central authority in colonial Punjab, but storm clouds were gathering further afield. Dissidence amongst Indian expats living in British Columbia, Canada grew even as Westminister urged the Canadian government to curtail the restrictions on immigration from India. Wary of how events abroad could inflame political turmoil in India, King George V, at his 1911 coronation in India, made prescient moves to uphold the Izzat of the Punjab with the establishment of the new capital city of India as New Delhi and a grant of eligibility for the Victory Cross to the native soldiers of the British Indian Army. Matters of honour were destined to come to a head in Vancouver three years later, just days before the outbreak of the First World War. This time, Punjabi loyalty would be tested by the Punjabi soldiers' kin. In Canada, intellectuals and radicals had combined forces to unravel the ties that bound Sepoy to Sahib. Many of the disaffected were veterans of the British Indian Army, whose faith in the government had been shattered by the realisation that their service and British citizenship amounted to nothing in the white realms of the Crown. The question of which faction of Punjab's warriors - loyalist or rebel - would prevail loomed large on the eve of war; if Ghadar operatives were able to instigate an uprising in the villages of Punjab, what they called the 'slave soldiers' of the Sikh regiments might well mutiny.

* * A Viceroy's India, Leaves From Lord Curzon's Notebook. London: Sidgwick & Jackson Ltd, 1984

A Call to Izzat

Within days of entering the fray, the British Expeditionary Force, having sustained grievous casualties, was on the retreat in Europe. With the very survival of Britain now at stake, nothing could be left to chance, so King George V, on rallying the colonies to war, imbued his appeal to the Punjabi-dominated British Indian Army with an explicit call to their Izzat. With the words, *"I look to all my Indian soldiers to uphold the Izzat of the British Raj"*, came the invitation to stand shoulder to shoulder with European troops. The appeal would resonate deeply with the ranks of the Punjabis. Despite having lost the Anglo-Sikh wars, Punjabis had not conceded to be the lesser soldiers of the Empire's sword arm. In the instances where the Khalsa forces, free from the meddling of their corrupt generals, had been able to illustrate their true mettle they had wrought havoc upon the British power unlike any native army before or after them. This was the case at Chillianwala in 1849, where Punjabis had stood toe-to-toe against Europeans in a battle where the British acknowledged they had sufficient artillery, cavalry and fully rested infantry but failed to defeat the Sikhs.

At the time, newspapers in London reported the battle had left the British laurels drenched with blood. Five regimental colours had been lost, the feared corps of Dragoons had retreated, and it was "doubtful as to which had sustained a greater injury from the conflict". Even the Royal Welsh 24th Regiment of Foot, unmatched in the annals of British military history as recipients of the most number of Victoria Crosses for a single action (11 would be awarded to them for their resolute stand at Rorke's Drift in the Anglo-Zulu war of 1879), at Chillianwala would suffer the indignity of losing both a standard bearing the Queen's colours and half of their numbers in a hasty retreat from the lions den. The events at Chillianwala, would scar the collective psyche of the British Army for years to come, after the disastrous Charge of the Light Brigade, when Lord Lucan remarked, "This is a most serious matter", General Airey replied, "These sorts of things will happen in war. It is nothing to Chillianwala."*. On the very same ground of Chillianwala, where their ancestors halted Alexander the Great's expedition to conquer the world, Punjab's courageous peasantry had once again proven they could better the greatest white power of their time.

In the decades following annexation, Punjabi regiments campaigned successfully across the globe to gain much Izzat in the public eye but were unable to erase the dichotomies within their ranks. While some British officers held friendly feelings towards the native soldier, a camaraderie without which a Punjabi-dominated army would never have supported a century of British rule, racist jeers from the rank and file would no doubt daily pronounce the colonial order of race. These reminders of inequality would take an ugly turn when Indian troops, on campaign in China, faced blatant racial abuse from allied European troops. In 1900, the British Indian Army, by now comprising some of the most decorated regiments in the Empire, had been prohibited from entering the Boer War. Instead, a nondescript army from the white colony of Canada was thrust into the limelight as colonial defenders of the Crown. British government policy would cut far deeper into the Izzat of the Punjabi soldier than any of Tommy Atkins (slang for British troops) pejoratives, such that when the orders were given that same year for deployment to China on an Allied mission to rescue besieged westerners, Punjabi troops would seize the opportunity to restore their Izzat.

The westerners, a ragtag assortment of diplomats, civilians and a small number of troops had become trapped in the British legation in Peking (Beijing) when anti-western rebellion swept across northern China. Chinese peasants, led by a mysterious society of superstitious rebels called the 'Boxers', on account of their martial arts skills, had ignited a revolt in 1899 with the murder of two priests at a German mission. When a German diplomat was also killed in the summer of 1900, German Field Marshal, Alfred Von Waldersee was appointed to head an eight-nation relief force comprised of troops from Great Britain, Germany, France, Austria-Hungary, Italy, Japan, Russia and the United States. Under Waldersee's command, the German contingent was impelled to restore national honour as the saviours of the westerners. Other nations on the ascendant at the turn of the 20th century, such as the United States of America, were under the same compulsion to claim glory for themselves. However, when the 1st Sikh Infantry of the battle-hardened Punjab Frontier Force made short work of enemy defences in a synchronised advance from the Chinese coast, they were able to pull ahead to be greeted first as the heroic liberators. Following the victory over the Boxers, embittered German troops garrisoned in Peking vented their anger over being outdone by coloured troops by harassing the Indian troops in verbal and physical altercations. Thus, upon the outbreak of war the sovereign's impassioned plea to the Indian Army to *"fulfill a sacred trust on the field of battle shoulder to shoulder with their comrades from all parts of the empire"* not only offered parity with white soldiers and an opportunity to win the Victoria Cross but, for the Punjabis, it was a proclamation to settle an old score with their white detractors on European soil.

In this quest for Izzat, Punjab's soldiers would find allies within the movement of Indian nationalists. Some Indian leaders, such as Mohandas Gandhi, believed support for the war would advance their cause for home-rule for India within the Empire, even as more extreme Indian radicals colluded with Germany to remove British power altogether. With the ranks of the British Expeditionary Force rapidly succumbing to an aggressive German war machine, the colour bar policy for Indians was dropped. The Lahore Division, en route to the Suez to replace British battalions garrisoning Egypt, Sudan, Malta, and Gibraltar, was instead ordered to sail on to France. British authorities had speculated that lifting the restriction would encourage

*** Woodham Smith, The Reason Why: The Fatal Charge of the Light Brigade. New York: E. P. Dutton and Co. 1960

support for the government and for the war amongst those preaching rebellion. If the Sirkar could give parity to the army, then India's demands for political equality with the white dominions was within realms of possibility, or so went the thinking of the time. For the professional soldiers of the Punjab, the best rebuke to the racists slandering their brethren in Canada as undesirable elements was to perform their duties and shoulder their responsibilities, rather than abandoning them at the precise time they could influence peoples' opinions for better.

The world's press would recognise the nexus between India's soldiers and nationalists within India's rally to Britain's side. The American Literary Digest (Volume 49 1914) would observe, *"The War in which Great Britain has become involved appears to be having the effect of making the Hindus lay aside, for the time being, the grievances that they nurse against the British Government because Indians are shut out of the management of their own affairs and out of Canada and other British Dominions, and is impelling them to offer loyal aid to the King-Emperor. The Indian rulers are sending cables to King George offering him their entire military and financial resources."* On landing in Europe, the soldiers of the Lahore Division were thrown into the thick of battle. With mother India behind them and despite being outgunned and outmanned, the Punjabis would immediately make their claim on Izzat with such contempt for death that their British officers "had to jump on them" to keep them in the trenches.

Izzat Redacted

By the time of the ceasefire and the Allied victory in November 1918, well over one million British and Commonwealth soldiers lay dead, scattered across battlefields straddling the shifting boundaries of a politically transformed world. Within Canada, the staggering human toll of the war effort is often brought home by the tragic story of Canadian George Lawrence Price, the last soldier of the British Commonwealth to die, killed just two minutes before the armistice. The first to be killed in action is said to be Britain's Private John Henry Parr, killed on the August 21, 1914. Somewhere between the fall of these two soldiers of the King, fell another 74,000 defenders of the Crown from India. During the war, the British India Army had earned widespread praise for their spirit, courage, endurance and skills, not only amongst the British officers who knew them well but across the rank and file of the Allied troops. However, after the war, upon their story being relegated to the footnotes of history, the truth behind the Indian contribution to the Great War could also be said to have become a casualty of war. Without the services of the Indian Army on the Western Front, both the British Expeditionary Force and Calais, the critical port of supply of British soldiers and munitions, would have fallen. Had the line of trenches that ultimately forced a stalemate to stretch south from the Flanders coast to Switzerland been breached, the war may well have been lost by the Christmas of 1914.

The vital contribution of the Indian Corps in Europe was summed up by General Willcocks, *"It was their good fortune to arrive just at the moment when they were most needed; just when our troops were using their very last reserves and fighting against terrible odds ... and even if they had never done another day's fighting their advent would have more than justified their having been sent, for they helped in some degree to save the Army in the hour of its great trial."* *** In joining the British Territorials and French reinforcements coming to the aid of the beleaguered BEF, Lieutenant-Colonel Merewether, the Record Officer assigned to the Indian Army Corps in France, asserted that their timely arrival had in effect "saved the Empire".

Some years later in 1927, the Rt Hon. Sir Frederick Smith Earl of Birkenhead, who deputed to IEF-A with Merewether, had coauthored the official record of the Indian expedition to Europe, proffered a reason for the Indian Army's devotion to duty. While unveiling the memorial to the Indian Corps at Neuve Chapelle, he compared the Indian infantry on the Western Front to the 300 at Thermopylae, whose valour he claimed was immortal adding, *"Whence, then, came this spirit of endurance and of high endeavour? It came from the twin sources of an inborn and simple loyalty, of an instructed and very perfect discipline. Like the Roman legionary, they were faithful unto death. They had accepted a duty. They discharged it. More cannot be said: more need not be said."* In remembrance, Indian soldiers were said to have been loyal to those whose salt they had eaten: the notion of duty as an obligation of salary had been established in ancient Rome with the amount paid to a legionnaire to buy the expensive but essential commodity, salt being the root of the word 'salarium' the Latin word for 'salary'. In making the King's shilling the focus of his eulogy, Smith had sidestepped the truth; the pact that united Indians in the rally to the Crown, the appeal for equality with the white dominions had become an inconvenient truth.

By the time of Lord Birkenhead's 1927 address, the huge debt owed to the Indian soldier by the British had been shrewdly brushed under the carpet in response to the growing Quit India movement. Given India's substantial role in the victory, expectations for greater political autonomy were running high amongst the general population. For all that, in March 1919 British authorities, instead of progressing plans for self-rule, enacted greater repressive measures through the Rowlatt Act and martial law. The Act was met with widespread anger in the Punjab and, in April 1919, in Amritsar, Indian troops fired on unarmed demonstrators, killing several hundred of them. The incident known as the Jallianwala massacre, inflamed the masses across the country, pushing nationalists to adopt a hard line position for total independence from Britain. It was the beginning of the end of the British Raj in India, and the Indian soldier would be left to bear the burden of the British betrayal. The soldiers of the Crown would henceforth be painted as mercenaries ready to trample their own people underfoot in shackled servitude to their imperial masters.

*****The Speeches of Lord Birkenhead, London Cassal & Company Ltd, 1929

****Willcocks, The Indians in France , London Constable and Company Ltd, 1920

Gone were the Punjabi soldiers' aspirations for personal and national dignity. After Jallianawala, the radicals were to be cast as the true sons of the soil, patriots fighting for the rights of all Indians. Before the war, Punjabi soldiers stood ex-communicated as undesirables in the west, and by war's end, with little support at home, they were to find little concession abroad.

In Canada, Prime Minister Robert Borden bookended the travesty of the Komagata Maru by refusing to lift the Continuous Journey regulation and reinstating the vote for British Indians. Despite being privy to the Imperial War cabinet's sterling accounts of the Indian soldier, Borden's only grant was to approve the entry of the wives and children of the few remaining Indo-Canadian males. By now, many had returned to India and only one South Asian had been permitted to enter Canada after the eviction of the Komagata Maru. In 1914, the Canadian-born lawyer of the Khalsa Diwan Society, Edward J Bird, had espoused the principles of Empire to extend beyond British ethnicity, that Canada's British-derived democratic traditions and institutions which stood for the freedoms of a broadly liberal and progressive society should have promoted the ideals of justice and opportunity for all. In WW1, Canada sacrificed 61,000 lives at the altar of war in its subscription to Empire. However, its doctrines around race would continue to shut out fellow British citizens, including those who had elected to stand with Canada as brothers-in-arms, while favouring immigration from even those who had stood against Canada at its moment of reckoning in the battlefield.

In the land of their birth, men cradled in the art of war, now beset with an identity simultaneously sinister and ridiculous, would be humbled by the heroics of those who preached nonviolence as the path to redemption. In the lands beyond the Indus, the pen wielded by Indian intellectuals seeking plum positions behind the desks of a new administration would prove mightier in rewriting history than the sword of the Punjabi peasant who had heroically sought the battlefield to prove his worth and that of his nation. Victory in the most significant global event of the 20th century had been won. Respect had been won but, with the new British and Indian nationalist agenda converging upon the King's shilling as the font of the Indian soldier's motivations for going to war, what was obligation - duty - and what was personal honour - Izzat - had all been rendered moot.

"The call to the stalwart Sikhs and other fighting races of India to rally side by side with other British soldiers in the battle-line in France has aroused enthusiasm in Hindustan which has no parallel in the history of the dependency. Ever since the British annexed the Punjab (the large province in the northwest portion of India) in the middle of the nineteenth century, the Sikhs have not confronted a European force in armed conflict. Not since the Indian Sepoy Mutiny of 1857 have the Moslem and Hindu soldiers fought European armies. Therefore, the warrior clans of India, whose battle traditions and exploits of valor stretch back to the misty morn of romance and chivalry, antedating anything of the kind that Europe possesses, are thirsting for the blood of Britain's enemies in Europe. A twofold reason for this desire is the Indian soldier wants to demonstrate his loyalty to Britain, and to prove to the world at large that he has mastered the occidental methods of fighting, and he has gained such command over the Western weapons of war and is so heroic and fearless that he is able to pit his strength and skill at arms against the crack regiments of Germany and give a good account of himself." The Literary Digest Volume 49 1914

"The Germans say that the Indians personally are much stronger and more nimble than German soldiers and it is therefore impossible for the latter to vanquish them in hand-to-hand fighting, unless the Indians are outnumbered." The Western Daily Press 31 October 1914

"The Indians who gave themselves to our cause did so at an even greater sacrifice than our own, for the meaning of the struggle did not touch them as nearly as it did us. To them the German was merely a savage with diabolical inspirations, a merely physical menace. The gospel of Treitschke did not trouble their philosophy. Honour – personal, communal and national – was the only reward they looked for."
The Times History of the War June 1915

AUSTRALASIA   CANADA   INDIA   SOUTH AFRICA

"The doctrine of a white man's country is one utterly intolerable especially for the subjects of the British Empire...if we allow the Magna Carta to be repealed and set at naught the will of any single section of our people, there remains no reason why the British Empire should exist, since its only title to existence is that it stands for the true principles of British freedom."

J. Edward Bird, Lawyer for the passengers of the Komagata Maru 1914

www.theglobeandmail.com article18830049

A gentleman's word is his bond. In wanting to gain a seat as equals at the table of Empire, the actions of India's soldiers in WW1 would not entail any act of sham, hypocrisy or treachery. India was the first to deploy its troops in the defence of the Crown and would ultimately field as many men in the war effort as all the other colonies combined, and by the end of the war, the all-volunteer Indian Army would suffer more casualties than either the largest white colonies of Canada and Australia.

GENTLEMEN THE EMPIRE

AFTERWORD

By virtue of remembrance, nations across the world have cast soldiers as modern heroes. In ancient myth, warriors fought evil as beacons of light designed to inspire greatness in others. In modern times it is the soldier who, devoid of all magic and mystical properties, proves himself a hero through deeds of courage in war. One hundred years ago the courageous acts of the Indian soldier were critical in delivering the allied victory, but their beacon came to be smothered by the mists of time. Thus the Great War Centennial was a historic opportunity for Canadians to commemorate those who lost their lives and rekindle that beacon and engage today's youth and diverse communities about the significance of their forefather's sacrifices in a seminal moment in the nation's history. This dialogue is especially meaningful for the Punjabi community who, having made Canada their home since the turn of the 20th century, have seen their proud heritage diminished by decades of bigotry. In an exclusively white narrative of the Canadian story, mass media has propagated many stereotypes detrimental to the community's standing.

Ultimately, in a growing number of cases, some Punjabi youth, having been pushed to the peripheries of society, are now looking for heroes amongst the anti-social fraternity. If mass media frames all the facets of 'ethnic' to stand in opposition to 'mainstream', why would these youth question the misdirected morals of criminal gangs offering belonging and empowerment? Whose ethics could resist the bonding, identity, protection, social status, thrills and financial rewards of a fraternity that snubs the club that consistently turned them away at the door? Recognising the Great War effort then as being multicultural and promoting diverse heroes for entry into the mainstream club of popular culture informs the disenfranchised that their community is valued for their contributions to society. It is a dialogue that begets mutual respect and trust. For Punjabi soldiers to stand on par with their brothers-in-arms in Canadian culture, as they once did on the battlefield, their heroic deeds must be narrated as a shared commonwealth history with the Canadian mainstream.

Having arrived in Canada, a land with which they shared a monarchy, flag and common British nationality (Canadian nationality was not enacted until 1947 and the Maple leaf flag was introduced in 1965), Punjabis expected to find some semblance of kinship with their fellow British subjects. After all, the Canadian establishment had for many years used pro-Empire sentiment to help establish a Canadian identity separate from our American cousins. The lay of the land that awaited them, however, was one where appearances trumped citizenship as a basis for nationality and rights. Fate first intertwined Punjabi and Canadian wartime destiny when, in the summer of 1914, Punjabis aboard the Komagata Maru were evicted from Canada. It was here in Canadian waters, far from the fabled battlegrounds of Flanders, that the raising of HMCS Rainbow's guns against British subjects could have set the Empire ablaze. At that precise moment, covetous German minds hatched their plans for world domination.

It is often said the greatest triumphs are those that are born of tragedy, comprising the backbone of an army that would soon become the only battle-tested colonial force ready for war. The Punjabis held the balance of power in their hands. Without them taking to the field on the outbreak of war, history may have indeed unfolded as strategised in Alfred von Schlieffen's master plan, with the taking of Paris in 42 days, and the war could well have been over by Christmas, as many speculated at the time. The Punjabis, instead of retaliating against the Canadians, chose to honour their oaths to stand beside their commonwealth brothers-in-arms and do their duty in the first battle of Ypres, even as the Komagata Maru sailed back to India. Six months later, the Punjabis would take the high road again when they were asked to reinforce a fledgeling Canadian Corps in its baptism of fire in Flanders. The men who arrived as 'friends in need' hailed from the heartland of the Sikhs that was also the home of the original Indo-Canadian community and the passengers aboard the Komagata Maru. In fact, by war's end, of the 498, 560 Punjabis who served in WW1, 300,000 of them put aside their grievances and enlisted directly from the districts of those aboard the evicted ship to shoulder an equal burden of war.

In this narrative, any Indo-Canadian youth encountering race as a barrier to becoming "Canadian" can see their community reflected in a military event lauded by curriculum, citizenship guides and commemorative events as a rite of passage and an assertion of nationhood. Within this inclusive counter-narrative, Punjabi and Canadian soldiers, fighting together against German militarism in a war of 'civilisations' are intimately connected, and, through that connection, Punjabis can be deemed to share both history and common societal values. In having helped shape the society we live in, the Punjabi community can be cast in a heroic light. The hero archetype conceived by society to possess universally admirable virtues can cut across the often-contradictory experiences of eastern and western influences on identity formulation that South Asian youth have to navigate amongst their families, peer groups and religious organisations. Engaged youth can frame these new heroes within the dominant British commonwealth heritage of the mainstream and also across Indo-Canadian and Sikh heritage.

As British subjects, Canada's pioneering community of South Asians used the idea of imperial unity to fight exclusive ethnic nationalism and to demand equal treatment throughout the Empire. When bigots did not want them wearing the same uniform or winning the same medals in combat, Indian soldiers put their bodies on the line, retrieving fallen white officers and winning gallantry medals by the thousands to vehemently refute any myth of white superiority in body or culture. Indo-Canadian youth can take pride in knowing that, from amongst the hundreds of ethnic minorities who call Canada home today, it was the Punjabis alone who stood tall as true friends in need when Canada took those first fateful steps in Flanders Fields.

As Sikhs, Punjabi youth can proudly assert their forebears displayed valour, devotion to duty and loyalty of the highest order. To rise to the challenge of fighting in a far-off land in a quarrel not of their making, Sikh soldiers imbued the sacred preaching of their faith as humanitarians and saint-soldiers. To defend liberty and the democratic freedoms of others, freedoms they did not have themselves, was in keeping with the spirit of 'sarbat da bhala', a principal that mandated selfless service not just to their own community but to humanity itself, a principle echoed by all Sikhs daily in their prayers. Their exploits on the battlefield reflected a devotion to confront tyranny as enshrined in the code of conduct of a 'sant-sipahi', a doctrine that neither permitted them to aid and abet their subjugation, nor allow them to resort to the radical's pursuit of rights denied as yet to even half the British population. In the catastrophe of the Western Front, they were consistently exposed to both the extreme folly of man and the most brutal elements of nature; lions corralled into the valley of death by inept generals practised in the stratagems of eras past found little mercy returning to frigid trenches during some of the coldest winters on record. When war demanded such acid tests of a man's character, it was the Sikh philosophy of 'Chardi Kalaa', the faith to bear tribulations as divine will and thus to find joy in adversity that testified to the courage of the Khalsa's indomitable crusader spirit and which helped change the course of world history, without plunder, murder or menace.

Such inspirational stories of Punjabi warriors yield new positive identities better invested in our society and renew a sense of belonging for the community. Studies have shown that those who possess pride in heritage, history and culture thrive in society; that is, of course, the advantage the white majority bestows upon its youth through a monopoly on classrooms, museums and films for its Euro-centric narrative, when corrupted identities serve only to draw minority youth into a program of their marginalisation and erasure. The immense sacrifices Indian soldiers made for the commonwealth require that their stories also be incorporated into memorial services, public monuments, and curriculums across these countries. Soldiers the world over throughout history have given their lives for the next generation, their today for our tomorrow. What a fitting tribute it would be to the Indian soldier then, if his story helped wayward Indo-Canadian youth connect with both their cultural identity and their Canada in a way that promoted school attachment, literacy, academic skills, self-esteem and better integration with a country whose cause they gave their lives for. In such equity, the community could find a sense of justice for the deeds of honourable men who fought for parity 100 years ago.

It has been said, "the arc of the moral universe is long, but it bends toward justice". For the Punjabi community denigrated in Canada as the 'other' for decades, there have been inklings of justice along the way. Through their remarkable endurance and devotion to duty, the men of the 47th Sikhs garnered a cherished royal appellation at the end of the war. For the accomplishment of being recognised as the only Indian regiment never to give up a yard of trench in any theatre of war, warriors who hailed from the districts of the Komagata Maru passengers became the Duke of Connaught's Own 47th Sikhs. It may be remembered that it was the Duke of Connaught's British Columbia Regiment that had been tasked to remove their kin from Canada at the start of the war. The long trajectory of this redemptive arc would also see an epilogue 100 years later, when Harjit Singh Sajjan, hailing from the ancestral recruiting grounds of the 47th Sikhs became the commanding officer of that British Columbia Regiment and, by the time of the centennial of the Great War, he would be appointed the Crown's Minister of Defence for the realm of Canada. This intriguing evolution should compel us all to look deeper into the past for lessons to help bend the arc further towards justice. If history is to serve a nation as memory serves a man, Canadians must overcome systemic amnesia and recognise that it was when nations looked past appearance as a predicator of citizenship, as in the 1914 call to 'Indian' British subjects to rally to the Crown, when hyphenated nationalities and colour bars were dropped, that the best characteristics of the human spirit, which transcend divisions of colour, creed religions and language delivered the victories that shaped our world for the better.

In remembrance then, it is not war that is commemorated but the ultimate sacrifice of honourable men who espoused our shared ideals and the common values of courage, selflessness, kinship and integrity. In the past, when the mainstream asked who the Indo-Canadians are and what have they done for the country, most clutched stereotypes designed to alienate and exclude. Going forward, in inclusive remembrance, Canadians could answer with the truth - they were our brothers-in-arms at a time when we needed friends the most. In wrapping the answer in the dignity of a warrior tradition - in duty, honour and Izzat - we can all help bend the arc towards justice.

Steven Purewal, November 2018

Author

<u>Steven Purewal</u> is a community historian, curator and Managing Director of Indus Media Foundation a non-profit Punjabi Cultural Society. Steven's work has been featured at The National War Museum, BC provincial legislature, rovincial museums, municipal venues and the Prime Minister's Reception for the Komagata Maru Apology in Ottawa. Steven lives in Surrey B.C. with his wife and three children. email:steven.purewal@imfc.org website:www.IMFC.org

Artist

<u>Christopher Rawlins</u> is a British artist and illustrator. Formally trained in art & design, he has worked as an in-house artist for commercial design studios. A passion for historical and military subjects led him to focus on commissioned artworks. His contemporary and modern techniques have earned him a devoted following. Christopher lives just outside of London, England with his wife Zoe and four children. email:info@christopherrawlins.co.uk website:www.christopherrawlins.co.uk

Photo Credits

M= main; T= top; TL = top left; TM = top middle; TR = top right; B = bottom; BL = bottom left; BM = bottom middle; BR = bottom right
All Photographs/images and artifacts courtesy of the author and the Indus Media Foundation Collection except as follows: Courtesy of the Nanaki & Sahib Nagra Collection (Canada): Pg 54BL 'Malik', Pg 92TR 'Vancouver Parade', Pg 97TL 'Landing of IEF-A' , Pg 101TL 'Turban Badge', Pg 105BL 'Outwhiskered', Pg 104-105M 'Indian Infantry carrying Maxims into action under fire in France'. Courtesy of the Avtar Bahra Collection (UK): Pg 101M '47th Sikhs Enroute', Inside back cover 'Kishen Devi Postcard'. Courtesy of Amandeep Madra & Parmjit Singh (UK): Pg 85M 'The Sikh Contingent'. With permission Royal Collection Trust/© Her Majesty Queen Elizabeth II 2018 2018: Pg 88-89M 'Diamond Jubilee Procession'. Sourced from Sarjeet Singh Jagpal 'Becoming Canadians' www.vancouver-historical-society.ca (Canada) Pg 92BL 'Sikh Singers'.

Key Sources

Indian Wartime Soldiers letters: Reports of the Censor of Indian Mails in France digitised manuscripts British Library IOR/L/ MIL/5/825/3
WW1 Casualty Information: Commonwealth War Graves Commission www.cwgc.org/history-and-archives/first-world-war/forces/indian-army
Statistics of the Military Effort of the British Empire During the Great War 1914-1920. London: War Office His Majesty's Stationary Office, 1922.
Divisional Artillery on the Western Front- Adjutant General Department, Section 6 War Diary 1917. Royal Arsenal, Woolwich, London, UK.
Indus Media Foundation & Simon Fraser University Workshop 'The Indian Army & The Great War' by Major Gordon Corrigan Nov 10, 2014.
Khalsa Diwan Society Vancouver BC Canada, Ross Street Temple: The Komagata Maru Museum. The Sarjeet Singh Jagpal Collection
House of Commons, Debates (Hansard) Canada.
All chapter notes provided online at www.DutyHonourIzzat.ca/Sources

Select Bibliography

Berton, Pierre. *Vimy* Toronto: McClelland and Stewart Ltd 1986.
Bingley, Alfred Horsford. *Sikhs, Handbooks for the Indian Army.* Calcutta: Superintendent Government Printing, 1918.
Budheswar, Pati. *India and the First World War.* New Delhi: Atlantic Publishers, 1996.
Cardew, F. G. *Hodson's Horse 1857-1922.* The Naval & Military Press Ltd, 2006.
Chhina, Rana and Dominiek Dendooven. *India in Flanders Fields.* Centre For Armed Forces Historical Research, 2017.
Dhesi, N.S. Sikh Soldier: *Battle Honours, Volume One.* England: The Naval and Military Press Ltd, 2010.
Doherty, Simon and Tom Donovan. *The Indian Corps on the Western Front.* England: Tom Donovan Editions Ltd, 2014.
Duckers, Peter. Reward of Valor: *The Indian Order of Merit, 1914-1918.* Jade Publishing Limited 1999.
Ferguson, Ted. *A White Man's Country: An Exercise in Canadian Prejudice.* Doubleday; First Edition edition, 1975.
47th Sikhs War Record: The Great War 1914-1918. Chippenham: Picton Publishing, 1992.
Grimshaw, Roly. *Indian Cavalry Officer 1914-15.* Kent: D.J.Costello Ltd, 1986.
Gordon, Corrigan. *Sepoys in the Trenches: The Indian Corps on the Western Front 1914-15.* Stapenhurst: Spellmount Limited, 1999.
Gordon, John. *The Sikhs.* Edinburgh and London: William Blackwood and Sons, 1904.
Greenfield, Nathan M. *Baptism Of Fire: The Second Battle of Ypres and the Forging of Canada, April 1915.* Toronto: Harper Collins Publishers Ltd, 2007.
Harfield, Alan. *The Indian Army of the Empress 1861-1903.* Kent: Spellmount Tunbridge Wells, 1990.

Head, Richard and Tony McClenaghan. *The Maharajas' Paltans: A History of the Indian State Forces 1888-1948*. Manohar Publishers; Box edition January 1, 2013.

Hickman, Pamela. The Komagata Maru: *Righting Canada's Wrongs*. Toronto: James Lorimer & Company Ltd, 2014.

Honours and Awards Indian Army August 1914-August 1921. England: J.B. Hayward & Sons Ltd.

Hudson, H. *History of the 19th King George's Own Lancers 1858-1921*. England: The Naval & Military Press Ltd, 2007.

Jagpal, Sarjeet Singh. *Becoming Canadians: Pioneer Sikhs in Their Own Words*. British Columbia: Harbour Publishing, Madeira Park & Vancouver, 1994.

Jarboe, Andrew Tait. *War News in India: The Punjabi Press During World War 1*. London, New York: I.B.Tauris, 2016.

Johnston, Hugh, J.M. *The Voyage of the Komagatamaru: The Sikh Challenge to Canada's Colour Bar*. Vancouver, Toronto: UBC press 2014.

Kazimi, Ali. *Undesirables: White Canada and the Komagata Maru*. Douglas & Mcintyre, 2012.

Kenyon, David. *Horsemen in No Man's Land: British Cavalry & Trench Warfare 1914-1918*. Great Britain: Pen & Sword Military, 2011.

Khanna, Prem and Pushpindar Singh Chopra. *Portrait of Courage: Century of the 5th Battalion, The Sikh Regiment*. Military Studies Convention, 2001.

Leigh, M.S. *The Punjab and the War*. Lahore: Sage-e-Meel Publications, 1997.

Longford, Elizabeth. *A Viceroy's India, Leaves From Lord Curzon's Notebook*. London: Sidgwick & Jackson Ltd, 1984.

Madra, Amandeep Singh and Parmjit Singh. *Warrior Saints: Three Centuries of the Sikh Military Tradition*. London, New York: I.B. Tauris Publishers in association with The Sikh Foundation,1999.

MaCmunn, George. *The Martial Races of India*. London Sampson Low, Marston & Co. Ltd, 1933.

Majumder, Rajit K. *The Indian Army and the Making of Punjab*. Delhi: Permanent Black, 2003.

Malik, H.S. *A Little Work, A Little Play*. New Delhi: Thomson Press (India) Ltd, 2009.

Mason, Philip. *A Matter of Honour: An Account of the Indian Army, Its Officers and Men*. London: Jonathan Cape Ltd, 1974.

Merewether J.W.B. and Rt.Hon Frederick Smith. *The Indian Corps in France*. New Delhi: Pentagon Press, 2008.

Metcalf, R. Thomas. *Imperial Connections: India In The Indian Ocean Arena, 1860-1920*. University Of California Press; October 2008.

Mollo, Boris. *The Indian Army*. U.K: Blandford Press, 1981.

Morton-Jack, George. *The Indian Army on the Western Front: India's Expeditionary Force to France and Belgium in the First World War*. Cambridge: Cambridge University Press, 2014.

Muthanna, I.M. *People Of India In North America (Part First)*. Bangalore, India: Lotus Printers, 1975.

Nasmith, George G. *Canada's Sons and Great Britain in the World War*. Toronto: John C. Winston 1919.

Nath, Ashok. *Izzat: Historical Records and Iconography of Indian Cavalry Regiments 1750-2007*. Centre for Armed Forces Historical Research United Service Institution of India, 2009.

Nicholson G.W.L. *Canadian Expeditionary Force 1914-1919*. Ottawa: Queen's Printer and Controller of Stationary, 1964.

Omissi, David. *Indian Voices of the Great War: Soldier's Letters, 1914-18*. Houndmills, London: MacMillan Press, 1999.

Omissi, David. *The Sepoy and The Raj: The Indian Army, 1860-1940*. Houndmills, London: Macmillan Press, 1994.

Roberts, Frederic. *Forty-one years in India From Subaltern To Commander-In-Chief*. London: Richard Bentley & Co, 1898.

Sandhu, Gurcharn Singh. *The Indian Cavalry: History of the Indian Armoured Corps Vol 1*. U.K: East- West Publications Ltd, 1982.

Simkins, Peter, Geoffrey Jukes and Michael Hickey. *The First World War*. Oxford: Osprey Publishing, 2003.

Singh, Amarinder. *Saragarhi and the Defence of the Samana Forts*. New Delhi: Bookwise (India) Pvt. Ltd, 2017.

Singh, Amarinder. *Honour And Fidelity: India's Military Contribution To The Great War 1914-1918*. New Delhi: Lotus Collection Roli Books, 2014.

Singh, Amarpal. *The First Anglo-Sikh War*. Amberley Publishing, 2014.

Singh, Amarpal. *The Second Anglo-Sikh War*. Amberley Publishing, 2016.

Singh, Harjeet. *India's Contribution to the Great War*. Pentagon Press, first published in 1923, Reissued 2014.

Singh, Kanwaljit and H S Ahluwalia. *Saragarhi Battalion: Ashes to Glory*. New Delhi: Lancer International, 1987.

Streets, Heather. Martial Races: *The Military, Race and Masculinity in British Imperial Culture, 1857-1914*. Manchester and New York: Manchester University Press, 2004.

Sydenham, George. *India and the War*. New York and London: Hodder and Stoughton, 1915.

Tan Tai, Yong. *The Garrison State: The Military, Government and Society in Colonial Punjab, 1849-1947*. New Delhi: SAGE Publications, 2005

Willcocks, James. *With the Indians in France*. London Constable and Company Ltd, 1920.

Additional resources at www.DutyHonourIzzat.ca/TeacherResources

WESTERN FRONT 1914: THE INDIAN CORPS ON ARRIVAL
INFANTRY BY COMPANIES (LAHORE & MEERUT DIVISIONS)

SIKH	17 ½
PUNJABI MUSSALMAN	12 ½
PATHAN	11
GARHWALI	8
DOGRA	7
RAJPUT	4 ½
JAT	4
BRAHMIN	1 ½
PUNJABI HINDU	1
MAHRATTA	1
Nepalese	
GURKHA	24

Sikh:
Punjabi Mussalman
Hindus / Jats / Brahmin

Lahore Division 1914 to 1915 Regiment 8 Companies / Class Company

Ferozepore Brigade
- 129th Baluchis: 2 Punjabi Mussalman, 3 Mahsuds, 3 other Pathans
- 57th Wilde's Rifles (Punjab Frontier Force) 2 Sikhs, 2 Punjabi Mussalman, 2 Afridi Pathans, 2 Dogras
- 9th Bhopal Infantry: 2 Sikhs, 2 Hindustani Muslims, 2 Brahmans, 2 Rajputs
- 89th Punjabis: 3 Sikhs, 3 Punjabi Mussalmans, 1 Rajputs, 1 Brahmans

Jullunder Brigade
- 1st Manchester Regiment (British)
- 47th Sikhs: 8 Jat Sikhs (Class Unit)
- 59th Scinde Rifles (Punjab Frontier Force): 2 Sikhs, 1 Punjabi Mussalman, 3 Pathans, 2 Dogras
- 40th Pathans: 4 Pathans, 2 Dogras, 2 Punjabi Mussalman

Sirhind Brigade
- 1st Highland Light Infantry (British)
- 1st King George's Own Gurkha Rifles: 8 Gurkhas
- 4th Price of Wales' Own Gurkha Rifles: 8 Gurkhas
- 15th Ludhiana Sikhs: 8 Jat Sikhs (Class Unit)

Divisional Troops (Combatants)
- 15th Lancers (Cavalry): 4 Multani Pathans (Class Unit)
- 3rd (Bombay) Sappers & Miners: Mazhbi Sikhs, Ramdasiya Sikhs, Hindustani Muslims, Marathas
- 34th Sikh Pioneers: 8 Mazhbi Sikhs & Ramdasiya Sikhs
- 5th, 11th, 18th Brigades RFA 109th Heavy Battery

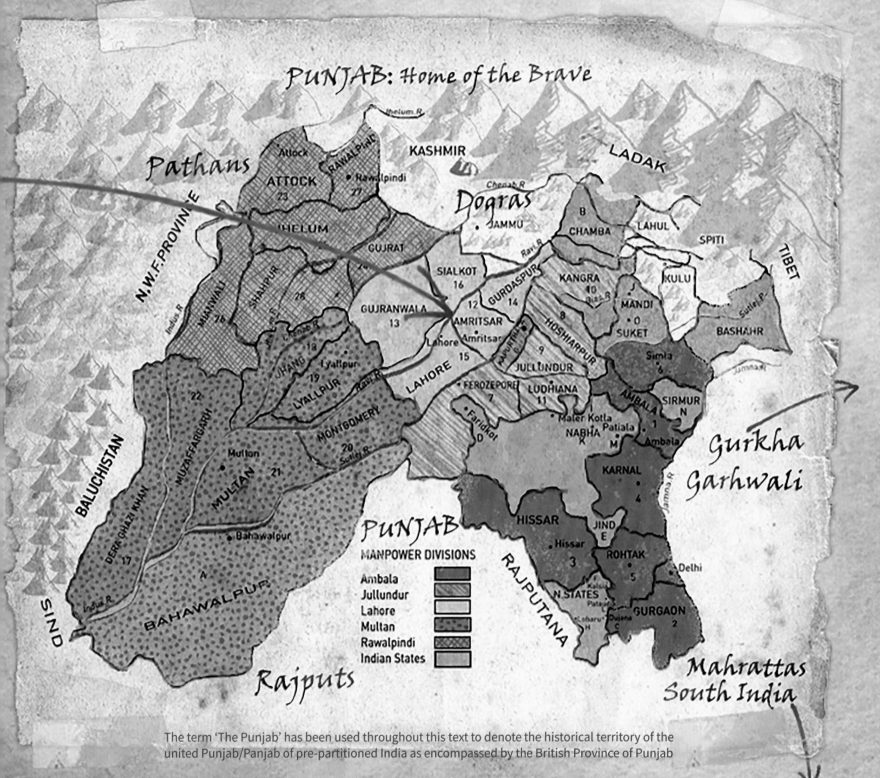

PUNJAB: Home of the Brave

Pathans

KASHMIR

LADAK

Jhelum R.

Attock

RAWALPINDI

Rawalpindi
27

Dogras

Chenab R.

B

LAHUL

SPITI

TIBET

ATTOCK
23

JHELUM

N.W.F.PROVINCE

JAMMU

CHAMBA

GUJRAT

Ravi R.

KANGRA
10

KULU

SIALKOT
16

GURDASPUR

Beas R.

MANDI

SUKET

BASHAHR

SHAHPUR

28

Indus R.

MIANWALI
76

Chenab R.

18

JHANG
19

Lyallpur

GUJRANWALA
13

12   GURDASPUR
14

AMRITSAR

Lahore Amritsar

Sutlej R.

8

HOSHIARPUR

9

Simla
6

Jhelum R.

LYALLPUR

Ravi R.

LAHORE

15

JULLUNDUR

LUDHIANA
11

AMBALA

SIRMUR
N

Gurkha

22

FEROZEPORE
7

Maler Kotla

MUZAFFARGARH

MONTGOMERY

Faridkot
D

NABHA
K

Patiala
M

1

Ambala

Garhwali

Multan

20

Sutlej R.

KARNAL

4

Jumna R.

BALUCHISTAN

DERA GHAZI KHAN

MULTAN

21

A

Bahawalpur

PUNJAB

HISSAR

JIND
E

ROHTAK
5

Delhi

MANPOWER DIVISIONS

Hissar
3

17

Indus R.

BAHAWALPUR

Ambala
Jullundur
Lahore
Multan
Rawalpindi
Indian States

RAJPUTANA

N.STATES

Loharu
H

Dujana
C

GURGAON
2

SIND

Rajputs

Mahrattas
South India

The term 'The Punjab' has been used throughout this text to denote the historical territory of the
united Punjab/Panjab of pre-partitioned India as encompassed by the British Province of Punjab

Indian Army Manpower Statement- Showing Punjab's Contribution by British District

Division who served.	District/State during War	Total men who served	Men enlisted during the War
Ambala	Ambala	10,254	7,400
	Gurgaon	20,181	17,700
	Hissar	18,400	16,000
	Karnal	6,819	6,530
	Rohtak	28,245	22,000
	Simla	2,213	1,996
	TOTAL	86,112	71,626
Jullundur	Ferozepore	20,539	18,315
	Hoshiarpur	21,153	15,871
	Jullundur	16,404	13,241
	Kangra	17,113	11,317
	Ludhiana	23,341	18,580
	TOTAL	98,550	77,324
Lahore	Amritsar	23,500	18,172
	Gujranwala	14,813	13,200
	Gurdaspur	19,204	16,809
	Lahore	10,800	9,299
	Sialkot	15,330	12,325
	TOTAL	83,647	69,805
Multan	Dera Ghazi Khan	1,047	1,037
	Jhang	955	911
	Lyallpur	8,266	7,928
	Montgomery	3,002	2,988
	Multan	4,700	4,661
	Muzzaffargarh	2,042	2,024
	TOTAL	20,012	19,549

Division who served.	District/State during War	Total men who served	Men enlisted during the War
Rawalpindi	Attock ...	18,851	16,002
	Gujrat ...	27,335	21,494
	Jhelum ...	31,881	21,336
	Mianwali ...	5,000	3,841
	Rawalpindi ...	36,292	23,629
	Shahpur ...	15,500	13,000
	TOTAL ...	134,859	99,302
British Districts*	TOTAL ...	423,180	337,606

Indian Army Manpower Statement- Showing Punjab's Contribution by Independent Princely States

State	Total men who served	Men enlisted during the War
Patiala ...	37,020	28,020
Jind ...	8,673	6,323
Nabha ...	7,000	5,000
Kapurthala ...	5,914	5,041
Bahawalpur ...	4,085	3,265
Maler Kotla ...	3,934	2,619
Faridkot ...	2,759	2,368
Dujana ...	1,266	955
Sirmur ...	1,207	775
Mandi ...	1,124	1,046
Kalsia ...	1,014	1,014
Chamba ...	499	499
Pataudi ...	450	450
Loharu ...	378	281
Suket ...	240	231
Total Princely States...	75,563	57,88

Punjab Total

Total men who served

498,560

Men enlisted during the War

395,493

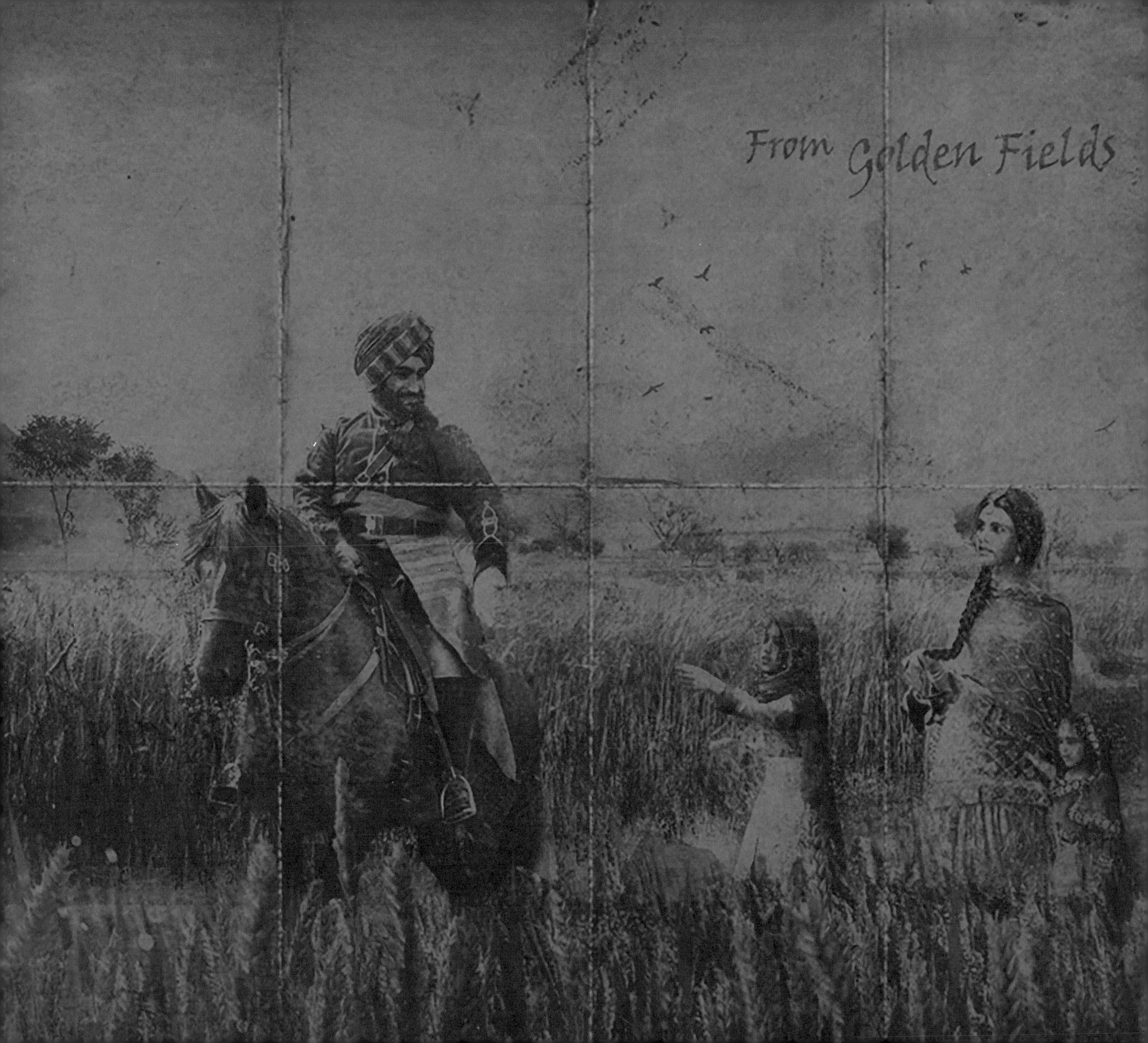
From Golden Fields